# More Praise for Unicycle

"This book contains some serious mathematics—smart, thought-provoking, and engrossing."
>—William H. Barker, PhD, professor of mathematics, Bowdoin College, coauthor of the textbook *Continuous Symmetry: From Euclid to Klein*

"A provocative book by a serious thinker, well worth the reader's time. We are essentially on the same page."
>—William A. Haviland, PhD, professor emeritus and founder of the Department of Anthropology, University of Vermont, coauthor of bestselling textbooks, including *Cultural Anthropology* and *Evolution and Prehistory*

"*Unicycle* is an important book. I am very impressed. It covers a lot of territory, and it is very thoughtful and even charming. The math and logic are understandable to the interdisciplinary reader. I agreed with everything the book has to say."
>—Esther Pasztory, PhD, professor emerita, Columbia University, author of groundbreaking books, including *Thinking With Things*, *Aztec Art*, *Teotihuacan: An Experiment in Living*

"An eloquent explanation, with spare logic and excellent argument. In my critical thinking class, my students study the core ideals of the Enlightenment; this book's world view gives me a position from which to triangulate between absolutism and relativism and illuminates all three."
>—David S. Cook, author of *Above the Gravel Bar: The Native Canoe Routes of Maine* and *Into the Civil War With the 3rd Maine Infantry Regiment*

"Looks fascinating."
>—Daniel C. Dennett, PhD, professor of philosophy, co-director of the Center for Cognitive Studies, Tufts University, bestselling author of books including *Darwin's Dangerous Idea* and *From Bacteria to Bach and Back: The Evolution of Minds*

☙ ❧

## Also by Paul Cornell du Houx:

### WHAT THE FARMER TOLD THE BARD, A NOVEL OF EROTIC PANPSYCHISM

"This rich, dense, playful novel of philosophical, historical, and metaphysical inquiry . . . The material is fascinating . . . The novel's chief attraction is Cornell du Houx's witty, daring, allusive prose . . . Imaginative vigor pulses through descriptive scenes in which characters encounter gods and Shakespeare's fairies . . . This book certainly brings fresh and unique material to the table . . . daring ideas and memorable prose."

—THE BOOKLIFE PRIZE BY PUBLISHERS WEEKLY

### YOGANOMICS SUTRAS ON THE TRANSFORMATION PROOF: NATURE'S PANPSYCHIST BALANCE, THE MORAL COMPASS FOR THE ECONOMY

"[The sutras] act like firecrackers in your intellectual reading consciousness.

"Cornell du Houx 'developed a math that lets us read the ethics of natural law within the environment.' This is a not inaccurate, but incomplete summary [in the afterword] of *Yoganomics*'s subject matter, which skates an enormous range of philosophical material. [The] afterword characterizes the contents as having 'the ancient and succinct style of the sutra,' indicating the sort of gonglike presence . . . that clearly underpins its ideas.

"For like a sutra, the text consists of numbered sentences . . . some of which have a vatic quality, others plainly conversational. They cover quantum physics, mathematics and pi; politics; various real and figurative modes of addiction; gender; the perils of climate change; the Tao; communist China; Plato; ranked-choice voting; and many more subjects, with recurring focal points involving socioeconomics, nature, environmental degradation, and the dangers of 'absolutes' in everyday thinking."

—DANA WILDE, MORNING SENTINEL, KENNEBEC JOURNAL, AUTHOR OF NEBULAE: A BACKYARD COSMOGRAPHY AND THE OTHER END OF THE DRIVEWAY

# UNICYCLE,
*the book of fictitious symmetry*
        *and nonrandom truth,*
                *or the panpsychist asymmetry*
                      *of nature's democratic pi*

———————————

Not exactly—

# UNICYCLE,

the book of
fictitious symmetry
and
nonrandom truth

---

or the

panpsychist asymmetry of

nature's democratic pi

Fifth Edition

Paul V. Cornell du Houx

Polar Bear & Company
Solon Center for Research and Publishing
Solon & Rockland, Maine

☙ ❧

> A major test of theories of the early universe is
> to account for the patterns seen in
> the cosmic microwave background (CMB).
>
> —Lee Smolin, *Time Reborn:*
> *From the Crisis in Physics to the Future of the Universe*

Polar Bear & Company™
is an imprint of the
Solon Center for Research and Publishing.
PolarBearandco.com, SolonCenter.org
The Solon Center is a 501(c)3 Maine Public Benefit Corporation.

Polar Bear & Company books are available at local bookstores
in many countries, or online, or at info@soloncenter.org.
Retailers may order via Ingram, ISBN: 978-1-959112-04-4.

Copyright © 2011-23 by Paul V. Cornell du Houx
All rights reserved. No part of this book may be reproduced in any form
without permission in writing from the author or publisher, except for brief
quotations for critical articles and reviews.
Library of Congress Control Number: 2011925682
First print edition 2011, ISBN: 978-1-882190-06-5
First eBook 2015, ISBN: 978-1-882190-20-1
Second paperback edition 2016, revised 2019, ISBN: 978-1-882190-28-7
Third paperback edition 2020, ISBN: 978-1-882190-93-5
Fourth paperback edition 2021, ISBN: 978-1-882190-47-8
Fifth paperback edition 2023, ISBN: 978-1-959112-04-4
Manufactured on durable acid-free paper in more than one country.

Illustrations: Photo of author in birchbark canoe, by Ramona du Houx; penny-farthing courtesy tobias openclipart.org "tobias pennnyfarthing"; *Original Face* enso courtesy K. Pfaff, in "Maze Tale" illustration by author; window by Emily Cornell du Houx; illustrations of set theory courtesy Dr. B. Sidney Smith. The unicycle in the back-cover image and elsewhere courtesy Gilby, gilby.com. Cover design by author.

The cosmic microwave background (CMB) image has been adapted to the cover design of *Unicycle*, courtesy of the European Space Agency and the Planck Collaboration. For the full image and more information, please visit: esa.int/spaceinimages/Images/2013/03/Planck_enhanced_anomalies.

The following description accompanies the cosmic microwave background image on the website of the European Space Agency. While not absolute proof, this recent evidence of nature's asymmetry provides context for the reasoning in *Unicycle*.

> Two CMB anomalous features hinted at by Planck's predecessor, NASA's WMAP, are confirmed in the new high-precision data. One is an asymmetry in the average temperatures on opposite hemispheres of the sky (indicated by the curved line), with slightly higher average temperatures in the southern ecliptic hemisphere and slightly lower average temperatures in the northern ecliptic hemisphere. This runs counter to the prediction made by the standard model that the Universe should be broadly similar in any direction we look. There is also a cold spot that extends over a patch of sky that is much larger than expected (circled). In this image the anomalous regions have been enhanced with red and blue shading to make them more clearly visible.[1]

---

# Contents

| | |
|---|---|
| Preface | xi |
| Author's Note | xv |
| Acknowledgments | xix |
| Of Myth and Reason | xxiii |

## I. Preamble

| | | |
|---|---|---|
| 1. | Samuel's Introduction | 3 |
| 2. | The Maze Tale | 8 |
| 3. | The Ancient Paradox | 10 |
| 4. | Definitions of Asymmetry | 14 |

## II. Changes

| | | |
|---|---|---|
| 5. | I Revisit the Transformation Proof | 19 |
| 6. | The Gnome and the Onion | 28 |
| 7. | Unpacking the Transformation Proof, Step by Step | 41 |
| 8. | Salmon Barbecue | 47 |
| 9. | Alice Disproves God and Deduces the Soul: Out of the Box of Everyday Awareness | 52 |
| 10. | Alice Disproves God and Deduces the Soul: Nonrandom Multifarious Polarity | 64 |
| 11. | Alice Disproves God and Deduces the Soul: Fundamentality | 72 |
| 12. | Samuel Passes the Torch | 77 |
| 13. | At the Pearly Gates, by Rolo | 79 |

## III. River of Asymmetry

| | | |
|---|---|---|
| 14. | Transition | 85 |
| 15. | The Lady of the Lake or The Rings of Pi, by Rolo | 87 |
| 16. | Context and Induction, by Lola | 97 |
| 17. | Totalitarian Math, by Rolo | 103 |
| 18. | Manitous | 109 |
| 19. | Samuel's Essay: Extremely Low Asymmetry | 115 |

## Contents

| | | |
|---|---|---|
| 20. | Samuel's Essay: Which Number Two Now? | 121 |
| 21. | Samuel's Essay: More About the Absence and Something About Set Theory | 123 |
| 22. | Samuel's Essay: The Largest Number Proof, Etc. | 138 |
| 23. | The Jinniyah and the Greatest Number, by Rolo | 167 |

IV. Aquilah and the Lamp, by Lola
| | | |
|---|---|---|
| 24. | Awakening | 177 |
| 25. | Genies in Bottles, by Rolo | 180 |
| 26. | Quill Pen | 186 |
| 27. | Aquilah's Essay | 191 |

V. The Tea-Room Scenarios
| | | |
|---|---|---|
| 28. | By the River | 201 |
| 29. | Infinity and The Book of Changes, by Rolo | 204 |
| 30. | Alice at Tea | 214 |
| 31. | The Gingerbread Variable, by Rolo | 228 |
| 32. | Molly | 236 |
| 33. | "The Sources of Plato's Opinions," from *A History of Western Philosophy*, by Bertrand Russell | 240 |
| 34. | Streams of Paradise | 244 |
| 35. | Atlas Speaks | 252 |

VI. Stirring the Pot
| | | |
|---|---|---|
| 36. | The Asymmetric Economy, by Anonymous Economist | 267 |
| 37. | Asymmetric Evolution, by Extraterrestrial High School Teacher | 279 |
| 38. | Philosophical Habitat, by Interplanetary Inhabitant of No Fixed Abode | 297 |
| 39. | Snagged by the Imperfect Democratic Tao of Pi | 320 |
| 40. | Nature's Democratic Counter-Pressures | 322 |

| | |
|---|---|
| Notes | 325 |
| Selected Bibliography | 329 |
| The Author's Story | 331 |

## Preface

Every book has its story, how it came together and found its way to readers, to used book stores, and beyond. A quality paperback with archival paper and plenty of glue along the spine can survive for centuries; an eBook is perhaps more vulnerable to deletion or deterioration in the long run, depending on the course of civilization. Both can be vital parts of the story.

*Unicycle* was initially assembled with some short stories from my primitive website, late in the dawn of the Internet. It contains a new proof that there are no absolute beginnings. So the first printing was misaligned, with errata fit for advance reader copies, even to the mistake of printing "first edition" on the copyright page. The eBook was the first finalized edition, and this preface is adapted from there.

None of these changes materially improve on the somewhat surprising deduction that moral facts can be found in nature, as the Founders hoped when they asserted, "We hold these truths to be self-evident." This declaration of natural law and human rights was signed in spite of the shock waves emitted by David Hume's revelation that no one had yet figured out a logic to connect ethics with nature, any definitive reasoning to tell us what we ought rightly to do as a result of what we observe around us. The shock of this moral disconnection from nature has continued today and competes with the courageous declaration to the contrary on which more than one democracy stands. With the explosion of technology, we need more justification than victory through economic and military power. There are moments of truth when we need to figure out the next step in time, so I hope this will be a contribution.

Meanwhile, fascinating developments in science are being published. Fortunately I am not a physicist, or I would be tempted to pull apart the narrative here, trying to fit in discussion of advances that I might understand. A book of deductions on nature's asymmetry is fed or starved by evidence, favorable or not. Asymmetry provides a cornucopia that requires restraint on my part.

I vividly recall my first sighting of *Lucifer's Legacy: The Meaning of*

*Asymmetry* at the local bookstore. There was no turning back after that. Gathered there was a history of scientific experience in evidence of nature's asymmetry. I loaded some onto *Unicycle*. Years later, I am tempted to unravel more than one chapter with a discussion of *Time Reborn: From the Crisis in Physics to the Future of the Universe*, using excerpts like this:

> [Leibniz's] principle of the identity of the indiscernibles requires that there cannot be two events in spacetime that have exactly the same observable properties ... This implies that our universe can have no exact symmetries. In fact it doesn't ... Whereas symmetries are helpful for the analysis of models of small parts of the universe, all the symmetries so far posited by physicists have turned out to be approximate or broken.[2]

Or this:

> From the perspective of the reality of time, it is entirely natural that the universe and its fundamental laws be asymmetric in time, with a strong arrow of time that encompasses increases of entropy for isolated systems together with continual growth of structure and complexity.[3]

I take my hat off to the scientists, while I try for some balance in bringing the fruit of their labor to foreign lands. But I will resist the temptation to get in that room with the physicists, cosmologists — I'll just take away the absence of symmetry, with asymmetry wherever I go. Otherwise my list of temptations to discuss would never end, including a recent article on Planck stars[4] and the possible bounce-back effect in black holes — or of the universe itself — which might go very nicely into the genie's essay in Chapter 27, where she connects the absence of absolutes with a fundamental polarity in nature's asymmetry. But trying to follow that "bounce" could unbalance a good number of chapters in this book with unnecessary speculation on the repercussions of asymmetry. But then again, the cosmic microwave background illustrated on the back cover hereto was irresistible. And now news has broken with evidence of gravitational waves [2015].[5]

It can be intoxicating to watch the evidence accumulate along with the interdisciplinary reasoning, especially when the stakes are culturally significant in fields more familiar to me, not to over-mention the political and religious aspects of natural law. Unless I am mistaken, *Unicycle* has succeeded in the long-standing attempt to build a deductive sequence connecting nature and ethics. So I hope to have sufficiently refrained from getting sidetracked. After all, one of the purposes of this book is to provide a tight enough deductive process to invite further study.

Solon, Maine<br>May 2020

## Update

"I'm going to stop updating this book." We all have a few expressions for statements like that—

Words resonate differently with changes in the cultural environment and may eventually change meaning as the language morphs. Words that might land with a clang and a thud may sing a decade later. So I have taken heart and added the word "panpsychist" to the title of this book, in the context of pi and the logic of asymmetry pertaining to the philosophy of mind. Philip Goff writes in *Galileo's Error: Foundations for a New Science of Consciousness*,

> In the dying embers of the twentieth century . . . not many philosophy departments in the U.K. had a panpsychist in residence. But the new professor at the University of Reading, Galen Strawson, was busy defending panpsychism as "the most parsimonious, plausible and indeed 'hard-nosed' position . . . about the nature of reality." This seemed like the place for me. I had no idea at the time, but the writings of Strawson, and a little later my own writings, would eventually lead to a full-blown panpsychist renaissance in contemporary philosophy . . .
>
> The roots of this revolution were the rediscovery, by Strawson and others, of crucial work on consciousness from the 1920s by the philosopher Bertrand Russell and the scientist Arthur

Eddington. I am convinced that Russell and Eddington did for the science of consciousness what Darwin did for the science of life.[6]

It was in 2007-8 that the pieces of the logic of asymmetry came together after years of walks along the Kennebec River in Maine and wild swimming. In many ways the reasoning emerged from short stories collected here and from my novel, *What the Farmer Told the Bard* (1996). So this prefatory update is another signpost to changes reflected in the book — in addition to Chapters 7, 39 and 40.

The changed cultural environment evident in the above quote cannot be disconnected from discoveries with science and engineering, like for example with the James Webb Space Telescope. Nature's asymmetry yields evermore secrets, the surprisingly large galaxies of the earlier universe among them. The asymmetries of the Big Bang are louder and brighter than ever, leading to fundamental questions about a universe in the absence of absolute origins — or any absolutes at all, as portrayed in this book. Meanwhile, particle accelerators bring us to the edge of a new understanding where reductionism calls for analysis that includes polarities also described herein.

A further quick take on the word "panpsychist" (qualifier and noun). It seems to have been introduced to philosophy in the sixteenth century by the rebellious Venetian philosopher and scientist Francesco Patrizi. While I am willing to throw in with the adherents to the wide range of ideas gathered by this rather antiquated-sounding term (to my ears) — if it resonates like a fine antique, that would be the genuine antiquity of its parts, back to the ancient Greeks and far beyond — I feel that it still shies away from a pantheistic perspective.

If the logic of asymmetry connects with people who envision a living landscape and its gods, the reasoning develops step by step into regions that are outside many a panpsychist philosopher's purview. After all, more than a few notes of the celebrated and multifarious embodiments of the god Pan intone the first part of the word and, together with Psyche, one named for the Breath of Life, call to us with the music of places unknown. And this is a good place to end the updates in the hope that the reader is encouraged to explore the following pages.

Rockland, Maine
June 2023

## Author's Note

At the end of his philosophical comedy, *Religulous*, Bill Maher says we must either "grow up or die." In pursuit of a few basic answers I have been attempting, somewhat paradoxically, to take his advice most of my life. When we stop growing up, we become the posturing "adults" I used to watch and wonder at as a teen. These adults seemed to think they had all the answers — and so many teens are pressured to look jaded, like they've seen it all. I didn't want to grow up like that. But I loved fairy tales as a child, and later on I realized that this was also called "folklore" (a more grown-up expression) and "mythology," which was religion when the human race was even younger than we are now. Isn't there some way to grow up and still believe enough for the stories to be true enough, so we don't have to leave it all behind and become "adults"? Adults who believe in fairy tales?

When I hear of a suicide bomber who murders men, women, and children with the idea that he or she will go to a paradise of ancient lore, it is like hearing something too horrible even for the Brothers Grimm or *Lord of the Flies*. When I hear a leader declare something like a crusade or jihad against another system of belief in folklore and mythology, I get that same feeling of children killing each other. In a sense, the terrorist, no matter how frightening, never got into growing up. While that may not be much of an excuse, lack of that particular excuse does not mean there is no shared responsibility. How many of our elders are responsible for the stories we tell?

But they are just stories, are they not? The power of what can seem nothing more than an idea or a fairy tale can be vast and projected over thousands of years by the force of human nature when it becomes religion. Without wishing to sound too responsible, I feel it's a matter of citizenship to tell each other stories in ways that clarify and question where the fiction might be — and the truth — and that leave opportunities for the next storyteller to come along. As a publisher it has especially been my mission to contribute to the process of growth that keeps at bay the self-arrogation of "absolute truth" that confuses our grownups and children alike.

I have been fortunate in having some teachers who were so good that I began to get the sense that it might be possible continuously to advance the frontiers of the discovery of the truth in fiction and of the fiction in reason. Experiences in literary analysis encouraged me to wonder if it might not be possible truly to identify the greatest fictions of all in our most powerful mythologies — even to the logical uncovering of God Himself as a character in a long-standing story. The fact that God is regarded by many as so obviously a fictitious character does not, of course, make it so. Meanwhile my love of mythology would not be satisfied with an empty character. The problem was worse that I had thought.

Characters must be believable. This means there must be truth in them. Otherwise their credibility is only based on our gullibility. That's not good enough for good fiction, let alone great works. I feared that to close the door on the credibility of the God of monotheism, for example, as mythology or otherwise, was to empty fiction in general of credible characters. Not because the character of God is so important to fiction, but any test that could be used to empty God of truth could be used on other characters as well. And what about us? Literature would become a paltry thing to be enjoyed only by the naïve or the cynical, who are in many ways closely related in decadence. How would the credibility of any individual survive? We can see these complicated interactions as we hear concerns about the infantilization of a proud American people dumbed down to a monoculture by cynical overachievers.

"King and country!" where God is king, is too often the result, with the rule of law in subservience. The problem has long been to find a *reason* for democracy, especially now to counter a culture of unreason. Violent revolution, though necessary in the Age of Reason, is no longer so rational an option with weapons of mass destruction.

But a logical reason for equal opportunity requires that elusive connection between nature and democracy alluded to in the Declaration of Independence as the "Laws of Nature and of Nature's God," where "we hold these truths to be self-evident," though we had not been able to prove them intellectually. Quite the opposite; philosophers cleaning up the reasoning of their predecessors increasingly identified errors in the attempt to draw ethical conclusions from observations of nature.

After many spare moments untangling these conundrums, I have finally got the following results to present for your consideration. The questions involved are fundamental enough to require a varied exposition, where God may no longer seem so prominent in the maze.

## Acknowledgments

Since this has taken a while to develop, the number of people who have inspired and helped me over the years is beyond my ability to count. I hope they at least suspect who they might be in remembering some conversations and give themselves the benefit of the doubt; so often assistance comes unexpectedly. And major acknowledgment must credit assistance in creating the conditions where I could commit spare moments to this pursuit.

The journey really got specific in the Department of Romance Languages at Amherst College; the memory of Professor Jeffrey J. Carre patiently listening to my weekly two-hour thesis presentations on what I proposed (and was thankfully accepted) as a new understanding of Gustave Flaubert has given me the invaluable confidence the years would require in my ability to both reason and doubt.

Economics, the other side of a double degree, seemed disconnected until I began to value the math as deeply as the fiction, economic or otherwise. Inscrutable economics was clarified as I meticulously built some primitive mathematical models; these called for some variables to be on the "outside" and some on the "inside" — of something. Even though this borderland was mysterious, it allowed me to realize that there was some serious politics involved in assumptions that had been confusing me. Clearing my mind in newfound meditation allowed me to more easily observe the arrival of these assumptions and question their provenance.

Ah, well if it was just politics, then I could relate to this economics, like I do to a novel. There were no intimidating imperatives, no absolutes that I just didn't get. All I had to do was follow the argument; it too had a plot. I could do that, step by step, if the steps were there. And if they were not there, then someone had messed up — and it wasn't just me. What a relief! Math became my friend. However, it had also become infused with un-math-like humanistic things; I was no longer sure what it was. Since the math in *Unicycle* is almost entirely in prose, the question remains. This is where I assume full responsibility for any errors in the book.

My profound gratitude for many reasons to Hubert Kueter, professor emeritus of German at Colby College, author of *My Tainted Blood*, and to Nancy Dhal Brooks.

Where the math and the narrative were so overlapping that I was unable to be sure of what I was doing, the author of *Continuous Symmetry: From Euclid to Klein*, William Barker of the Bowdoin College Math department, encouraged me with the notion that I was indeed doing some "serious mathematics," as he described it. I am still cagey about identifying myself as doing anything of the sort. Even so, emboldened, I began to wonder if this might be a mathematical novel and what, if anything, that might mean.

The very idea that this is a novel at all can be contested on the grounds that it is a gathering of short stories and essays. But I lost that argument to the individual characters who are providing the fiction, as well as the nonfiction.

David Cook, author of *Above the Gravel Bar: the Native Canoe Routes of Maine*, reoriented me with his book and encouraged me with his lifelong teaching experience.

As for the curious borders between math and philosophy and the structure of the reasoning to follow, I am grateful in more ways than I can specify to Norton Starr, mathematics prof. emeritus of Amherst College. I am certainly not the only student who has been inspired by his responses and the invaluable time he has given in addressing unformed ideas with an open mind. He was famously there for students when I was an undergraduate at Amherst and responded wholeheartedly three decades later (as though I were still at the Zoo) when I needed guidance in the vital initial stages of getting it written down. And to one of Prof. Starr's more recent students, thank you Beau Alessi.

When the eminent anthropologist William A. Haviland, read the manuscript and commented in detail, it was a threshold in bringing this project to fruition. My deep gratitude to Bill and to Anita de Laguna Haviland for their helpful comments and for their support over route and carry.

To Dr. Nikolai Dejevsky, author of *A Myth of Messina: Echoes of Russian Richmond*, thank you for reading the booklet entitled *River of Asymmetry*, which provided the early draft for *Unicycle* and for helping to set me on course with the benefit of a lifetime's experience in publishing and Oxford scholarship.

Thank you Charles Ferguson, Colby College Prof. emeritus of

French and Italian. Where would I be without your help in the big picture and the smallest details?

My gratitude to Dr. Diané Collinson, author of publications including *Fifty Major Philosophers*, for help and encouragement with the manuscript.

Many thanks to Prof. Daniel C. Dennett of the Center for Cognitive Studies at Tufts University for giving time to *Unicycle* and offering encouragement, in addition to granting permission to publish excerpts from *Darwin's Dangerous Idea*.

For allowing me free use of sizable sections of their writing, my thanks to Prof. Sam Nelson of Claremont McKenna College and to Dr. B. Sidney Smith. The excerpt on pantheism is provided courtesy of Prof. Michael Levine of the University of Western Australia. News, written by Kitta MacPherson, is provided courtesy of Princeton University Office of Communications. The excerpts from *How to Read Hume* by Simon Blackburn are provided courtesy of Granta Books. Excerpts from *A Different Universe: Reinventing Physics from the Bottom Down* by Robert B. Laughlin are provided by permission from Basic Books. And thank you, *Discover Magazine*.

A tip o' the hat to the artist Justin Williams; not sure where and how this book would have happened had he not left his cabin in the woods to rebuild this house by the waterfall, long before Cornell du Houxs arrived in Maine and projects together were launched.

To my children, Rebecca, Emily, Alex, and Adrian, who grew up with this project, thank you for the questions that children ask and adults sometimes try to answer and for the increasingly specific application of academic skills you gained over the years — here is the product. Emily took on the extra burden of reading and rereading the manuscript as it grew, providing key written comments to which I responded with new chapters. I don't think I should include our cats past and present by name, but I encourage a trip to your local shelter, certainly if you want to write. To Ramona, this book, at last!

## Of Myth and Reason

One more thing before we begin. The idea of a mathematical novel with fairy tales might yet be unsettling. I would therefore like to thank David S. Solmitz, author of *Piecing Scattered Souls*, and posthumously his father, the philosopher Walter M. Solmitz of Bowdoin College, for helping to introduce my interdisciplinary attempt, with the following excerpt of a chapel talk given on December 5, 1961. Walter Solmitz, survivor of Dachau, begins by saying, "The professor's privilege is that he may ask more questions than he can answer himself." Then he warms up and relates a tale of a frog king, concluding as follows.

> And now there comes my professional question: Is it true that sometimes some humans remind us of some animals — and some animals of some humans — in their looks and in the way they seem to act?
>
> Is there any significance to that? And as my friend's appearance made me see better the fairy tale of the frog and the bewitched prince, can conversely the fairy tale help us to see appearances better and to look through appearances?
>
> Of course, we are scientific in our thought, we must be scientific, and make the scientific distinctions, but cannot the fairy tale complement and supplement our everyday, scientific outlook?—
>
> Let me, with the omission of some steps, which might have made my thought easier to follow, still jump to a few reflections on this.
>
> The philosopher finds it sometimes desirable to supplement his critical thought by the free play of the imagination. Plato tells also some fairy tales, and he tells one about the life hereafter, and the choice one has to make himself of the form in which to spend one's next life. One who was a singer in this life chose to be a nightingale in his next life. A fighting hero who had gone through some tragic experiences in this life chose to become a lion in his next life: so that we may say that Plato saw in a lion

a tragic hero who had despaired too much to become a human again.

And is it by chance that Nietzsche, in describing the transformation and metamorphoses through the individual's phase of the lion, must create for himself the freedom to be free for new creations?

And in one of the masterpieces of contemporary prose, Hermann Hesse, the Nobel Prize winner of 1946, describes what happened to him one July day in 1955 while he was working in his garden. While he was standing and breaking wood and was lost in memories of his childhood and the parrot they used to have at home,

> Suddenly like a golden flash from the blue sky of the summer morning, something came shooting down, bright in yellowish green, whizzed past my head . . . came flying back, set down on the branches by my feet — and was a parrot. "Yes, where are you coming from?" and it was only good that I still knew the parrot language from my childhood.

And after a detailed description:

> Never had anything happened to me as fair, as unlikely and like a fairy tale as this visit that lasted perhaps for ten minutes — this visit from the virgin forests of distant lands, the virgin forest of my distant childhood in which I still knew the language of the birds.

Is all this only by chance? As is it by chance only that since ancient times the Aesopian fables have used lions and mice and ants when they wanted to characterize outstanding human characteristics? And what about the comparative behaviorist and psychologist? The current issue of *Scientific American* has an essay with drawings of animals whose style would fit any fairy tale or fable book — and which ends with a moral teaching as a conclusion as would fit any Aesopian fable. And since ancient times have not the astrologers described humans as lions or black widows or scorpions and the like?

And is it then by chance that we ourselves in our everyday talk speak of Adenauer as a fox, or ourselves as pigs, of others as chicken, or somebody as catty, or a wise owl, of others as funny birds — and furthermore of the Russian bear — and of some people even as polar bears?

Is it not true, is it not strange that sometimes we may say something essential about a human being if we see him as that "kind of animal" that he is. Might it not be true that just when we do that, at the same time, we become all the more aware of the transcendental — of the kingly soul in the animal form?

What is it that is behind these strange correspondences and tensions between the animal and the truly human animal? What is it that makes us truly human animals? What is it that makes us truly human? What is it that sets us free? What is it in us that wants to be set free?

The professor — freed here from the scientific rigor and the scholarly discipline of the study and the classroom — allows his hopes free rein. And his hope is — which is always a teacher's hope — that the questions he could raise but not answer, the quests his generation has not yet been able to fulfill, will be taken up by you to put you into the mood, open your minds and hearts, to the possible realization that at least the human lion and the human lamb will get along in peace — and in this sense let me extend to you the season's first greetings and far-reaching warm wishes.[7]

# I. Preamble

Titania:
And the quaint mazes in the wanton green
For lack of tread are undistinguishable
. . . . .
The spring, the summer,
The childing autumn, angry winter, change
Their wonted liveries, and the mazed world,
By their increase, now knows not which is which.

—Shakespeare
*A Midsummer Night's Dream*

# 1. Samuel's Introduction

> Looking back at the worst times, it always seems that they were times in which there were people who believed with absolute faith and absolute dogmatism in something.
>
> —Richard P. Feynman,
> *The Meaning of It All: Thoughts of a Citizen-Scientist*

Philosophers from the earliest times have used dialogue and fictional narrative to explain themselves. There is good reason for this and specifically for attempting to find a balance between fiction and nonfiction when writing about subjects that are meant to be logical. It's more than a question of making it interesting to the reader. It's a question of making sense at all in the long run.

One reason for this has to do with the absence of absolutes. Such an absence is the unifying theme of these stories and essays. They are part of a common sense, logical process, proving definitively that absolutes do not exist, nor do they make sense in any language, including math.

Far from empowering our words, absolutes tend to water them down and make way for the various relativisms, which have further reduced the significance of words to a weird kind of power struggle, capable of lapsing at the state level into brute force. This book offers a fresh standard of reason to help us get beyond postmodern relativism and absolutist fundamentalism, which, while appearing to be fiercely on opposite sides of the culture wars, open back doors to each other, encouraging false choices on a road to nowhere.

What emerges from the reasoning to follow, instead of relativities and absolutes, is a balancing polarity, as in a waterfall and a millpond, where the impossibility of an absolutely flat surface on the pond above allows the water to fall onto the millwheel. This is more than a metaphor.

Why, one might ask, is it necessary for there to be no chance of an absolutely flat surface for the relationship of waterfall and pond to work? That is one of the questions — where science breaks into philosophy — addressed here in fiction and nonfiction.

Looking into the factual presence of a pond, and then into the poetic world of metaphor reflected there, one might ask, is there such a thing as absolute fiction, disconnected from the facts? The very question itself, presented to the imagination by the stories implicit in the shadows and lights of the pond, is one of nonfiction.

What about absolute nonfiction? Just the facts? Pure reason? A waterfall with no history that is open to interpretation? Just the falling water — particles of physics — with no chance of inspiring the imagination? Empirical evidence completely cut off from a consciousness that might wander and ask questions?

Using fiction and nonfiction, we will see how they are inextricably linked and must both be used in some way in order to prove the connections specifically, giving us a useful sense of direction. We will explore how logic, as a language including math, becomes hopelessly paradoxical in the absence of fiction. And that fiction cannot leave reason behind.

We will see that it is enough to be sufficiently logical for the purpose at hand, but only when leaving open the door to a magic garden with a light shinning through. This will be shown using a logical key to the nature of change; we have called it the Transformation Proof. It is a proof by contradiction, where a fiction is used to highlight the reality. The reasoning is assisted in this case by the fiction, so it does not become fiction itself. The logic is reinforced. They interact and, as may be the case when one has a story, truth is carried along in the telling. Our logic assures us that we can leave no story entirely alone.

The maze of short stories and essays that combine to form this book will demonstrate that as long as she can stop short of absolutes and universals, nature can achieve her extreme degrees of specificity — and true power. As members of the natural world, for us to fail to do likewise is not only self-defeating but imprecise. We can share in the source of nature's truth in our words by abandoning the assumption that we can achieve absolutes or that they even exist, except in myth and fiction. This is not a reduction of possibilities, but an augmentation, a step on the way beyond supposed absolute limits.

In the process of reading our reports, mythical and factual, we hope you will find that the theoretical concept of the absence of absolutes has an important connection to everyday life. The collection of fiction and nonfiction together will demonstrate that we need both in order to solve some of the oldest puzzles. In particular, the Transformation Proof will be applied to the question of whether anything is absolutely random — of importance not only to probability and statistics and the evolution debate, but to the question of whether there is a basic, moral direction in life, a truth to be followed. And is that truth democratic?

Then there is the question of whether anything, including an absolute god, can be beyond everything and in some way unknowable. Alice has the answer, with a new and definitive disproving of God while deducing in the same breath the existence of soul. Witnessing this feat of unravelling the logic of change expressed in the Transformation Proof, the authors of this book were finally able to organize their project.

Key to the discovery of any fundamentally democratic sense of direction in nature is the question of absolute symmetry itself, of importance also to our everyday sense of beauty, truth, and proportion, as well as being of concern in physics, astronomy, and math.

Here we will be distinguishing between an absolute and something that is just about absolute — such as the difference between absolute symmetry and other uses of the word "symmetry." This is more than a quibble. We will explore reasoning that shows that the difference is one of all or nothing, where to assume the absolute is to assume away everything.

Going beyond absolutes, we will explore infinity in a new way, demonstrating that the absence of absolutes rounds off infinity or "flattens" it to a specific but changing degree.

Among our conclusions we will briefly address a core issue of economics to demonstrate the ethical existence of "adverse demand" and that the value of one's currency and the health of the economy are dependent on investing in the equal opportunity of one's fellow human beings and in the natural environment.

Not surprisingly, when deciding on the presence or absence of something as fundamental as an absolute, we can say something about the fundamentals of any field where the qualifier of "absolute" might make a difference. Arriving in this way at the tangle of relativistic thinking that bedevils the foundations of every field — when you get down to underlying philosophy — by clearing away absolutism, we can avoid some confusion arising from the dependency between relativism and absolutism, a dependency that shows up even in the more subtle arguments of the relativists. One result will be that when we hear the word "absolute," we can listen for the relativistic echoes associated with it and find a way through with a better sense of direction.

We will not be traveling every river in every region of philosophy, down every forest path and canoe carry into the backcountry, however compelling the view. Some fiction will be provided instead, and some essays on how this philosophy relates to some key aspects of the current mixed-up state of philosophical affairs, one that has weakened — even with the best of intentions — the legacy of the Enlightenment.

Clearly I am stirring the pot with this introduction. This book is only meant to be a preliminary report on one of the first turns in the process of stirring up a subject that should become even more relevant, in as wide a variety of ways as can be connected by thinking asymmetrically — that is, where nothing is absolutely final and everything is connected, not in every way, but in specific and characteristic ways that are often repeated but never absolutely exactly. So even though we will only touch on a range of subjects, we will have to be sufficiently specific to make contact between them at such a fundamental level.

The relevance of asymmetry is one of survival — if to think symmetrically in absolutes is to invite destruction in ways large and small. Indeed, the Transformation Proof demonstrates why true symmetry and asymmetry are mutually exclusive. So the question of personal balance arises as well; balance in the absence of absolutes brings along its own ethics to bridge the ancient divide between what is and what ought to be, a disconnect that has been considered by many thinkers to be absolute. We will discover that absolutes, while haunting relativism as effectively as they bolster absolutism (or objectivism), allow for the randomizing attitude that "anything goes" while usurping a better understanding of true balance.

One of the main problems for humans in attempting to find a standard of behavior is the question of how to find even a shred of ground outside one's subjective consciousness — some locale like the one Plato hoped for "outside the cave," where the view would qualify as objective and worthy of respect as being true. Although Plato framed the question in absolute terms, there is a tremendous amount of sympathy for this quest throughout the ages. We will revisit the question, not as one of being inside and then outside a "cave of illusion," but rather of "waterfall and pond," where a river of asymmetry can be deduced, one that speaks to us from within our skins of places beyond.

In this process of unfolding an idea asymmetrically — not being one that is approached absolutely directly, but in a more roundabout, natural manner — the first story we would like to introduce is the generic maze tale. As one reads a maze tale, one tends to identify with the ways it can be translated and resonates with one's own experience. The basic structure of the ups and downs of life is clearly present. But there is an endless variety of possible experiences to be had along these well-worn pathways. The following trek is extremely spare and based on a typical design found on ancient coins from the island of Crete.

One of the most universal symbols on Earth, mazes, including labyrinths and spirals, appear on standing stones of megalithic sites such as Newgrange in Ireland, on the floors of cathedrals such as the one at Chartres in France, and Native American art. Mathematicians express them as fractals. Their intrinsic asymmetry allows for feedback and cybernetic liveliness. The continuity of these designs over time, like eddies in the river, reflects a diversity of ideas, many of which are lost, but which have carried forward a basic structure with an opportunity for more applications of new ideas. We will carry on with this theme of the maze, with gratitude for a tradition that allows us, even in spite of itself, to embark on an ever-changing adventure.

But we will try to avoid travel by unicycle; such elevated symmetry requires a degree of specialization and skill that we gladly enjoy as spectacle.

## 2. The Maze Tale

Sire, there is no royal road to geometry.

—Euclid of Alexandria to Ptolemy I,
according to Proclus

As you approach the center, expectations are raised, but if the balance is lacking you are crushed as it turns out to be a rung in the maze where you move on, around and out, not to the center but towards the middle of the rungs! You now have the opportunity to find balance anew and continue on the journey. As the Book of Changes, the I Ching, says often: "perseverance furthers."

Then a leap of hope arises again when the rung curves round and inwards — towards not just the middle — and, yes, inwards, inwards once more towards the imagined goal. The center is in sight just over that hill or beyond the valley —

But no! The turn goes the other way. You travel out once more, this time to the very edge, way out on the outer rung of the maze. You might think that this is indeed the center, for you might gather perspective on the maze as a whole, whereas at the center it might be difficult to see the whole. You might also delude yourself as to whether you have truly arrived just by being on the journey. Then again, isn't the mission, the quest, what it's all about? You move on and on.

Then round the next bend, there it is: the center is before you and before you know it, you are there! Of course, perhaps you might have gone directly in from the start? But that's another story.

# 3. The Ancient Paradox

"Tell me, then,
Who is the potter, pray, and who the pot?"

"Well," answered one, "a potter once was I,
And now my clay with long neglect is dry;
But fill me with the old familiar juice,
Methinks I might recover by and by!"

—*The Rubaiyat of Omar Khayyam*

After having wound the spring with this preamble, the narrator will take a fairly direct route into the heart of the matter. We will encounter the Transformation Proof and the way it unravels a fundamental paradox. This paradox is a problem that has afflicted humanity since long before Heraclitus of Ephesus, who, paraphrased by Plato (and then by the rest of us), said no one can step in the same river twice. As Heraclitus thought everything is changing, he would agree that the same is true of every step along what my mathematical friends have referred to as the *rungs* of the mazes in the wanton green.

Why "rungs" and not, for example, "pathways"? You can count rungs like the units of a number line, and yet they are not rings, rings being too symmetrical to make a maze. But these rungs are also *not* rungs. They are rungs when viewed more edge-on from the outside. But the rungs become one path as you walk it. Here we encounter an intimation of that ancient paradox that can be summed up in the question: winding labyrinth or maze of choices?

Right away this labyrinthine pattern presents us with the symmetry of paradox. If it is a true paradox and its symmetry is pure, we will never find the way out. It would be just as though the rungs were perfectly closed rings. And this book, as the reader will discover, would never have been written. So where is the paradox of labyrinth within maze or maze in labyrinth?

## 3. The Ancient Paradox

The famous labyrinth of Knossos on Ancient Crete is a mythical maze, where one could easily get lost by making "poor choices." Down that path one would encounter the Minotaur. Nowadays we often distinguish a labyrinth from a maze, as being a continuous, winding path with no choice. But then, the path one actually takes inside a maze of choices is itself a continuous labyrinth. Are we doomed by the Fates to find the Minotaur? And what of the choice (if any) to enter the labyrinth at all? Isn't that a station in the complex maze of life's choices?

Some traditional turf mazes of Shakespeare's England are still around, being recut and walked time and again; mazes of many kinds are gaining some popularity in the world at large. In keeping with the Transformation Proof, towards which we are pre-ambling, where asymmetry is the wedge that pries open every paradox, we will choose just the word "maze" to include all varieties of the labyrinthine enigma.

The familiar mystery of paradox is also summed up in the French saying, *plus ça change, plus c'est la même chose*. Taken literally, "the more things change the more they remain the same" would describe an impossible self-contradiction where things would be actively immobile. But in everyday speech, we are not being asked to be so obvious or absolute. Although there is some fatalism in this expression of repetition without progress, surely the hope of learning something from experience is also somewhere in the depths. So it's a question of how we should understand changes past, present, and future. Oftentimes a good paradox is pleasing to behold, even as a certain resignation echoes with the sentiment. But it's a complicated feeling.

At one extreme the saying does seem to allow for a novel sort of eternal conservatism where nothing changes at all, while at the other extreme the changes are so fast that nothing is really ever new — or even possible, so jaded are we. Optimistically, we are encouraged by this old aphorism to find true value in the balance of change, so that when we find value and quality, we can progress. But, plus ça change...

Sir Isaac Newton, Gottfried Leibniz, and subsequent builders of the calculus pored over some specialized aspects of the paradox of change. Of particular interest was the concept of "instantaneous change," which we will consider asymmetrically in this book. Fortunately they did not have to solve that fundamental question in order to obtain a workable math that transformed our world.

Today the meaning of change has arisen at the heart of one of the key elections in the history of the United States. As we thread once more the maze of change, we will find some important clues as to what this change might mean.

The history of philosophical thinking about paradox, self-contradiction, and change has so many complexities that we can easily forget that this reality is familiar to us all on an everyday basis. To stay fresh, while faced with the challenge of considering such a deeply explored and ephemeral subject, we will not further encumber ourselves with the weight of its history, but proceed instead somewhat as though we are meeting it for the first time. For it can too easily take on a hypnotic and serpentine appearance. Indeed, change has been worshipped in caves and labyrinths, as though the paradoxes can be scattered like demons by faith. But our purpose here is not to weave illusions, at least not unconsciously. Nor do I want to underestimate the depth of the illusions surrounding this subject. I suspect that it has found its way into some of our deepest cultural programming, providing meanwhile opportunities for fiction. So although the way on offer here to understand this maze of reasoning is not as complicated as many more familiar complexities, it requires repeated application for lack of habit. We need to build it a habitat. In the process, we have decided to front load this book with the unifying logic in the next four chapters and then develop the consequences in the tales and essays that follow, as much as to say, have a look at this reasoning (Chapter 7 is a useful summary), and when you have delved into the theme, come back and check it out again in the environment of the book as a whole.

Far from being the end or even the beginning of the story, the logic of the Transformation Proof is like tying a new kind of knot to coordinate a whole network of ideas, the language and philosophy of asymmetry. In the way that a knot allows us to get a better idea of how the rope behaves, our proof shows us a fundamental continuity of meaning. Basically, if it cannot be knotted, then you can't call it a rope. This knot shows us a rope with strands like stem cells, with signals of creative potential. This is a language so natural that it is encountered again and again by nature's creatures, which are instinctively attuned to its broadcast — whether or not they encounter the knot! But if we who have assembled these stories and essays were to leave the Transformation Proof to the end, you might wonder all the while how such consequences could ever be proved, and your skepticism could justifiably increase. By the time you reached the proof, if you ever got there, it would very likely be regarded with a baleful eye, possibly with good reason.

Everyone's shared asymmetric habitat is such that nobody ever got this first time round, if only because there is no absolute first time, according to the Transformation Proof itself. So if it happens to speak to you right away and make sense, it is most certainly because you have been working up to this expression of it in some way already, as we have been doing in this preamble. We are all here in the maze. Now for the story with the proof — after a brief introduction of the following definitions.

# 4. Definitions of Asymmetry

That the universe is lopsided appears to be critical
for our existence.
It is also perhaps the greatest of the outstanding mysteries.

—Frank Close, *Lucifer's Legacy: The Meaning of Asymmetry*

Asymmetry is defined by Webster's *New World College Dictionary* as "lack of symmetry." Webster's definition of *symmetry* is "similarity of form or arrangement on either side of a dividing line or plane," and "correspondence of opposite parts in size, shape, and position."

At first sight, symmetry is easy to find wherever we look. Your window might be a rectangle divided into four panes — though each pane will frame a different part of the view out the window. So the view through the symmetrical window would be asymmetrical. Technically speaking, symmetry is often described as happening where some operation leaves the object in question unchanged in some way — even though that changing operation is connected to it. Symmetry and paradox often go hand in hand.

## 4. Definitions of Asymmetry

The window has symmetry about the vertical axis, for example, dividing it in two. This can be described as a reflection about the vertical axis or a translation where the two left-hand panes would look the same if they were slid over somehow to replace the right-hand panes. Of course we know that such a theoretical operation in practice may not work out so simply. The pane would have to be removed, and the glass of one pane might be cut to fit exactly the original square in the window and might not fit so well if reused to replace the opposite square, especially with some warping and weathering of the frame. So although "symmetry," loosely speaking, once we start looking for it, can be sighted just about everywhere, from the flowers to the leaves to the blades of grass to the sharpest technologies, when we take a closer look — or when we stand back — things can get complicated and less than ideally symmetrical.

There are many handy categories of symmetry that we learn about in math class. For example, we will be referencing the symmetry of repetition or translation, which one finds in a ladder or a repeating series, where any rung or unit appears to be translatable to the next position without having to undergo any change. There is point symmetry at the center of a circle, where we set the point of our compass in order to draw the circumference. The point is symmetrical as it does not seem to change in any essential way — even as the compass needle turns in the paper. Then there is the symmetry of a flat surface that does not appear to have any variations. Wherever we are on the surface, it is the same as any other place with respect to any other place (or even with respect to some coordinates). The surface is entirely homogeneous. This raises more than a few questions and paradoxes right away — like where are we? Are we anywhere at all?

There are symmetrical equations in math that are used in what has been called a "language of symmetry" or group theory. The question remains as to whether any of this "symmetry" is really sufficiently symmetrical to merit the term, even — or especially — when it is in the psyche of the mathematician in the guise of "pure math."

In order to address these and other related questions, we will qualify symmetry with such terms as "absolute," "pure," or "perfect" and use them in this way interchangeably for variety. We will consider "absolute" or "perfect" symmetry as having such uniformity as to give rise to no differences, changes, or variations, whether through a given operation or not. Anything else is asymmetric.

# II. Changes

> Not only for strength, but for beauty, the poet must, from time to time, travel the logger's path and the Indian's trail, to drink at some new and more bracing fountain of the Muses, far in the recesses of the wilderness.
>
> —Henry David Thoreau
> "Chesuncook," *The Maine Woods*

# 5. I Revisit the Transformation Proof

> If nature should turn out not to respect this symmetry, then everything that we understand, our theories, and the sum of all experience would require us to go back to the drawing-board.
>
> —Frank Close, *Lucifer's Legacy: The Meaning of Asymmetry*

To his sudden question about symmetry, I replied that you have to start somewhere, and I think the easiest place to start is with the question of absolute finality. If you can show that absolute finality makes no sense, then the paradox of absolute symmetry — or absolute anything, for that matter — makes no sense either. I tried to relax in the traffic of the approaching town, mindful of the old story of the two guys who ran someone over while discussing awareness.

"Yes? Continue."

My mind went blank. Then Fortune smiled. "If an object is absolutely final, it cannot change at all, ever. It cannot even change from one part of the object to another, okay?"

There was a pause. "Right—"

"It might be hard to imagine such a thing, but the main thing is that it can't change at all, ever. It's final."

"Right."

"So let's take an Object A. If Object A is in a relationship with Object B, and A is absolutely final, then B must be absolutely final as well. There would be perfect symmetry between them with respect to their finality. The question is why."

Again my mind went blank. And there was traffic. I drove on. Then I remembered the only other time I had been asked to summarize the reasoning — what had I said next? "Here's the thing: If B ever changes, then the relationship between A and B changes.

"If A is in a new relationship, then A has changed in some way.

Something about it has changed — it has the new characteristic of being in that changed relationship.

"Now get this: every part of it has acquired that new characteristic. Every part is new! Does this mean that just a slight change in B changes A completely? A would no longer be A. If it can be completely transformed and still be A, we have a paradox. If slight changes cause absolute changes all the time, where are we?"

"Yep."

"How do we recognize it as A anymore? Is there some part of A that is unaffected by the change in the relationship, some essential core, or some level or degree of its characteristics that can remain untouched by the change? What about its overall appearance? In fact, unless it changed absolutely and completely, some part would seem to remain unchanged. Can A change absolutely and still be the same? Can anything remain outside a context of change? We'll definitely have to get back to that one later. Especially as there are relationships in math between, say x, y, and z, where x and y will change while z seems to remain constant."

"Yep."

I took a few moments to recover my sense of direction, so we wouldn't get lost in the traffic. Then I struggled on, "The main thing for now is that in order for A to remain absolutely unaffected by the change in the relationship, A must be disconnected from the relationship. That is to say, there must be no relationship. If there is any relationship at all, then any change in the relationship will involve a corresponding change in the character of A. A cannot logically be totally disconnected from the change and still be in the relationship. This goes for any part of Object A.

"So if there had been from the start any part of what we thought was Object A that was somehow not in the relationship, we must discard it. For the purposes of this reasoning, we might as well refer to that part of A that is in the relationship as A and the other part as something else. Likewise, any part that *might* remain unchanged is not a part of Object A."

"Yep. Talk about reductionism. You can logically reduce down to your most basic fact of a change somewhere and the reasoning will grow back up from there. It's the logic of a seed in the ground."

Not having understood what he was talking about and for fear of losing the thread, I just kept going. "So every aspect of A would be affected by a change in B. The one cannot remain final if the other does not. Therefore, if one side of the relationship is final the other must be so as well. And there would be perfect symmetry between them with respect to their finality. So that deals with the original question of why either A or B must be final if the other is."

I paused for effect and put the gear stick into fifth. Then I realized I was being tested. Perhaps I could relax into student mode and proceed to answer as best I could. "Now the question is, what could avoid being in a relationship with something that changes?"

"Right! If nothing can, then — since change is a fact — nothing is absolutely final.

"Furthermore, we could then say that any object that is absolutely final cannot be in a relationship with any object that *might* change. The mere possibility of a change in B means that A cannot be absolutely final and unable to change, ever. The potential allows the open-endedness."

I took his excitement as a sign that I had passed at least part of the test. He continued. "Even the possibility of the slightest change in one side of a relationship preempts the possibility of anything else in the relationship being absolutely final.

"This goes to the question of the identity of objects, people, and things of all kinds, imagined or otherwise, and of course even the open-endedness itself. We haven't defined what we mean by an object. But if this reasoning can be generally applied, in the absence of absolute finality, the identity or character of anything we might consider or dream up is not absolute. We can't be boxed in like that.

"And in the absence of the final state of absolute immobility, all things are in a state of change, but not absolutely. Absolute change would be another absolutely final condition — and the absolutes we are considering are absolutely absolute, and that means final. So there's a balance of change—"

Silence.

"Of course," I ventured, "there is still the question of whether a thing can be absolutely unrelated to something else, or is there?—" I was losing the thread in the traffic.

Abruptly he changed the subject.

Later he surprised me with this: "But you have just shown that no object can ever remain absolutely unrelated."

"I did?"

"Yep, as long as *anything* in a potentially changing relationship is never finalized completely, nothing at all will ever be able to escape a relationship with it absolutely. Any instance of perpetual open-endedness guarantees open-endedness everywhere. A relationship is everywhere inevitable, no matter to what degree any other particular object is finalized, removed, or tries to close itself off. There's no escaping the open-endedness of the other side of the relationship."

I could see that I was now going to fail to keep up with him. He was finding my limits on this arcane subject to date. I was becoming concerned, because I thought I had had it figured prior to his arrival. I thought I had done my homework; it was important for the meeting that was to take place.

"Substitute anything you like for A and B and your reasoning remains true," he continued enthusiastically. As far as I was concerned he could have been saying anything at all. I almost hoped his absorption in his favorite subject would disguise my ignorance. "Reduce your object to the slightest changing element, and the whole thing is affected logically."

"Logically?" I asked feebly.

"That's the bottom line that makes sense of what otherwise seems just a paradox."

We drove out of town.

A silence was now accumulating to the point where I was feeling intellectually exposed. He was definitely figuring me out. I took the initiative. "So, assuming there is no escaping the open-endedness, how do we know the open-ended potential to change won't just come to an end? How can you guarantee that it's perpetual?" I pretended I was asking just to refresh my memory of this slippery subject that he seemed already to have grasped — but in my confusion, how could I know if he really knew? Our relationship was changing again.

"Because," he persisted, "there was no absolutely exact beginning. All beginnings are in a current and historical relationship with actual and potential changes. Substitute A for the beginning and B the present. B changes, so A cannot be absolute. The current phenomenon of change in objects guarantees the absence of absolute finality or perfect exactitude anywhere. That's part of the mystery of change. Its reach goes beyond — always, eventually — because all it needs is to be potential change. Current change in B preempts finality in A — no exact beginning."

## 5. I Revisit the Transformation Proof

"But how do we know the potential is always there?"

"Because it is in a relationship with actual change. It's an unbreakable relationship, to the extent that the potential is part of the very nature of change, its power. Change is like electricity; it has potential and kinetic aspects, in a kind of polarity."

I must have been showing signs of despair, so he tried to come to my rescue. "Getting back to the question you were getting back to — How do we know we aren't stopped by the paradox of every part of A being changed beyond recognition by a single degree of change in its relationship with B, because no part of A can remain unaffected or unchanged, effectively changing everything in A? The short answer is that the power of change breaks through the paradox."

"How?" I reminded myself that I was still in the driver's seat, at least literally, and took refuge in the priority of survival on the road.

"To see how it works, peel away every aspect of A that might seem to remain unchanged until you get to that essential aspect that just changes, what you defined above as simply A. Now we can ask what that means — *just to change, only change.* Does it change absolutely? If so, then as soon as a change begins to take place, A becomes something else by disconnecting absolutely. The change is so instantaneous that, as you said, there is no process of change whatsoever, to the point were it would be a self-contradiction even to call it 'change.'

"But let's complicate things a little more and say that A is mysteriously transformed absolutely into what we will call 'Object C.' The transformation places it outside that relationship between A and B (where even a potential change in B allows for a potential change in A and vice versa). We now have the situation where C has something in common with those 'false' aspects of A that were 'peeled away' because they apparently never had any relationship with B. C *never* had a relationship with B, because, as we said, being completely disconnected means no relationship at all, ever. And if C never had a relationship with B, it *never* had a relationship with A, because it could not have a relationship with A without being related to B, with which it has none."

Then there followed this exchange:

Me: "But why does C no longer have a relationship with B?"

Him: "Because B is related to A and C is absolutely disconnected from A. If it were related to B it would be related to A. So it can't be related to B."

Me: "Okay, but B has changed, say to D."

Him: "That just adds a step beyond the relationship between A and B; C cannot be related to D because it would be related via B to A."

"Another way to look at it is that in order for A to transform absolutely into C, C must have an absolutely final characteristic as far as the transformation goes — the transformation without process is where C came from entirely. C was entirely the result of an absolute disconnect from its previous condition of being A. So C is absolutely final where that break happens. There is no process of change. As we have established, an object that might change (B) cannot be related to an object that is absolutely final."

Me: "Okay, but A no longer exists—"

Him: "You mean A *never* existed! Sure, there is the fiction of a relationship between A and B, where A has changed magically, for the purpose of the proof by contradiction. We are assuming an instantaneous change from A to C, so as to reveal how that plays out in a context of change. But the absolute transformation blows all history and everything away, except for itself.

"The magical transformation assumes the absence of a process in the change from A to C. In order to discover the would-be annihilation involved in such magic, we can still imagine Objects A, B and C. In other words, even as A instantaneously becomes C, A is still something to be reckoned with. Also, even with A out of the picture, like I said, B still has the characteristic of change that connected it to A, and C cannot relate to that.

"What we discover is that the mysterious transformation from A to C does logically means that A never existed, because it means that C is so absolutely disconnected from A that to become C denies the past condition of being A. This would also deny the past relationship between A and B. So B was never B as such, with all the characteristics of being related to A. And so on and so forth with D or anything connected to it. We can infer that any absolute transformation is mutually exclusive with any environment of change, and that to assume such a transformation assumes the absence of all other existence, assumes it all away.

"When we started out on this proof we said that being completely disconnected means no relationship at all, ever. We were referring to C being disconnected from A, but we can now make this statement in a more universal way. Any object that disconnects absolutely or changes without process has no relationship with anything. This makes it mutually exclusive with anything else. Either it alone exists or the world as we know it exists. They cannot inhabit the same context."

That was the nitty-gritty. This was where he got all his seemingly flat statements. He proceeded to lay out a few more. "The result of all this is that if change is absolute where A is concerned, as soon as there is an Object B with any potential to change, there never was any possibility of an Object A. The very conditions that would set up a relationship between A and B where B might change are preempted. No aspect of A would be possible in such a relationship. The chance of B changing preempts the chance of A happening. For A to happen it would require the possibility of something of A continuing to change during a change in B."

His having to remind me seemed to mean I had failed the test in some obscure way, except for the fact, I reminded myself, that I was in such good company in society, in the world in general, that it hardly mattered. In fact the global implications for us all reinvigorated my interest and banished any lingering guilt of the "dog-ate-my-homework" variety.

"Therefore," he concluded with another inference, "to say that an Object A can change absolutely is to say that the object never happened at all. This is the proof by contradiction, the Transformation Proof."

\* \* \*

But it was only the beginning, as I listened for more. "If we want to assume some absolute attribute in the nature of change, we are left with the absolute condition of symmetrically final objects in a world of change where the absolute finality cannot relate to any of the changes they are related to by being in the same world — an impossible paradox."

"So what it means, 'just to change,'" I chimed in, as though I had been with him all along, "is that change can't be in any way absolute, so any relationship where change is involved cannot involve an absolute." After a pause, I inadvertently said, "Aha!"

"Yep, that's the power of the open-endedness. What we get is some kind of balancing effect, a breaking symmetry before absolute extremes that never actually happen, because they are preempted by the disintegration of the near-symmetry. Change is what actually does happen, in the absence of absolutes, whether we like it or not. Things can't get to the absolute of discontinuous, instantaneous transformation on the one hand, nor do they remain absolutely constant on the other. If things did get to such finality on either hand, we'd have pure symmetry in logic. But we don't, thank goodness, not any more than we do in the rest of nature — nature being proved to be connected to these words. But that's another story—

"It's as though change allows for the creation of a whole new object that still looks substantially the same — change includes sameness as part of its process. The aspects of A that we 'peeled away,' when we assumed, for the purpose of the argument by contradiction, that they were not changing, those peelings were parts of A after all. Change would not exist without the sameness; that phase is part of its nature — the phase of potential. That's how every part of an object can be affected by the change in a relationship without otherwise appearing to change. No absolute template is required. The sameness is refreshed throughout by changing relationships and potentials showing up to take part in the action. Otherwise there could be no seeds and no growth. No object could ever happen. Amazing power of creativity."

"Creativity?" I gulped for air. Somewhat overwhelmed.

"This is not a matter of redefining change to include its opposite. We underestimate the power of change when we think it only does the obvious by bringing about something different. Change is also endurance. To say that something either changes or it doesn't is to invest the nature of change with an absolute and build in a paradox. Change breaks potential paradoxes, where a thing seems not to change while still being in a relationship where nothing is left unchanged. Change is by nature a symmetry breaker.

"In order to sustain itself, the paradox would require absolute unchanging finality — like an absolute ideal or template, whereby the object can be recognized again and again, even as its relationships change every aspect of it, including all recognizable characteristics. The paradox requires absolute separations between parts changed and unchanged, whereas real change requires overlapping degrees and open-endedness, vagueness that can sometimes lapse into fiction and mythology where it can be specific again. Without the vagueness there are no degrees of precision. That's the truth. Vagueness is just another degree of precision.

"The paradox gets us nowhere, logically or otherwise. It has to give

## 5. I Revisit the Transformation Proof

way to the logic that makes sense and provides further insights into the nature of change. Change has to break all paradoxes and symmetries before they happen, because it has an asymmetric leading edge, like a seed in the ground. The relationship of that logic builds or grows with every change throughout all parts, including the ones that appear not to change. The relationships also recede. Change is full of illusion. It can take you places you have never imagined. I call that a kind of creativity.

"Of course we could just confine this to the way the language is used to reason. But I think the asymmetric leading edge could unravel the whole fabric of life, so to speak, with explanations and understanding, and refresh it! All the way from within the reasoning itself, out into the physical universe of which it's a part. The pervasive asymmetry shows up in all sorts of places, including this new logic of yin and yang, the polarity of change.

"So the answer is no."

"No what?" I asked.

"No — nothing can remain unrelated to change, remain outside a context of change."

We turned north, heading for the Old Canada Road.

"So why didn't you tell me this from the start?"

## 6. The Gnome and the Onion

Every narrative has mazelike sequencing. In the story of how I became aware of this generalization, it took many trips through the maze before I could get a balance on the identity of the "seed" or essence of the maze — or of any other object. In order to get a feel for the problems surrounding this issue of changing relationships, you are invited to join me, Samuel, in retracing some of my steps on this already well-worn path, visiting anew some old dead ends along the way.

I really thought I had this thing nailed down. I figured that any potential change in B potentially changed every aspect of A, requiring A to remain open-ended. It had to. Any aspect left out of the potential changes was not in the relationship between A and B. I was closing in on the center of the maze.

Then suddenly A disappeared. As though I had taken a hairpin bend in the road, every aspect of A had changed, nothing was left unchanged — it had changed completely.

Even if initially it had changed only somewhat, eventually it had shed all that was not truly defined as A, and the remaining essential A was all changed, every aspect — at least, that was how I imagined it at this point in the maze.

What I had recognized as A was gone, leaving an unrecognizable chimera — a beast of another kind. All because of the slightest change somewhere. Touchy critter!

I gazed around the room and beheld the ancient paradox. It seemed to be everywhere. The room was now visibly a section of the maze of my repeated attempts to understand, so involved it seemed in the logic of change.

There was the table I had made of driftwood pulp logs. I had taken a chainsaw to rip them lengthwise and used a nice old hand plane on the rough inside surface. The legs were reinforced with natural wooden knees of trees long since fallen into the lakes and rivers of Maine. The half logs were held in sequence, like a wooden xylophone, their flat sides up, their semicircular sides down along oak branches also ripped and planed then connected to the legs with those natural knees, in memory of the way the trees had grown them.

I collect interesting wood for boat building and furniture. If some of the pieces ever come together as a part of a boat or a piece of furniture, it always seems to be part of some greater unknown object. Each small log along the table is a standard four feet long, once cut to match the long-gone requirements of the paper mills. Was my table a part of some greater plan outside the machinations of the mill? Many of these logs, usually four to six inches in diameter, had got stuck on their way down the Kennebec River, heading for the pulp vats. Every summer more pulp logs mysteriously reappear and come to rest on the riverbank as driftwood.

So there was the table, along with its history, now a piece of some maze or other and some rhythm of life. My logic had not made it disappear. It was no chimera to me. But it was now a paradox because ancient logic said it should have disappeared or perhaps never have appeared in the first place. Each piece was still there, in some very obvious way unchanged. Should I discard those obvious pieces after all the work in putting them together to make a table? Was the only way to truly achieve the essence of the table to remove each unchanged component — to effectively destroy it? No matter how much I might clap and wave my hands and play the magus with a magic wand, no change in wand B would cause any obvious aspect of the table to change. Yet there was surely some relationship between my hands and the obviously sturdy table I had made. My logic said that any change in Object B must cause a change in every aspect of Object A.

In my own story, I watched the supposed center of the maze disappear as I headed out into the middle of the rungs, trying to understand this thing. I had "nailed" a table together with wooden dowels, nothing more. Was there any essence to this wooden object?

I paced up and down the room, went outside into the garden to look at the tomatoes and think.

Over where the mint was growing wild and standing a yard high, one of the cats was curled up in a wheel of fur, nestled in there like a sleeping maze of peace and comfort, a touch of mythology in the garden. Essence of cat.

I didn't know where I was in my story of the maze, which might be one way of describing what it's like in the middle of the rungs, I thought. I tried to break the reasoning down again:

Dead-end thought sequence #1: After a change in B, essential Object A is changed, leaving *nothing of itself unchanged* — to change absolutely and basically disappear, leaving something else in its place, or maybe even nothing left at all. Either it was now absolutely there or it wasn't — an all-or-nothing sort of thing.

So Object A would in some way have an absolute, essential characteristic. But what sort of an absolute changes? Isn't that a self-contradiction? Aren't absolutes supposed to be final?

Perhaps not always. But if they are not final, doesn't that mean there can be no absolute or complete transformations? Without that finality, how could anything finally begin to change? No essential aspect of any object could even begin to show any really definite change without an absolute beginning somewhere. I could not have planed a single shaving off the essential pulp log, whatever that was. Paradoxes and more paradoxes!

Maybe the middle of the rungs is paradoxically a good symbol for the center of the maze? Could this be the true meaning of the quest: just keep going, even though there is no real direction? "The path is the goal" or something like that? Just drop the mind and go beyond, take the leap of faith, or something? Spring from the maze? What maze? As far as I could tell, it was just as much there as not, while the table, the tomatoes, and my cat in the mint could at the moment be nothing but present and accounted for. If there was an essence to everything, my convoluted path should be able to take me there, I hoped. But in spite of its apparent logical predictability, it seemed to be invisible. Complicated paradox.

The cat looked up, having sensed my rather close attention.

Dead-end thought sequence #2: The absolute characteristic of essential Object A might totally change with the change in B, but at the same time, in a totally unrelated way, it might have remained the same, according to a Platonic template. Would I have to accept that absolutes exist that are totally unrelated to each other? There would be an unchanging, eternal template for essential Object A (forget any discarded, unrelated parts of A for the moment). And there would be an essential Object A that changed absolutely. How could the eternal absolute act as a template for the changing absolute? In some respect they would be entirely different. Paradox. I would have to fake it and just say that the changing stuff is not real — a time-honored tradition — but my cat disagreed. Even illusions are real illusions, I reassured her, and left it at that.

In these two laps of this labyrinth of paradox, I was confronted with a double beast at least: the chimerical, changing absolute essential Object A (of sequence #1) and the bull-solid absolute half-human, half-fantastical Minotaur (of #2, at a stretch), all claiming to be king. What comedy of errors could we make of this? I had to agree with them in a way. Can't we just get one absolute around here! I struggled to keep it together — so to speak. Even my puns were having trouble getting off the ground. I was at a loss for words.

Neither of these was the beast I was looking for. *My* Object A made sense. It did not have parts that were in no relationship to each other while being in a relationship — head of bull and body of man, chimera or whatever. It did not arbitrarily "get real" outside of Plato's imaginary cave of illusion where humans dwelt in bondage.[8] It did not have aspects that could be categorized out of existence while being made a part of the issue — more chimeras, human or otherwise. I was willing enough to make a leap of faith and leave reason behind, but what reason was there to leave? It seemed I had long ago made many leaps and was just trying to find common ground or a place to land, or at least to rest a while. It seemed very odd to me that religions asked for leaps of faith from us rabbits and frogs, or from us monkeys swinging from rung to rung without knowing the why or wherefore. Somehow we had acquired some skill in leaping and swinging, but we sometimes missed. Leap again! we are exhorted.

Again I wondered whether the "middle of the rungs" where I was now hung up somewhere between things was perhaps the actual center and essential meaning of Object A, represented by the maze. A sort of existential and somewhat nauseating place. Or perhaps a golden paradox to grok forever and a day. Yes this was it! And isn't this where the leap of faith is supposed to really happen? Was it happening already? Was I being blessed and too dense to know it? Was this the unearned salvation of Christian lore? Or was I getting a little seasick on so many waves?

Then, I remembered, as though from an echo, that the reasoning says that at some level at least there can be no absolute finality, no absolutes at all. Let's hang onto that level, to this rung, and see where it leads. If B changes, A does change, and change exists. Whew! Nothing that is in a relationship with potential change can be absolutely final. It's still true in some sense, at least logically in a language I can understand. Doesn't understanding matter? I did not try to leap out of the maze as a means of untangling it. I just clung to one side of the ancient paradox — looking over at the question on the other side: Can anything be unrelated to change?

*　*　*

My experience of the center or essence of A had been a misunderstanding, an illusion. Something had disappeared or failed to appear. I had missed something. I had made a mistake. I had unwittingly built in the assumption of an absolute in a way that had me going in circles and skipping to other circles, as though I had been programmed to leap first and ask questions later. This was itself understandable, given the number of questions that arise with the human mind. Whatever allowed us to take hold of the next thing and put one foot in front of the other did not contradict itself by preempting us with a stream of questions that had to be answered first. It had some logical consistency.

To entertain the possibility that I might be wrong was itself a confirmation. I began again to reconstruct the reasoning that kept slipping away. My situation and misunderstanding in the middle of the rungs now seemed appropriate as a metaphor for the way things are. Between the two beasts, I expected to get a clear view of the Alpha Grail soon.

I kept going, refreshed by a sudden turn inward.

Then another turn inward toward the center.

Still no Object A.

Now, with my increasing introspection came what seemed like a turn for the worse, yet again, and I moved out, out onto the outer rung of the five-rung maze.

I began to count them. Were there five? It depended on where I started counting and how I counted the center pathway. This got me out of myself a bit. Sometimes there seemed to be six. Traditionally, there are sometimes said to be seven. In other words, in some indisputable way, Object A (if represented by the maze) was changed by the change in perspective, or in relation to B; that was a basic fact of reason, especially after you stripped off all those unchanging layers down to — what? Something. Whatever it was, it was a manifestation of the nature of change.

Around the next bend, as though shining from over the horizon, Object A was making an appearance like daybreak, where the symmetry of absolutes — like the sun bisected by the horizon — begins to happen. But as it continues, the perfect symmetry is preempted according to the reasoning that in a relationship that might change, all parts remain open-ended. None are sufficiently finalized to conclude a perfect symmetry. True openness preempts us from concluding absolute finality. Open to and from what?

Hanging onto this side of the ancient paradox, the essence of A is asymmetric. Change is asymmetric.

The sun continued to rise in the center of the maze, opening up as I watched from the outer rung. Then it began to look like a black hole at the center of a galaxy — present but not. I stayed and watched, shunning the paradox, in awe of the view, wondering how I could still experience it.

Moving along the outer rung of the maze, I tried to get a balance on this asymmetric understanding, as I began to view the maze as a whole, using it as a means of orientation. Everywhere it was changing, even as it was being itself. If I assumed the absence of absolute finality, it had to continuously become itself, or morph with continuity into some related object. It had to keep up with the changes that kept its integrity; either that, or sort of melt away — but never just vanish. In order to become something else in all the changes, it had to become itself for a while. It seemed magical for a thing to change completely while appearing to remain the same. But in the absence of absolutes it would not change completely, nor would it remain in any way exactly the same; change would have a heartbeat, a circulatory system, where successive changes led to the maintenance of every object. Existence that fell short of either stasis or of absolutely radical, random and chaotic change must have a beat — as it bounces off the impossibilities of either pole ever being achieved.

But as I moved round towards the bottom of the maze, the path seemed to disappear. What if an absolute could coexist with change? What if change itself could be absolute?

The suspicion had returned. If an object could change instantaneously into something else — then what? It would also be true that absolute finality could inhabit a context of change, as is commonly accepted today: Was I so far out on the edge, coming to the end of the last round, that I would now just drift out, away from the maze? Was I drifting back into the dead-end thought sequences above? And was I leaving society? Friends? Relationships? Was that how I was changing up here on the edge of the North Woods? Unable to see the forest for the trees, with nothing but slogans and sayings? A postmodern remnant, about to return to city headquarters?

Yet again, with the help of tangible examples like the driftwood table, I peeled away every aspect of A that might seem to remain unchanged until I got to that essential aspect that just changes because B changes, what I had defined as "simply A." Again I asked what this means — *just to change, only change.*

To change with absolute finality might not be such a logical contradiction, after all, if the change were by nature an absolute finality, an unmediated, instantaneous, transformation from being Object A into being Object C. An intuitive truth of nature — something perhaps supernatural — meant to supplement and somehow assimilate our logic. So what if one day, for no reason, the sun never rose again? To date, our science has not been able to rule it out.

Can A change absolutely with such finality? Then the words of a friend came back to me: "If so, then as soon as a change begins to take place, A becomes something else by disconnecting absolutely. The change is so instantaneous that there is no *process* of change whatsoever — to the point were it would be a self-contradiction even to call it 'change.'"

In case this had begun to sound like nothing but words, he had decided to "complicate" the thing, as he put it, and assume that A is mysteriously, absolutely, and instantly transformed into what we will call "Object C." Then he gave me the proof by contradiction, by assuming the magical transition. How did it go?

The absolute transformation places Object C outside that relationship between A and B. We now have the situation where C has something in common with those "false" aspects of A that were peeled away and discarded because they apparently had never had any relationship with B. They had never changed when B changed, so they couldn't be in that relationship; remaining absolutely unchanged meant that they have an aspect of absolute finality. A is stripped down to its essential nature and changes miraculously into C. The absolute disconnect of this "change" means that C also shares that aspect of absolute finality.

And neither did C ever have a relationship with B, because, as we said, being completely disconnected means no relationship at all, ever, with *anything related to A*. So C never had a relationship with A after all. And, as we said, if C never had a relationship with A, it never had a relationship with B, because it could not have a relationship with B without being related to A, with which it has none. In other words, if A were itself, A could not be itself, so nor could it relate to another Object B that might change. End of proof. It makes no sense and goes nowhere to assume that any change can be absolute and unmediated. The mediation cannot in any way be absolutely final. And this mediation is a connecting object in itself. Absolute finality is mutually exclusive with change.

I'm paraphrasing some of the conversation with my friend, not to get lost by substituting too many alternative words. So one result of all this, he had said, is that if change is absolute where A is concerned, as soon as there is an Object B with any potential to change, there never was any possibility of such a mysterious Object A. The very conditions or *context* that would set up a relationship between this instantaneously changing Object A and Object B, where B might change, are preempted. No aspect of this Object A would be possible in such a relationship. The chance of B changing preempts the chance of this mysterious Object A happening. For Object A to happen it would require the possibility of something of A continuing during a change in B. "If we want to assume some absolutely final attribute in the nature of change, we are left with the absolute condition of symmetrically final objects in a world of change where the absolute finality cannot relate to any of the changes they are related to by being in the same world — an impossible paradox."

So, I had said, what it means, just to change, is that change can't be in any way absolute, and the relationship between A and B cannot be absolute either, in a changing context. Change cannot happen if there is an absolute involved in the process and its relationships. If an object tries to remain forever unchanged while another might change, the attempted absolute finality must fail. There are no absolute essences.

There are two mutually exclusive worlds: one ruled by the conditions assumed for the purposes of the Transformation Proof (and where A and B can exist in a relationship of pure symmetry, each having an absolutely final aspect to repeat exactly) and the other is the real world of asymmetric change.

I had written some notes when we had got to our destination. I misplaced them. Then I found them, filed away somewhere. Now I'm writing this down, and of course this isn't the exact way my friend had said it, word for word. In order to get to this point where I could reliably get it straight, I had had to go through the maze over and over. This is the story. My friend's name is Rolo, by the way. He had gone to visit one of the ancient Indian camp sites. I remained here by the brook for obvious reasons. The next time we got together over this proof, I raised the question of the supernatural. Has it escaped the reasoning? I wondered. He suggested we ask Alice.

\* \* \*

A word about proofs: A logical proof is a way to develop understanding of the language and our assumptions. The Transformation Proof helps us to understand what it means to say an object is "absolutely final." We have further developed the language so that when we say something is so absolutely final, we have to say that it is unable to relate to anything like an Object B that might change. The proof makes our language more specific. So we don't say for example that something finally stops and then continues, without being aware that what we really mean is that it sort of stops and then continues. Otherwise, if we don't leave open the logic of our sentence with words that assume a "sort of" along the way, we begin to compound some major errors and confusion down the road, and we lose precision.

Life can certainly be ironic, but not truly paradoxical — a key distinction. By being able to say "sort of" we allow ourselves the opportunity to be highly specific as well.

\* \* \*

The absolute we have been dealing with here is one of finality. Absolute finality is required for a truly instantaneous and unmediated transformation where Objects A and C have nothing in common — the one just "becomes" the other. That is what we were investigating — whether change could happen that way or if it had to be messier and perhaps even more mysterious. Now we have a choice. If we want to use reason, we must also explore change as a phenomenon of continuity without any absolute finalities, like a narrative; whereas if we want absolute divisions of change, we must forego reason at the most fundamental level.

* * *

We must also change the way we traditionally use formal logic, where every statement has an opposite: statement "A" and statement "not-A." When this "classical logic" assumes absolute symmetry between the opposites, it self-contradicts. With such a built-in contradiction, it is difficult and ultimately impossible to explore the relationships between the opposites. If the opposites are assumed to have absolute symmetry and thereby be in perfect opposition, then there is no way to arrive at the opposite from either side of the absolute symmetry of their opposition; the given conditions are absolutely final. No more can be said or done. We saw what happened when we tired to use the reasoning that said A could magically turn into something that was absolutely not-A (being C). We can now say that if there *is* a relationship between opposites, then the opposition is asymmetric, opening up the logic of change.

* * *

This reasoning, by its open-ended nature, can go in a lot of directions — not any direction, as we will see. But it does have endless potential. *Actual* and *potential* change are themselves in a relationship (A and B) where they keep each other open-ended, so the potential to change has no beginning. And this potential cannot be separated from actual change without losing meaning as potential change.

No beginning? Can an object acquire the potential to change? Could this situation where there is no absolute finality have arisen out of one where an absolute finality or beginning existed? This has been covered already by substituting A for an absolute beginning and applying the Transformation Proof. But I found myself asking it again, even so.

All things must already have had the potential to change. Otherwise an object could be absolutely final. You can't have the condition where an absolute A *does* happen for a while and then B has or acquires the potential to change, allowing A to change absolutely out of its absolute condition. Not going to happen — never did — as far as our language is concerned. We will investigate the reach of this language in the chapters to follow.

So our reasoning tells us that change cannot be absolute. And that no absolute can be in a relationship with anything that changes. Change observably exists; absolute finalities do not. The fact that I continued to go over the Transformation Proof in various ways began to answer the question of whether I was becoming too absolutist with the proof. In a most curious way, by being specifically logical it was positively allowing statements to be made without end. Once I realized this I began to leave it alone.

\* \* \*

Instead of spinning out of the end of the maze, I rounded a sharp bend inward, turning into the avenue leading to the center, and Object A appeared like the Holy Grail in all its overflowing layers of complexity before me.

I approached, and it gained the clarity of a specific object, rather than a more generalized, abstract form — I found myself looking at an onion. This is the story. Believe it or not, a gnome with a shovel jumped over one of the rungs I had traveled. His manner of arrival seemed offhand, almost random, but then he dug a hole and planted the onion. He then saluted and vanished like a particle in an atom. The onion grew a green sprout out of the ground as I watched. Were the layers infinite? What would that mean in this newly rediscovered context, where infinity is rhythmic? What sort of rhythm is open-ended? I assumed it must be rhythmic because of the polarity of change, the heartbeat of potential and active change. If I left this place, how would I return, and when? Could I ever leave completely? No!

That sounded absolute. I shuddered at the thought. Were we about to go round again?

No! Of one thing I was convinced — I could not return absolutely exactly to the same place again. Not with reason intact. I was in no place sufficiently exact to do so. And for that very reason I was able to know this place to this extent — to a far greater extent than any absolute finality would allow (which would be not at all).

I looked at the onion sprouting green shoots in spurts of growth, the way nature rhythmically changes, and imagined it where it lay buried, imagining the open-endedness everywhere throughout its

## 6. The Gnome and the Onion

layers, allowing it to be as it is, "becoming," as they say in the ancient practice of yoga — like the lotus symbol — but never as an absolute, to give an old image a new look. What sort of asymmetric meditation is this? *What would the mystics and worshippers do without their absolutes?* I wondered. Would they be left with music, dancing? I shuddered again at the thought of being too categorical.

As I turned and departed, I was reminded of the waterfall and the pond at the end of the garden, here in Maine, where the still water of the millpond breaks and falls — just at that smooth edge on the old milldam, so smooth and replete with the impending, chaotic falls.

I left refreshed, imagining the invigorating ionized air that goes with a waterfall — and thankful to be in a state where nature is being welcomed all the way back onto main street.

I was beginning again, always a part of rhythmic changes, while the water fell in foaming jazz rhythms in my mind, where the beat is stretched almost to the point of absolute chaos. I returned from the garden.

As I set to work on this writing, I realized that the reasoning through which I had been traveling could only function by being open-ended, even so far as to be in a recurrent relationship with fiction. There was a deep polarity at work, turning the millwheel of reason; the mechanical logic lived. I needed to know more about it. Why are reason and narrative so entwined?

\* \* \*

The impossibility of absolutely generalizing on Object A, the grail, the onion, or any other specific thing, imagined or otherwise, kept coming home to me as the Transformation Proof opened up. The essential character of every object permeated whatever it turned out to be — all layers of the onion had that essential "onion-ness" in various ways. If another object was in question, I would have to go with that and describe it accordingly, and differently, right down to the point of leaving well enough alone or perhaps being at a loss for words. Generalize? Universalize? How?

Sometimes it's good to leave things unsaid; when you stop trying to nail it all down, things can start to make sense. A few words might even fill up with meaning, might even overflow with it — even to excess!

But hadn't I generalized by saying you can't generalize on any object? Or by saying earlier that change cannot be absolute? I was heading back into that rung of the maze. Absolutes do not exist? Hadn't I inadvertently used a universal absolute? What is it to say it's impossible to generalize?

I thought back on the way the seed reflects the maze through the nature of change, whereby the object is refreshed by its essence and its essence is redefined. Wasn't it possible to make a general statement about all the tomatoes in the garden, for example, and have that particular remark be a one-off event in a sequence of language — an event, an object in itself, unique, while being in a web of changing relationships, refreshed before ever becoming absolute? It needn't be the absolute gospel truth on those tomatoes. Couldn't this be applied to any generalization? To say absolutes do not exist is not to use an absolute. It identifies a universe of complexity. In order to generalize, we must realize that we are really just leaving off being more specific, leaving a loose end — the very refutation of absolute finality and universal absolutes. So the generalization is all the more true by virtue of its specific relationships. *It's just another degree of specificity*, without which the wide spectrum of precision would be lost. The whole maze seemed to resonate, and I was on yet another rung than I had feared, as though I had leapt right over that rung and into mythology.

Do Absolutes exist? I could now confidently answer the question with a resounding NO, a negative with waves unfolding with new significance connected to new ways of understanding why it is true. These unfolding patterns told the story of the myth of absolutes.

# 7. Unpacking the Transformation Proof, Step by Step

We know there is asymmetry, observable in nature. How do we know it is everywhere to the exclusion of any pure symmetry? Here's another look at the Transformation Proof, step by step.

1. Let's assume a perfectly symmetrical Object S (maybe pretend it's a box) — alone, all by itself.
2. Next, imagine we now have a relationship between Object S and some asymmetrical Object A — perhaps a broken box.
3. As a result, pristine Object S can no longer be defined as being absolutely symmetrical and alone.
4. Because it is now an Object S that is in association with asymmetrical Object A; together, they form an asymmetric unity.
5. The character of S has changed by association with A.
6. The identity of S has changed.
7. The symmetry of S is in some respect broken, fractured, altered.
8. In fact, any aspect — including any physical part — of Object S we choose to observe will be in a relationship (however indirect) with asymmetric Object A and will therefore lose its pure, absolute symmetry as an object, material or otherwise.
9. The asymmetric change subtly and not-so-subtly penetrates to all parts and aspects of Object S.
10. The assumed Object S in association with Object A is now something other than the self-contained, exclusive purity it once possessed.
11. Even so, Object S observably maintains an identity in the relationship.

12. The identity of Object S is changed but not annihilated, because asymmetry is open-ended and cannot be absolutely, symmetrically pure and final, closed off.
13. Object S can be changed but not absolutely, when it becomes asymmetric in the relationship.
14. Now, this relationship between the two objects cannot both happen and simultaneously not happen.
15. By the definition of absolute symmetry, Object S is either associated with Object A or not.
16. Asymmetric Object A is not defined as being absolutely exclusive that way.
17. As soon as Object A shows up, Object S has already ruled itself out.
18. We must drop our assumption of the existence of a "perfectly symmetrical Object S (or box)," according to this proof by contradiction.
19. Asymmetry and pure symmetry are mutually exclusive.
20. If any asymmetry exists, then there can be no pure symmetry.
21. The absolutely perfectly symmetrical Object S would not happen in an environment where there are any Objects A.
22. As long as there is any question of a relationship between any Objects S and A, Object S is preempted by any asymmetry.
23. Conversely, if S somehow happened prior to A, the asymmetry would be preempted; there would be nothing but pure, absolute S.
24. If Object S already exists, then nothing asymmetrical can find any foothold; it has no way to arise.
25. Object S in its pristine state can only endure in the absence of Object A; it could only have a prior existence, as such, in the absence of any asymmetry.
26. By observation, we know asymmetry is already pervasive in nature, in the universe.
27. So, it is "too late" for any absolute symmetry to happen, in space, time, or otherwise.

28. Furthermore, we can define pure symmetries as absolutes, and all perfect absolutes are pure symmetries.

29. Therefore, in the absence of any single pure and absolute symmetry, we are left with nature's observable, multifarious, asymmetrical pluralities and polarities.

30. In the absence of the finality of absolute symmetry, all asymmetries are connected; there is nothing to separate them absolutely, nor do they merge into pure symmetrical homogeneity.

ଔ ଓ

## Notes Further Unpacking the Transformation Proof

- Extremely low asymmetry is often mistaken for the existence of absolute symmetry.
- The natural asymmetries include the theoretical (albeit extremely low) asymmetries fundamental to math — we cannot meditate, think, theorize, reason or conjecture outside of nature.
- Human animals, especially in Western cultures, have been and still are very hung up on separating mind and body, with ideas of purity of soul, purity of math and logic.
- Curiously, the logic of asymmetry conjures fiction, where the reality of an environment in the absence of pure symmetry functions to enable us to imagine absolute symmetries and other fantasies — while building something solid.
- Consider, for example, a number line or series of repeating units: If nature does not repeat with absolutely symmetrical exactitude, then something mysteriously creative is happening between repeats.
- This is why we can observe repetition as rhythmically alive and musical.
- This creativity can go so far as to build new sequencing and

objects, but not without preceding patterns.

- So science, math and the humanities need each other, need imagination, to make sense.
- No series can repeat without nature's creative connectivity, the same connectivity that brings leaves along the branches of trees and petals round the flower, and let's not forget history — it sort of repeats.
- So, in the absence of absolute symmetry, nature produces similarities and differences with asymmetric connectivity.
- The most powerful physical barriers are not exempted from the logic of asymmetry.
- When any two things connect, they must at some point, in some way, truly connect, that is, merge completely but asymmetrically.
- Because, otherwise they will never honestly, truly, connect at all — we would be allowing for the interference of an (impossible) absolute.
- In the absence of absolutes, nature's asymmetry allows the greatest nuance and precision.
- Only the surface need make the slightest contact for any presumed perfect symmetry to be already broken throughout, as Object S is everywhere preempted.
- This is true for all things; this is how consciousness flows and takes physical shape.
- Consciousness has physical, panpsychist connectivity.
- There is no point symmetry at any beginning, ending, or in-between — no pure fulcrum of balance.
- Nature's true balance is what is actually happening in the absence of any absolute end or beginning and in the absence of perfectly symmetrical balance.
- Nature flows because it is never absolutely stopped.
- Asymmetric polarity in motion takes place between order and chaos, without any absolute poles at either end.
- There is no pure and random chaos and no perfect order along the River of Asymmetry.

## 7. Unpacking the Transformation Proof, Step by Step

- No perfectly pure and homogeneous flow, either.
- The more pressures build into (the absence of) a fixed, absolute pole or central position, the more counter-pressures will develop away from the impossible symmetry.
- Polarities are ever-present in asymmetric flow.
- Nature cannot stand perfectly still.
- Pressures for absolutes must be countered.
- These counter-pressures may happen in the most subtle ways, near and far, or they may become violent with immediacy.
- It is the absence of absolute dead ends that allows extraordinary subtlety and precision to develop.
- The logic of asymmetric change improves Darwinism and deals with the theory's strange paradox of life and consciousness having to arise from mere algorithmic, biochemical operations.
- Consciousness is asymmetric and physical.
- It's not all a dream, nor just a machine.
- The asymmetric quality of consciousness cannot be kept out anywhere; it is neither prior nor subsequent to matter.

☙ ❧

*Sunlit Stillness into Asymmetric Chaos*, by author

# 8. Salmon Barbecue

I was not alone in finding the reasoning difficult to handle, manage, and recall. Rolo sympathized when he said, "This thing was and still is so slippery a dragon that I kept thinking I had overlooked something. I would find myself reworking through it all again and again, scale by scale. I kept seeing it in different ways, though some of the differences were slight. Eventually I realized that one major problem in recovering the reasoning was that it is difficult to relate to in the cultural environment where my thinking tools were fashioned and where I was trained to use them. So I tried to make up some story, a fable, to give it at least a small place to live. It seemed that everywhere around me the world was dominated by absolutes. Absolutes — or the hope of absolutes — are favored and promoted in a myriad of ways. And the promotion did seem to have solid positive attributes, giving a resounding NO to my logic — so I returned to Maine, the lakes and rivers."

While I appreciated the emotional connection to his experience with this subject, I couldn't forget that he was including far more than the few logical steps outlined above. Rolo's post-doctoral studies in mathematics and his superior understanding of the implications of the logic of change had me asking him repeatedly why he wanted me involved in this book, except as a publisher.

Rolo got his name in the circus. In school he was drawn to clowning around in class. He would say that clowning was a sacred Indian tradition with many tribes. This hardly ever failed to cause at least some hesitation with whoever might be questioning his antics, especially since Rolo is an Indian. He was residually ambivalent about his origins. The residue of a broken levee somewhere, a resistance overcome by the flood of understanding later in life. A flood, a torrent, calm waters over the dam. This was an area where I had little confidence in questioning him, and I couldn't be sure if his occasional ambivalence was a similar lack of confidence or not.

With his undergraduate degree in math and physics, he had traveled to Europe, where in Italy he apprenticed himself to a clown. His skills included the unicycle and the great motorized monocycle, whence his name — Rolo. There he met Lola. They were an act, Rolo and Lola, husband and wife.

He had brought me a manuscript entitled *Zen and the Art of Monocycle Maintenance*.

"Why not?" he had protested. "It's a three-ring act. First you've got the jaw-dropping magic of *Zen and the Art of Archery*. Then comes *Zen and the Art of Motorcycle Madness*, a balancing act of romance and reality on the high wire where the madman (spoiler alert) turns out to be as sane as you or me. Then comes the clown on the monocycle — a clown, sitting on this humping great motorcycle engine inside a big fat wheel."

"But it's basically a math book! It's not really funny—" Once that was out of my mouth, I realized I was involved. My experience as an editor had been overridden by a deep passion that kept surprising me.

Rolo looked at me wisely. "You see! You're going to rewrite it for me."

"But how?"

"I could train and equip you, all right. If that's what you want. In fact I might have to. You've got a double degree in economics and French, with a good grounding in calculus and statistics. You're trainable, you're interested. It's possible."

"How long would it take?"

"You'd come out with a PhD. Probably in philosophy. We could work with one of the universities where I used to teach."

He was serious? "You're telling me that I would have to give up my writing and my publishing company because you can't write the book? Wouldn't it be easier for me as editor to help *you* write it?"

"How's that going to help me put the math together with the fiction you seem to want?"

"Well what sort of a book are we talking about here, anyway?"

"Well, just what sort of logic do we need? You know, formal logic? math logic?"

"Absolutely formal?" I reflected back to him.

That's when we decided to meet up in Maine at this place away from it all, in a town at the edge of the woods, beyond where the lights go out as you head north, and the stars get bigger. Certainly it was arguable that the paradoxes unraveled by the Transformation Proof were the result of excessive formality, whether in reasoning or otherwise. We decided to unwind for a while.

* * *

Now we had just finished chopping some wood for the barbecue pit by the waterfall. We watched it fire up until the heat rocked the lowest branch of the oak tree.

Later, when the coals were right, we put a whole salmon on the grill. The ladies showed up with bread, wine, and cheese, right out of *The Rubáiyát* of Omar Khayyám, that astronomer, mathematician, poet, and sometime drunkard, depending on your view of metaphor and poetry. It was warm out, and Alice was wearing a genie vest and Lola always had something of the circus about her to go with her dark skin and black hair. But the book of something beneath the bow was still missing.

Later on Lola suggested we just start putting Rolo's short stories into the book. She was persuasive.

Finally I asked in exasperation, "So which one goes in next?"

"Well what have we got so far?"

I gave her the folder, and she sat down on the porch and skimmed to about here.

Rolo ambled over and looked over her shoulder. "So you *are* writing it!" he exclaimed with a roar. As he leaned down and read more closely, he realized it was fiction, based on true events.

Alice just kept contemplating the coals in the semicircle of stones.

I raised my hands in protest. "How do you know it's even a book?"

"Now dear!" said Lola to Rolo, acting out the part of Mrs. Rolo from the circus days. She stood and smoothed his graying locks, playing the love game of "husband and wife," which amused them and baffled others — stopping him from reacting.

She turned to me, "The one about the Lady of the Lake. Then we'll talk asymmetric arithmetic. Rolo's been overcomplicating the thing. It has to grow, don't you think? He'll never figure out the further reaches of the reasoning without allowing it to reach out — in fact, we are going to deduce that it is physically impossible to think what needs to be thought before one takes some physically important steps that may not even have anything obviously to do with the reasoning."

Coming from her, with the Italian accent, and the way she was playing with Rolo, this had seductive undertones; we were seduced into acquiescence.

Then Alice, still seated and watching the coals, said, "This possibility of a change in B, it means that B cannot be in a relationship with an Object A that has an absolutely final characteristic, such finality being the case if A disconnected absolutely in order to change instantaneously into C, without any open-ended, connecting process. The potential change in B means that there is no potential for magical A to be in the relationship. The sheer fact that B might change is enough, because if B did change then A could never have happened in the relationship at all, ever. Its absolute characteristic would disqualify it, since a change in B requires a change in every aspect of A, and A would have an absolutely unchangeable finite characteristic in contradiction. Such finality is absolute and for all time. It could never turn out that A had been in a relationship with B.

"So absolute change self-contradicts, as A could never have got into that situation to begin with. Seems kind of obvious sometimes, other times not. Any theory that assumes an absolute or unmediated transition is out of sync, not only with reason but with nature, I'll bet. If B is the head of the salmon and is flipped by the same 180-degree rotation about the axis of the spine as is the tail represented by the letter A, which undergoes a corresponding rotation ordinarily considered to be symmetrical, then the transition fails to be absolute and is in fact asymmetrical. This shows up in the fact that the skin of just one side of the salmon is partly fused to the grill and will make a great surface for cooking the other side. Symmetry transitions in group theory don't take this failure of absolute finality into account. As a result there are all sorts of problems in dealing with infinity, the flip side of finality.

"Group theory can describe flipping a salmon in general and to some specific extent, but the more we have to describe flipping this particular salmon, the more difficulty we have. The trouble in dealing with infinity means trouble in pinning down the specifics. This shows up in quantum field theory and the problems with the Big Bang theory. But now what we have done is we have flattened infinity, so to speak, that is, if you imagine infinity as a circle—"

Lola and Rolo stood arm in arm listening to her almost as though she were talking about them. Meanwhile I had begun the process of flipping the salmon on the barbecue. "I can take a hint," I said, standing back with the spatula and the large spoon, preparing to try again without interruption and without dropping the fish into the fire.

I flipped the salmon — all of it was still on the grill. No big bang or yells of shock and flying coals. With a sigh of relief, I said, "Why don't we leave off on the math and science for a while?"

"Okay," she said, happily. "Tell you what, I bet you I can disprove the existence of God before that salmon is done."

We were so well convinced by what followed that she later obliged us with the following essay.

# 9. Alice Disproves God and Deduces the Soul: Out of the Box of Everyday Awareness

First a logical quickie: IN the absence of absolute finality, nothing completely separates one thing from another. Therefore, all things are connected in some way, and we have fundamental continuity as a basic reality, or a basic rationality, at least — before we jump to the conclusion that reality is always rational.

In the absence of absolute finality we can continue to reason in a variety of new ways and build on that foundation. But first we should further distinguish between the language that describes the way things are and the way they actually are (which includes the language). If we have found that it is illogical to use the language to include the assumption that absolute finality exists, does that mean we have discovered that nothing is in fact absolutely final?

We might say that nature would have to be illogical to have any absolute finality, but is nature logical? I'm going to assume that nature, including the universe, is real enough to be called "real." This isn't a "what is reality?" essay, as such, though it is uncovering what is true.

Logic is connective in that it shows us when there is something that does not fit in some way. Nature has fit things together in ways that might seem simply juxtaposed or even mysterious, but they are related by the fact that they all exist. Whichever way we might want to define nature itself, we have at least one word to include anything nature might do or include. We can put it all under the heading of "existence." This is the same sort of universal discussed in Samuel's story of the onion. Existence need not be an absolute simply because it in all-inclusive, especially if everything it includes has no absolute finality. It's just a description of the way things are: they exist. They are in a changing state of existence, according to our language.

Nothing does not exist. Non-existence is not an option in our asymmetric way of thinking, because non-existence would have to be completely separate and symmetrically opposite to existence. Pure symmetry does not exist, nor does nothing, nor does zero. The language of the logic of change we are using allows us to imagine nothingness (with symbols like zero), and that ability to fantasize allows the freedom to realize the rational fact of the matter — that there is no nothing. This is one example of how the logic of asymmetry recognizes the fact that logic cannot function without fiction. Math would be lost without this ability. This seems a bit obvious sometimes, but not always. When the scientists and mathematicians start to fantasize about nothing, or when we build dream worlds with zeros and imaginary dimensions, it is easy to get confused if we deny there is any fiction in the reasoning. We need the ability to conjecture the impossible in order to produce the proof by contradiction, for example. This places fiction firmly among the things that do exist, but it is important to the integrity of the fiction and nonfiction that they be respected as different though related beasts.

For our purposes here, I would like to use the word "Nature" to mean all that exists. For entertainment in the midst of this reasoning, I will capitalize and personify Nature. If she turns out to be God in some mysterious way, so be it.

* * *

Now, in order for Nature to present us with absolute finality in spite of our logic, she would have to find a way to escape from the all-inclusive word, "existence." She would have to find a way to both exist and not exist, without being caught by the simple reasoning that nonexistence is not an option, as far as our language, logic, and understanding are concerned. Nature would have to be beyond understanding in some respect — very mysterious, supernatural. She would have to be forever beyond the reach of our consciousness in a way that would allow a perfect separation to exist. If our consciousness were ever to access Nature's characteristics beyond that mysterious barrier, we could then bring along our language and include those characteristics under our heading of all things that exist. Our consciousness (whatever that is) would be a connector.

But do we need to bring consciousness into the discussion at this point? No.

The question of whether our language is surpassed by Nature's mystery — or any mystery, divine or otherwise — is a question of whether there are things that are not accessible to that language, things that could never be spoken of in any way. If there is a universal connectivity, we should be able to find a way out of the box of our language (and even our individual consciousness) to contact with it a greater reality. But let's not get ahead of ourselves. First, since we are starting only with the language of the logic of change, we need to make some logical connections. We need to speak in terms of the relationships and changes of the Transformation Proof. We are wondering if there can be a supernatural mystery that can remain aloof from the asymmetry of our language. We have a logical language continuum established by the sheer proof itself, and we are using it to speculate here.

The Transformation Proof says that no absolute finality can be in a relationship with any object that might change. It follows that in order for any Object A to avoid a relationship with B where B might change, A must stop B from changing. So in order for any supernatural object to avoid a relationship with an asymmetric object, it must put and end to the asymmetry. And it must do so without being in any relationship with it, ever. The supernatural object is blocked by its own paradox — according to our logic. How do we break out from within our language?

Answer: No asymmetric object (including our language) can be finalized absolutely from within or from outside or from anywhere in any way. This is because it has a manifold nature where relationships exist within it that keep it "refreshed" and changing. Any attempt to finalize completely any aspect of it is doomed by the fact that there are other aspects within it that are in asymmetric relationships with that aspect under consideration for finalization. This multiplicity (that is within the language) is the very nature of its asymmetry. Without such asymmetry, it would achieve pure symmetry as one homogeneous object. All asymmetric objects, indeed all things, have this changing, mazelike structure. They have an internal spring action in the relationships of the layers or aspects described by Samuel. (We will consider the implication for infinity of this mazelike spring later in this book.)

What this means is that a changing asymmetry is connected and therefore communicates, indeed broadcasts beyond the changing boundaries of any open-ended object, by virtue of the fact that the asymmetric object redefines itself rhythmically, again and again. The effects are like the ripple of the pebble being defined as thrown into the pond. The effects undergo changes themselves, but they are fundamentally irresistible, being impossible to completely finalize. This broadcast happens among all the changing relationships in existence, even between existence as a whole and all of its parts. In this way existence can expand beyond any universal horizon that may occur at any moment, according to the way it happens to change. It may also change in a more self-contained way. It is all that is, and nothing, supernatural or otherwise, can escape its potential. The merely potential relationship is already a relationship of some kind.

We can now use our language with confidence to describe another way that the paradox of the would-be supernatural object blocks it from happening: It cannot save itself or close itself off from these polarities or waves of change. The first inability is one of being inhibited from an active attempt; the second is the inability to be defensive.

Therefore, (1) would-be supernatural Object A cannot put a final end to Object B, and (2) it cannot stop asymmetric B from having a relationship with it, because A cannot escape the effects of the changes, however remote they may be. In this way the potential effects are accompanied by actual ones. Continuous potential change guarantees the inescapability by ensuring open-endedness.

I am loth to say anything about the inescapability of responsibility that goes with this idea, so I'll take it no further.

Here is where we go beyond the confines of the logic itself: Because the reasoning of our language is itself asymmetric, the effects of its changes go beyond its words and reasoning. Put another way, no matter how inarticulate we are, we can always speak of — or at least reference — things beyond words and things we know extremely little about. We can smile knowingly about this.

So Nature cannot escape being touched by a relationship with our Transformation Proof. The reasoning holds true in that things beyond the logic are in a relationship with this reasoning and share in what we might call an asymmetric "Field of Action." Asymmetry is *fundamentally inclusive*, extending to all existence. In fact, pure symmetry being nothing, Nature could not have boundaries if she did not have fundamental asymmetry to specify and include them. The inclusiveness is more fundamental than the exclusiveness of any boundaries. The democratic opportunity that we can infer from this will be addressed more fully in another part of this book. Asymmetry will always get out of any box, somehow. But what about us? What about our consciousness?

This may seem a bit obvious, but let's not take it for granted that we are in any way aware of what we are saying!

We have concluded that there is an asymmetric continuum in our language, based on the above reasoning, our ABCs, and the Transformation Proof. Does this mean that consciousness shares that continuum? Where are we in the asymmetric field? Clearly our consciousness exists. It must be asymmetric. Therefore: asymmetric consciousness, without absolute finality, is immortal in some way. Interesting. For now, let's just make the following points.

\* \* \*

If our language is an expression of consciousness, the language continuum is a characteristic of our consciousness itself. If we agree with the reasoning, it must be the way we are aware in that respect, not just the way our language technically works. The fact that it is our consciousness that is organizing itself logically means that the logical conclusion that nothing is absolutely final pertains to our awareness. That is how we are aware. Our consciousness is therefore asymmetric in being aware of the Transformation Proof itself. As we have seen, the proof says that nothing can escape open-endedness. If this is the way my consciousness is in respect to the proof, then the rest of my related consciousness is asymmetric. My awareness is a field of asymmetry within the wider Field of Action and existence.

Stated in another way, if we understand and agree with the proof, then the proof is a description of the way we are aware in that respect where we agree with it. That one asymmetric respect is all we need to extend the asymmetry of the proof to the rest of our consciousness. The proof is a fact of which we are aware. If we go into denial of the fact, the fact remains. If it is revisited and found to be otherwise that previously thought, if it is discovered that we were under an illusion, then it never was the fact as such. On the other hand, if it is true, we may revisit it and discover that there is more to it than we had thought; we might experience its growth, as would be expected from the nature of its degrees of connected, open-ended asymmetry.

Whatever becomes of the fact of the proof, it is part of the asymmetric continuum in the maze of our consciousness. The image of a maze is used here as a more complex idea of the "box." When we "get out of the box," we realize we are in the maze, so to speak, an asymmetric field with ripples. To get away from the fact of the proof, we would need to disentangle ourselves from that maze. This is logically impossible from an asymmetric rung of the maze where the proof resides, a rung that keeps asymmetrically connecting with the rest of the maze wherever we go. It's this open-ended asymmetry that allows us to get outside of ourselves and deduce a greater reality (not necessarily in that order).

But what if we are under an illusion and think we understand the reasoning when really we do not? After having thoroughly investigated it, to ask ourselves if we are witnessing an illusion is like asking if the other objects that we witness are illusions. Then what is real? What is reality? This is like asking, Am I aware of what I am witnessing? At some level this is a good question, but when it gets to the point where someone is asking, "Is Object A really Object A?" I for one have very little time for anyone who argues that they are not at all aware of what they are saying or witnessing. They are simply contradicting themselves. I witness a contradiction and know that I can follow the reasoning that I am using. This does not mean that the reasoning cannot go deeper than I know at present, as just previously mentioned. It does not mean that I cannot make mistakes or be under an illusion. I just don't ask myself if I'm really proposing Object A when that is what I am saying I am doing — enough! That would indeed be a self-contradiction and that is that.

Going the other way, going deeper, we can conclude that what we are calling the Transformation Proof is not exactly new. It must be something every civilization comes to conclude sooner or later, in the Field of Action, in the universe.

* * *

Another point (or two) I would like to make about getting out of the box is that we can consider consciousness as a part of existence that inhabits an environment in Nature, even though we are not sure exactly what this awareness is. In fact, the uncertainty is in some vital way a salvation, being the asymmetric lack of finality. All we need to know to include consciousness in existence is that logically it is not nothing.

We have deduced that in the absence of absolute finality, our consciousness is open-ended — everlasting in some way. And from my consciousness' point of view, there is no final separation between consciousness and anything else in Nature. Even physical objects that I observe cannot be absolutely separated out from my consciousness. And this turns out to be true of all objects in the wider field of existence — none of them can be cut away absolutely. We will consider further what this means about consciousness and matter, later.

The proof says that nothing is absolutely final. But is this always the case from every other perspective? Could my consciousness just think it cannot be kept out, when in fact it can be entirely excluded forever, even if that might not make sense to me and to those who agree on the reasoning of the proof?

Reapplying the reasoning above, the answer is: If my consciousness does not and indeed cannot entirely limit itself, its open-endedness can connect with other asymmetries in an open-ended field of consciousness that has the potential to be in some way aware of anything eventually. Its asymmetric open-endedness makes it impossible to exclude it forever. The merest question in the direction of any elusive object would bring about a relationship along with its characteristic degree of awareness, however slight it may be. Insofar as the field of asymmetry does not block itself (and it cannot do so absolutely), my consciousness has the potential to eventually become aware of anything that tries to block it. And as I have discovered, my consciousness has no final end. This does not mean that I *must* become aware of everything eventually! All that is needed for there to be an *existing* relationship between my consciousness and anything else is the *potential*. In fact, if I were to become omniscient, that would build in a kind of symmetry that we will have to consider as we further study the question of God. What we want to emphasize here is *potential* and *opportunity*. That's where the relationships really happen.

And one thing more: Other people can have a look at the proof and decide whether or not they go along with it. There are of course many possible reactions. If one does not find an error in the reasoning, one can agree with it — or not. Or one can resist the proof without trying to find an error. In the later case, one is excluded somewhat from using reason in dealing with the proof, but not excluded from the effects of the open-ended asymmetry. This is how the mystic who rejects the mind as inadequate is cornered by the mind at a bend in the maze. Hitherto this cornering of absolute mysticism had not been achieved in philosophy. The mystic has had an escape route through the paradoxes of a mind that uses symmetrical thinking. The mystic has used the illusion generated by a mistake in understanding. This illusory habitat has allowed the mystic the luxury of using false reason to build paradoxes and discredit the mind in favor of an illusory absolute. This "falling into illusion" or "samsara" is what true mysticism warns about. To forego reason altogether is the "leap of faith" and has more than a touch of madness. Just because there is a lot of chaos in the mind does not mean it does not offer the opportunities the mystic is really looking for in the universal Field of Action — or just sitting by the waterfall and the pond.

\* \* \*

Given that it is an empirical fact that we are aware of the reasoning, the awareness or consciousness is a fact of life, not to be too repetitive. But it is a fact that is also a bridge between the subjective — and often romantic — individual and the objective and seemingly external reality. All these observed phenomena, whether we classify them as inside or outside of us, exist in the context of their relationships. As soon as we can establish asymmetry in an empirically observable object and connect to the Transformation Proof, we have found a bridge to a most interesting pathway from our consciousness into the natural environment that it inhabits. This is sort of an out-of-the-body experience. Clearly we inhabit Nature. Our consciousness is part of the way Nature is. Anyone who tries to resist the open-endedness of the consciousness in their environment (unless they can find a fatal error in the reasoning) will be unable to close off their consciousness forever.

As consciousness explores existence, all obstacles would eventually be encountered — including any that might seem absolutely impassible or unknowable, even as new obstacles may emerge. An obstacle means that something is blocked. When it blocks consciousness, it becomes knowable in some degree and forfeits the possibility of any absolute exclusivity. No part of any obstacle can block endless consciousness and remain forever absolutely unknowable. Even if the obstacle tried to remain hidden or aloof, it would have to have a relationship with the consciousness it was avoiding and would become an obstacle to the basic questioning of an open-ended attitude. That relationship would eventually give it away and subject it to the possibility of exploration.

Either there is an obstacle that can be encountered or there is no obstacle at all. An unknowable obstacle or unknowable object of any kind is a self-contradiction when faced by open-ended awareness that progresses asymmetrically from one thing to the next, without end in time, space, or otherwise. The language of asymmetric reasoning can therefore make true statements about the way things really are. This is possible because of the observable way our awareness works in conjunction with the unknown. Our consciousness can be open enough to admit of an asymmetric unknown, beyond which no further unknown can be unknowable. This is the way science can progress.

Looking at it from another way round: In order for there to be an unknown that is beyond the reach of asymmetric, open-ended consciousness, the language of that consciousness would have to be *entirely* disconnected somewhere from the environment the language is being used to describe. Such a discontinuity would be absolutely final. Because the Transformation Proof describes asymmetry as mutually exclusive with absolute finality, any such finality anywhere puts an end to the asymmetry of the language of consciousness altogether. The imposed absolute finality would impinge on the proof in an absolute way, meaning that it would disprove the proof for all time and circumstances. It is too late for that. By the proof, any absolute finality is mutually exclusive with any change. Any potential of a relationship where absolute finality might interfere with the asymmetry would mean that the whole language would already be entirely disconnected from the whole environment that it is used to describe. In its own terms, the language would not even exist, would never have existed. Clearly, as I write, this is not the case. Any contact between our awareness and its environment makes for a continuing relationship whereby the awareness can bridge any divide and progressively, asymmetrically, investigate any object or obstacle.

There are many things that are way beyond our comprehension. But given enough time, understanding can be transmitted and grow. As long as there is no absolute finality in our consciousness, nothing exists to stop the continuing contact with successions of realities. All obstacles can become bridges to further understanding, because of the asymmetric quality of consciousness. The asymmetry of consciousness guarantees that it always has the capacity to continue in some way. This is a kind of immortality, a gift of the nature of change. Fortunately, it is accompanied by fundamental opportunity, even though we get boxed in or lost in the maze.

By reasoning that the language of consciousness itself is asymmetric, we can conclude that Nature and the whole of existence share this open-ended quality. We can reason our way out of the box. We can understand the world beyond our skins. So we can empathize.

In order to block consciousness absolutely, Nature would have to put a final end to the asymmetry of consciousness. By the sheer fact that our language does in fact exist, we can conclude that Nature herself and all existence must be asymmetric and mutually exclusive with absolute finality.

And nothing in existence can totally block asymmetric consciousness. Every wall of exclusivity can be breached. The presence of asymmetry anywhere means that nothing can opt out of it or remain untouched by its logic in a supernatural realm. This disproves — with reason and the repeated scientific evidence of Nature's rhythmic asymmetry — the existence of universal Platonic ideals and theological descriptions of God as surpassing understanding. But we have not disproved God, yet. If He, She, or It exists, we have only proved that God is intimately knowable.

* * *

There is yet another way, yes, that we might know that not only Nature — however she may be defined — but all of existence is incapable of putting an absolute end to asymmetric consciousness. Our reasoning so far says it cannot be done. As we have just seen, it becomes a question of the *relevance* of the language used in the reasoning. The word "relationship" is the key here. In order to escape the universality of the reasoning, an object would have to be able to escape a relationship with a continuing, immortal consciousness. This would render the object irrelevant to consciousness. As far as any consciousness is concerned, the object would be irrelevant to the point of nonexistence. It would never interfere in any way with anything in Nature or anything at all that any entity might ever become aware of or inquire about. It would be irrelevant to the most fundamental questioning. Nothing of any consequence — including any language — could exist like that, or amount to an absolute. In the absence of any language to make sense of absolutes, we are left with the language of asymmetry as an integral part of Nature.

The absence of absolutes in Nature would explain the overwhelming evidence of Nature's asymmetry. A scientific hypothesis and any eventual theory need to be testable time and again; this reasoning has been born out already by all scientific experience to date, as described in *Lucifer's Legacy: The Meaning of Asymmetry*.

Another breakthrough in evidence, announced in a press release entitled "Fermilab Scientists Find Evidence for Significant Matter-Antimatter Asymmetry" made *The New York Times*.

> Physicists at the Fermi National Accelerator Laboratory are reporting that they have discovered a new clue that could help unravel one of the biggest mysteries of cosmology: why the universe is composed of matter and not its evil-twin opposite, antimatter. If confirmed, the finding portends fundamental discoveries at the new Large Hadron Collider outside Geneva, as well as a possible explanation for our own existence.
>
> In a mathematically perfect universe, we would be less than dead; we would never have existed. According to the basic precepts of Einsteinian relativity and quantum mechanics, equal amounts of matter and antimatter should have been created in the Big Bang and then immediately annihilated each other in a blaze of lethal energy, leaving a big fat goose egg with which to make stars, galaxies and us. And yet we exist, and physicists (among others) would dearly like to know why.[9]

Witness the mutual exclusivity in the words "less than dead." Here is an excerpt from the Fermilab press release.

> The dominance of matter that we observe in the universe is possible only if there are differences in the behavior of particles and antiparticles. Although physicists have observed such differences (called "CP violation") in particle behavior for decades, these known differences are much too small to explain the observed dominance of matter over antimatter in the universe and are fully consistent with the Standard Model.

If confirmed by further observations and analysis, the effect seen by DZero physicists could represent another step towards understanding the observed matter dominance by pointing to new physics phenomena beyond what we know today.

. . . . .

"Many of us felt goose bumps when we saw the result," said Stefan Soldner-Rembold, co-spokesperson of DZero. "We knew we were seeing something beyond what we have seen before and beyond what current theories can explain."[10]

In 1998 the philosophers Andy Clark (University of Edinburgh) and David Chalmers (Australian National University) published the essay, "The Extended Mind," in the Oxford philosophy journal, *Analysis*. They attracted considerable attention in answering the question of where the mind stops and the rest of the world begins. Using the often repeated example of two individuals who make their way to the same address (the Museum of Modern Art in NYC), one storing the information in her brain's memory, the other, impaired by Alzheimer's, using a notebook, Clark and Chalmers described the mind as a system that includes parts of its environment.[11] We can now back up such observations with a basic logical connection. We can reason that an asymmetric continuum pervades the whole of existence. We can extend to all of existence the reasoning that shows why it is impossible for Nature to forever block the continuous asymmetry of awareness.

Curiously in order to disprove God we need to disprove absolute chaos. The two are linked in the nature of the fallacy of absolutes.

\* \* \*

It is about here in the reasoning that I, Samuel, interrupted with the large fork to poke the sweet potatoes which had been wrapped in aluminum foil and tucked among the coals. I felt a regular devil and briefly imagined Alice giving such a talk in a roomful of philosophers with everyone dressed up in Halloween costumes. After letting her in on my thoughts, she continued with a fairly credible imitation of the coldhearted laugh of the mad logician.

# 10. Alice Disproves God and Deduces the Soul: Nonrandom Multifarious Polarity

It may appear that we have already disproved the existence of the absolute deity, or at least cast doubt on its existence by the unreasonableness of assuming such an absolute. But we have limited ourselves to a discussion of absolute finality, without showing how the absence of such finality specifically preempts the possibility of the mysterious Godhead of monotheism.

There are powerful and scholarly arguments to the effect that a God with characteristics in common with those created by Him "in His image" (as the Bible says — namely, we humans) cannot reasonably be expected to be all powerful, all-knowing, loving, and still not act to prevent the horrors endured by humans in natural disasters — even if evils such as genocide can somehow be blamed on human ignorance, frailty, and sin. If that sentence was a bit lengthy, it is because it has to stretch to cover many volumes of scholarly work concerning God and the problem of evil and suffering.

The arguments against a loving all-powerful God allowing such deep misery to happen have great force, but they depend on a shared understanding of love. The proponent of this "God's love" must intellectually and emotionally share in the "love" of the opponent to a sufficient degree for the opponent to win the argument. In the course of this book, we will develop the asymmetric reasoning into what we might call "love's logic," where reason and love are intertwined and interdependent like the waterfall and the pond. Not only will this further dispel the contradiction of a loving God who will not help the stricken, but it will solve the riddle of the God who is maintained to be so mysterious as to escape being an absolute with all the finality that goes with such a definition. For example, what if Nature is God?

## 10. Alice... Nonrandom Multifarious Polarity

My two good friends Samuel and Rolo have already alluded to a curious polarity that must be deduced in the absence of absolutes. This further step in the reasoning is especially important in preventing the escape of any would-be god from the (impossible) limits of being an absolute — escaping into some kind of infinity or cosmic consciousness. The polarity that I am about to describe will prevent such an escape, proving that it is impossible, there being no God to attempt it, should He so wish. Here is how it goes.

As we have seen, the absence of absolute finality leaves us with no exact repetition. Exact repetition depends on perfect finality; otherwise what exactly to repeat? We cannot sort of repeat something exactly and argue that it is worthwhile to continue to try to make sense. Absolute symmetry depends on exact repetition. Likewise absolute randomness depends on exact repetition. Asymmetrically speaking, we find that nothing is random. This means that existence is going somewhere. This already sets up a kind of polarity of direction.

If perfect randomness does not exist, pure chaos does not exist either, as chaos is random.

An irony of randomness is that it requires the "perfect order" of exact repetition, for anything to have just as much chance of happening one way as another. The chances must be perfectly symmetrical in order for, say, a coin to have a truly fifty-fifty chance of landing heads or tails. We tend to identify such symmetry as being perfectly ordered when in fact it would also be completely chaotic. Exact repetition is nonexistent and shares the nonexistent characteristics of perfect order and absolute chaos. These two states would be poles apart if they existed. In their absence, another kind of polarity arises. Because nothing goes to the extent of being random chaos or to the extreme of perfect order, everything in existence happens in between.

We can observe that there are tendencies towards chaos and order. But in the absence of the extremes, we can reason and observe that there is a polarity that prevents the extremes from happening. The presence of an asymmetric continuum also ensures that the tendencies themselves are not ultimately kept from one another, so a polarity can affect the entire system of tendencies. In the absence of the extremes of absolute chaos and perfect order, we have an elastic polarity that maintains the tendencies in-between. This can be found as a physical tension on the continuum in the Field of Action.

We have deduced that the finality of absolutely constant conditions does not happen. This changes, for example, the classical concept of inertia, insofar as the concept assumes that an object at rest can theoretically remain so forever, or that it can remain forever in motion in a constant manner, such as a straight line or a single speed. In the absence of any absolutely static condition, everything is always changing by degrees; complete immobility does not exist, and nor does absolute or constant motion. Either condition on its own would be absolutely unique. This means that the more an object tends to remain as it is, the more pressure will build to move it away from that condition. How and when that pressure reaches the threshold of noticeably acting upon the object in question is itself a question of the nature of the object and its environment. Whatever might be the way that Nature moves the object away from achieving any absolute, she will do it eventually — and never in exactly the same way, nor in a completely different manner.

Rolo, who is currently being patient and waiting for his salmon, reminds me to give Albert Einstein a mention. It seems that any discussion of inertia calls forth some aspects of relativity theory, special and general, not to mention much further the question of what Einstein meant by an absolute, since the theory uses a math that assumes absolute symmetry. This assumption itself would not adversely affect the day-to-day workings of Einstein's and Hendrik Lorentz's transformation symmetry. After all, humans have evolved with major assumptions of absolutes and made one dramatic and practical discovery after another. So I will leave the question of how the absolute symmetry of relativity theory relates to the unsolved issues of symmetry, randomness, and infinity in quantum field theory, not that I could take it any further without starting up Rolo's monocycle. But I can't help mentioning a conversation I once thought I had read about. Einstein and Heisenberg, I thought it was, were arguing. Finally Heisenberg said something like, "Look, my friend, you accuse us of describing the world as random and you say God doesn't play dice. Well your theory is just as random because it depends on symmetry." And that was that, I thought. The progressive Jew had got trounced by the Nazi sympathizer. Having failed to find any reference to this conversation again, I have come to believe it was another conversation I had read too quickly while trying to figure out a few things. Even though it may never have happened, it encouraged me to challenge the accepted wisdom about the virtues of symmetry. And Einstein now seems to be right about the dice. They are always loaded. So would God use them? Albert Einstein's ideas about the character of "God" are yet another story, as referenced in the famous "God letter" to Eric Gutkind, where he writes that, for him, Einstein, the word "God" is "nothing more than the expression and product of human weaknesses." With precision he states this as an opinion. I wonder what he would have discovered had he attributed this same weakness to the idea of pure symmetry.

\* \* \*

Thus far we can deduce that between the more orderly and the more chaotic circumstances of existence, conditions are always changing according to a fundamental polarity. This polarity is not unlike the concept of the Tao, as sometimes described.

The polarity does not fundamentally necessitate a move that has the objective of attaining one extreme or the other; rather it ensures the avoidance of the absolute condition, merely because that condition cannot happen. The more an object is pressured into an extremely symmetrical condition, the more the polarity will manifest itself. The rate of manifestation from a potential to active condition has its own polarity that ranges from the predictably gradual to the extremely, almost randomly, sudden.

The more an object attaches itself to the futile attempt of achieving an absolute state, the greater the risk that it will lose the integrity of that position — even resulting in destruction. It is self-destructive to attempt to establish an absolutely unique position. The seeds of destruction are planted in the attempt. This is a curious kind of polarity because it acts in the absence of a polarity of perfect extremes. The genie of asymmetric polarity is as fundamental as the continuum from which it is conjured, when would-be absolutes threaten to attempt the impossible, as in the case of the various systems of belief in the absolute deity of monotheism, or any such godhead, monarch, dictator, or philosopher king.

Given the balancing asymmetric polarity of continuous change, the more a single consciousness tends to focus on all existence while assuming itself to be the exclusive center and origin of existence, the more it will build pressures for change away from such a constant and symmetrical condition. If God were the only god and did not assume Himself to be so, He would of course be mistaken. If such a god existed, he would be in an impossible situation. But the self-destruction is not only in the assumption.

No center of intelligence could ever have established itself as an absolutely unique god that sees all and knows all, having created everything. Even the attempt would tend to self-destruct. Certainly for any consciousness to think of itself in such terms is self-destructive. What most psychologists would agree is true can now be applied to consciousness as a whole. Likewise, just using language to assert the existence of a single creator god is irrational and potentially destabilizing in its paradoxical exclusivity.

In the absence of an absolute god, we have *immortal conscious intelligence*. This is a definition of soul. In the absence of a unique and absolute First Cause (as taught by Aristotle and his followers down the centuries), we can deduce a multitude of souls living in interrelated individual rhythmic patterns, some more harmonious than others, throughout existence.

\* \* \*

Philosophical reasoning about existence can lead us to draw conclusions about Nature that overlap with physical sciences. This has the advantage of subjecting the reasoning to scientific experience — a reassuring result of the way science developed historically out of philosophy.

As we have seen, one major implication of the absence of exact repetition is that there are no completely unique objects or events. Such isolation of identity would have to be perfectly final. Instead we find that things tend to develop rhythmically, in patterns of related objects. Things emerge with and from other things, often through what scientists and mathematicians call "symmetry breaking." But these thresholds of emergence are where *near-*symmetry is broken.

This somewhat Taoist way of analyzing Nature is a holistic divergence from reductionism. *A Different Universe: Reinventing Physics from the Bottom Down*, by the Nobel Laureate Robert B. Laughlin, gives examples of this emergence and the emerging understanding of it. Laughlin puts it this way.

From the reductionist standpoint, physical law is the motivating impulse of the universe. It does not come from anywhere and implies everything. From the emergenist perspective, physical law is a rule of behavior, it is a consequence of more primitive rules of behavior underneath (although it need not have been), and it gives one predictive power over a limited range of circumstances. Outside this range, it becomes irrelevant, supplanted by other rules that are either its children or its parents in a hierarchy of descent. Neither of these viewpoints can gain ascendancy over the other by means of facts, for both are fact-based and both are true in the traditional scientific sense of the term. The issue is more subtle — a matter of institutional judgment. To paraphrase George Orwell, all facts are equal, but some are more equal than others.[12]

One of the most familiar examples of emergence is the way the Newtonian laws emerge from the quantum world, which behaves according to different laws. The lack of ultimate ascendancy allows us to say that each emerges from the other. We are faced with a question of which facts we wish to emphasize, which involves social pressure, hence the reference to Orwell. This calls for fiction!

Reductionism has proved a wonderfully powerful tool, but it is not the only one. Reductionism is a good thing as long as it remains a tool and does not become a monocultural force. Having reduced the world to particles with a language of mathematics that is so symmetrical and Platonic, we now have reason to believe we have pushed the culture that depends on our technology deep into romanticism and religious mythology. When Laughlin references Orwell, there is an asymmetric polarity lurking where an overly symmetrical culture has produced not only a quest for extreme order in a "theory of everything" but the other impossible dreams of capitalism, runaway romanticism, anarchy, and their attendant inequalities.

This might go some way to explain the profound denial in a technological century where science in the hands of religious extremists is being used to attack reason. Fortunately, an open-ended asymmetric Field of Action provides opportunities to respond in a balanced and powerful way.

Rhythm and pattern, in the absence of absolute constants, can call forth a change. Depending on the circumstances, the change can be extremely abrupt. But it does not come out of nowhere. A continuous condition of extremely slight emergence as Nature compensates for the units of a pattern that repeats with extremely close and constant sequencing can build a disruptive counterbalancing event. It is as though Nature is being forced to fill in between the units of the pattern so minimally — to allow for some inexactitude in the extreme precision of the repetition — that she needs to express herself more freely. When and where this happens would depend on the patterns of all relationships in existence, but would therefore allow for a traceable connection between events and a degree of predictability. Asymmetric connections exist even through the slimmest areas of emergence. Areas of emergence are variously predictable by the extremes of organization and exactitude in physical laws and their domains.

The illusion of singular, one-off objects, events, and domains can always be broken. The one continuous thing in this process is change itself, whether it's change out of or into emergence, emergence itself, or otherwise. Change is not absolutely random nor totally organized; we can discover its logic and the logical conclusion that its logic goes with fiction. We can also consider that in the absence of exact repetition, consciousness must be creating something in the process of change, whether cultural or more environmental. There is a creative emergence at work. In the absence of exact repetition, something observably new is always happening to some degree.

Laughlin describes the new dawn of emergence like this

> As I have lived inside theoretical physics and become familiar with its ways and historical currents, I have come to understand the von Klitzing discovery to be a watershed event, a defining moment in which physical science stepped firmly out of the age of reductionism into the age of emergence. This shift is usually described in the popular press as the transition from the age of physics to the age of biology, but that is not quite right.[13]

The Nobel Laureate Klaus von Klitzing discovered the quantum Hall effect. As Laughlin says,

> The quantum Hall effect is, in fact, a magnificent example of perfection emerging out of imperfection . . . If the quantum Hall effect raised the curtain on the age of emergence, then

the fractional quantum discovery was its opening movement
... The fractional quantum Hall effect reveals that ostensibly
indivisible quanta — in this case the electron charge $e$ — can
be broken into pieces through self-organization of phases.
The fundamental things, in other words, are not necessarily
fundamental.[14]

Other ostensibly fundamental constants, Laughlin informs us, include Planck's constant $h$, and the speed of light $c$. Likewise any emerging perfection would not be absolute.

Here, at the border of science and philosophy, the example of such a relationship between a high degree of perfection on the one hand and the more chaotic imperfections on the other suggests our now familiar asymmetric polarity of change.

# 11. Alice Disproves God and Deduces the Soul: Fundamentality

Is the asymmetric continuum that runs throughout existence more fundamental than consciousness? Or to put it another way: If consciousness cannot ultimately be kept out of anything, are all things already in some way alive?

The continuum is basically connective, and so is consciousness. This we have established. Also, we have seen how consciousness, being asymmetric in nature, has the capacity to apprehend and thereby connect anything eventually. This means that it cannot be fundamentally less connective than the whole continuum. In order for the continuum to outreach consciousness it would have to be prior to it in time or space, or extend behind some fundamental obstacle to consciousness. Consciousness would have to have had a beginning or an absolutely final characteristic, putting a perfectly symmetrical facet onto its asymmetry, *an asymmetry as fundamental as the whole continuum itself.* Such a basic beginning or symmetry, such an absolute dead end, would be an absolute finality in an asymmetric environment, and that is impossible, according to the logic of change. It would be like the continuum having an absolute beginning.

So how can there be a difference between consciousness and the continuum as a whole? It did not come after or before the whole continuum anywhere in time, space, or any other aspect of existence that might provide an obstacle. It is just as fundamental and just as connective. Where could anything have distinguished itself outside consciousness itself? The answer must be that nothing could have asserted its existence before consciousness got to every part of it — permeated it. Consciousness must therefore be the very same variety of substances as the entire continuum or Field of Action. This means that awareness is a physical phenomenon. This emphatically does not mean that all material objects are insubstantial illusions, as characterized by Platonic philosophers and others. Quite the contrary. Physical consciousness that is built up in complex objects has built-in limited choices, in the short to medium run. These options become evident as science unravels the physical nature of things. In the long run, free will wins out. The implications of this are, of course, numerous.

And I might add, the idea that the human body and the "things of this world" are fundamentally debased and separate from the Ideal, the soul, or the City of God, as described by Saint Augustine, is a powerful, long-standing, and destructive illusion that we still struggle with today. There is no such categorical and hierarchical half-human division. There is no Minotaur, as Samuel has pointed out.

But before we go any further we need to clear up a loose end. Why isn't any particular asymmetric object, like Samuel's driftwood table for example, just as pervasive as consciousness? If consciousness can be everywhere, why not any other asymmetric thing? The answer is that the asymmetric boundaries of the table are not able to go where consciousness goes, without losing their identity. Consciousness can simply be aware of asymmetries without ceasing to be consciousness. It's potentially as subtle as anything it finds, so nothing is beyond its asymmetric reach. This is because of its ability to wake up and learn (and learn and wake up). If it finds an obstacle, it can learn all about that obstacle by following the asymmetries. It can learn about its own nature, so no asymmetries can avoid its own asymmetry. We can learn about the table, but the table cannot. Until the table somehow transforms into a robot with a learning program, it's a one-way street on the continuum.

But we do have a profound reason why experimentation with Artificial Intelligence has been successful in programming robots to learn from their mistakes. The lack of pure randomness in Nature's sense of direction means that trial and error is not a zero-sum game — the bot learns because there is a meaningful path to take. The direction or polarity of the physicality of consciousness is important.

So we can learn something about learning; the cutting edge of the learning process is asymmetric. This can be translated with a variety of inferences. But basically we often learn best when we approach somewhat indirectly, by lifting a corner somewhere and finding a pathway, by finding an edge, a hook, or an end to unravel. Having education drilled into us can be counterproductive, for example. Not that drill is not sometimes important as a counterbalance in coordination with other activities or to deal with chaotic circumstances like warfare. We make specific discoveries about individual things in coordination with Nature's asymmetric horizon, like a balance of theory and practice.

Although no object except the continuum of consciousness can connect everything, the continuum allows every object to be connective in the context where it is found. There is no object that is not of the continuum, so everything in existence is the way physical consciousness is aware and unaware to various degrees. This awareness invites further exploration. Meanwhile, next time you gaze with affection at a trusted piece of machinery, your car, boat, or plane, or just a special object, consider the possibility of some genuine empathy there. And a good piece of sculpture might genuinely seem to come momentarily to life, or to inspire stories like those of Pygmalion. Consider also that all things have traces discoverable from afar.

The idea that everything is somehow alive or directed is, of course, ancient, and we can reason that it demonstrates instinctive wisdom. By the same token, odd versions of the idea of an invisible hand of God or otherwise have been developed into some strange notions with powerfully superstitious effects that require time and knowledge to disprove effectively. Recently it has resurfaced in the concept of "intelligent design." To the extent that we have established that existence is a multifarious, conscious continuum with a nonrandom sense of direction, we have confirmed some sort of intelligent design in Nature, but obviously not the sort of infallible, unique intelligence that the term was coined to imply. It is no more true to claim the existence of one absolute creator than to say, for example, that every part of your body has its own separate soul. Both positions are akin to the paradox that teams the psychology of anarchic chaos with the perfect order of dictatorship; neither absolute is possible, given the logic of change. Put slightly differently, fundamentalist monotheism predictably turns into a runaway paganism, as the attempt for absolute unity breaks into corresponding chaos and conflict. The depth of the denial precipitates the illusions needed to run from the truth. This has not been helped by a community of philosophers who have until recently all but given up on the search for the truth, a quest that is a natural instinct and a common-sense thing to do.

We can now reason that the absence of absolute symmetry is the fundamental problem for monotheism. No object can be absolutely one of a kind. There can be no single, solitary, eternal instance of anything, even though many relationships are distant. Any prolonged tendency towards a single and exclusively unique center of intelligent awareness of all things cannot happen without developing vast, self-destructive, breaking near-symmetry. Scientists investigating this may find it liberating, depending on the extent to which their science has become a belief system.

Given the impossibility of an all-knowing center of life, we can observe that there is a host of different kinds of intelligences and connected fields of awareness. In the absence of absolute finality, none of these can be entirely separated from the immortality of consciousness as a whole — an immortality which its asymmetric, open-ended and emerging nature fundamentally guarantees.

We can conclude that the more any center of awareness is open to and expresses the fundamental polarity of change in its mazelike rhythms, the more involved it is with the basic nature of immortality itself. Conversely, in the absence of absolutes, the more the center of intelligence or awareness tries to become a single, symmetrical center, denying its connected, mazelike structure, the more it will tend to lose integrity and risk the disintegration of its identity by trying to live an illusion — effectively trying to be the monotheistic god. Also, it follows that the more one tries to "be God" — or be with or merge with God — the less one senses the immortality of the soul and the more one fears delusions of death. This would explain how extreme religions successfully manipulate followers by using primordial fear.

Moderate religious attitudes avoid this syndrome by accepting and respecting other lifeways and desiring to live peacefully together. I would make the distinction between an absolute monotheism that is dependant on the need to convert and conquer — and therefore weak and unstable — as compared with open monotheism where a personal preference in religion is regarded as a contribution to the community. Open or moderate monotheism is welcoming, helpful and inclusive, without being coercive, probably what Jesus, as he is often represented in the Bible, is all about — like a god of love. The Pagan roots of monotheism demonstrate a natural polarity in action and cannot be denied, from Christmas trees to Easter bunnies.

All centers are fundamentally asymmetric. The immortality that allows a center of awareness to be a soul that survives the body at death would be achieved because that centrality is organized as an expression of one of the fundamental poles of existence in relation to some expression of the other. This ensures that the soul never achieves the symmetry of being the entire polarity in one. It is in this fundamental asymmetry that the soul finds immortality and the open-ended creativity to explore. The soul is a maze. Simply, the more self-centered one becomes, the more one closes oneself off from eternal Nature — another ancient belief brought to light with reason. And a serious reason for a sense of humor in not taking oneself too seriously. The more symmetrical and homogeneous one becomes, the more unconsciously foolish one becomes. The lack of self-awareness, wit, and depth that goes with absurd posturing is often accompanied with the kind of aggression that cannot easily empathize.

In the absence of absolute polarity, it is the curious nature of this manifold polarity that neither pole can itself be a center of pure symmetry. If it were, the polarity would end and there would never have been anything at all. The polarity is an eternal, changing relationship, where the identity of self has the opportunity to grow in the discovery of the balance in thought and action. We need to learn about love to progress.

## 12. Samuel Passes the Torch

After hearing the substance of the essay that she would later write for this book, we began to clamor with the objection that Alice had said she wasn't going to get into the nature of soul and that she ended up doing just that, and why didn't she just say she was writing about love?

"You're so intellectual!" said Rolo.

"Look who's talking! You're so intellectual you've forced us to write this book," she responded flatly. "And this isn't the end of it! I was right to restrain myself from romance. Though I did go on a bit, I'll admit — but I said I'd do it before the salmon was done and I did — so there!" She was looking now at me.

There was a brief discussion about whether we should review the ABCs of the Transformation Proof again, but no one could countenance it, in writing or otherwise.

The salmon was in fact done by the time she had finished speaking. Alice is a good judge of the state of the coals.

As we all watched in silence, I asymmetrically translated the fish to a platter held by Lola. Alice got the big fork and removed each sweet potato, checking for tenderness.

The river meanwhile carried on its unselfconscious conversation with the rocks in the whitewater below the dam, as though remembering where a sawmill had powered a small boatbuilding business, of which there was no trace now but the few rusty ends of iron that I'd hammered flat years ago.

Alice had carefully placed the last sweet potato on a plate, and we realized that we were now listening to the water. There was assurance in the flow, and we quietly admitted to each other that it now seemed more than just imagination.

"You did it," said Rolo.

"Yep," I said.

"She did," Lola chimed in. "The river agrees."

It was understood that we weren't referring to the potatoes.

"So who speaks the language of the river?" I asked self-consciously, but they were listening again, and my question went by like the bubbles on the moving surface, bubbles and foam lit by the sparkling moonlight, springing from the base of the falls.

My question had been superfluous for sure, and I tried to get to the real question. "Alice, will you continue narrating the book?"

"Okay, if the others don't mind," came the somewhat distracted reply.

Everyone seemed agreeable with hardly a word, and we brought the salmon and sweet potatoes up to the porch and onto the driftwood table.

"Well, if you don't mind, Rolo," said Alice after a while, savoring a soft, juicy flake of barbecued salmon in her mouth, "I would like to introduce a fictional character to narrate the story of the Pearly Gates."

"Okay," he said, "but why?"

"Good point."

"But don't you think it might be a bit much to follow so soon with that story of mine, your having just disproved the existence of God? Shouldn't we intellectualize in the clouds a bit more before we come in for a landing with some hard fiction? I could always offer up some tasty morsels of mathematics." He passed along the broccoli.

"I think Alice has brought us home," I suggested.

She looked at me with the blue eyes and sweet, thin lips, lightly turned in a smile, and dabbed them with the edge of a napkin. "Since this is your home, Samuel, what a nice thing to say!"

# 13. At the Pearly Gates, by Rolo

Let's reenter the fictitious world of dreamland and myth to see what happened when God himself was hanging out at the Pearly Gates in conversation with St. Peter.

Along comes a cosmologist, after a long and distinguished career. God interrupts the conversation to draw the gates closed so Peter can do his thing. The professor looks up at the those gates and sees the great cross that is formed where the two gigantic doors close seamlessly — well, the trained eye of this scientific observer scans the workmanship and sees an irregularity. Out of habit he just happens to point it out to Peter who discovers the slight irregularity in the seam where the gigantic doors close at the Pearly Gates and doesn't get the point. But he becomes suspicious. Not of the gates but of the scientist.

"Is this a problem?" Peter asks indulgently. "I'm sure it won't interfere with your entrance to Heaven. This is quite routine, you understand. A quick check of the record is all we require." And the saint is about to open a huge volume that he carries with him on duty at the gates. But the scientist can't take his eyes off the slight break in the seam, high up on the great white Doors of Heaven, the Pearly Gates. Peter is distracted by this and can't get to the man's record without asking him if there is anything else.

"No . . . it's just that I didn't expect this . . ."

"What did you expect?"

"Well," and the guy sort of looks ashamed, "perfection, of course," and he looks around at the fluffy clouds and such, and adds, "if you see what I mean. You know, Heaven."

Peter frowns into the book of personal records. He thinks for a moment. "You are right. We'll just fix that." He calls out to God who is on the other side of the door listening. God's always on the other side of something listening, isn't he?

"I'll fix it!" shouts God. And sure enough the crack along the seam disappears and disappears and disappears — is God a perfectionist? — until the doors are such a perfect fit that they close seamlessly, literally seamlessly.

"Thanks," Peter calls out. He didn't hear God say, "How's that look?" So he shouts out, "Thank you! The flaw is completely gone! Thank you, God!"

No reply.

Well, the long and the short of it all was panic. Panic on the part of the scientist because he quickly figured out that the doors would no longer open. In fact they could no longer be seen, just a Great White Wall between the Pearly Gate Posts, which were more like towers. Panic on the part of Peter because he was shut out of heaven. Panic on the part of God because he was no longer in heaven, but in prison.

Then the scientist resorted to his old engineering instincts and tried to keep his head. Peter, on the other hand, hadn't had much practice for a couple thousand years. He stood there pale as a ghost. Then slowly the scientist realized that there was something wrong with the generally accepted idea of absolute symmetry. He looked up at the great seamless cross, where the doors used to meet to form the central post and realized that he had been mistaken; there was a flaw in the math back home. There was no absolute symmetry. There couldn't be, not really.

If there were such perfect symmetry, then nothing would have remained, and they would never have arrived at the gates to begin with. Then he realized that God might be quite upset because it was increasingly apparent that he wasn't the ultimate. If he had been the ultimate, then he could have pulled the doors closed with such pure symmetry that not only you couldn't tell the left door from the right door, but you wouldn't be able to tell the left side from the right side! And where would you be then? Nowhere much. Certainly not in Heaven. God would have been so powerful as to preempt his own existence, which would be so self-contradictory as to be powerless. So the doors were just jammed, fused shut.

Why? one might ask. Isn't an exact reflection what symmetry is all about? Or an exact center? Remembering the flaw, the irregularity in such a context, the scientist realized that the only thing that allows us to know where the one door ends and the other begins is the fact that we can't tell exactly where the one ends and the other begins! It's the irregularities that show up. Without them nothing would show up.

That's where we get texture and form. "We can feel where we can't tell exactly!" he exclaimed, as though awakening to a heavenly dream. "We can explore and explore that uncertainty, that rough edge! We can smooth it and smooth it! We can discover it! Because it is so uncertain, so lacking in absolute perfection, lacking in it to the degree, the degree . . ." He trailed off into thought. "To the degree of freedom!"

To put it another way, what we usually refer to as "symmetry" is really a slice of a moving process, like opening a book, turning the pages from right to left, or left to right, and then holding it open at the chosen page. There appears to be symmetry along the spine, but that symmetry has different sides and is really just a stage in a sequence of steps that continues after you put the book down.

While such thoughts passed though the scientist's disincarnate mind, Peter was turning from white to red as storm clouds formed out of the fluffy white ones. The scientist thought of the cycles in the weather, and with a private flash of lightening imagined the rings of pi opening up continuously, being unable to secure any absolute circle anywhere. The idea of original sin was turned on its head, as he looked up at the way the irregularity that had allowed the gates to function had been turned into the obstacle of doors jammed by God.

"Reincarnate me at once! I want to explore this cycle of imperfection some more. I've got work to do; my lab is waiting!" The words tumbled out. He had never been a believer in reincarnation.

"Reincarnation!" exclaimed Peter. "Never!" Then he simmered down. "Not so fast! The door is still jammed. Since you know so much, perhaps you would be good enough to unjamb it for us?"

"Only God can do that," came the reflexive reply. "He does have enormous power and He is the one who jammed it shut." Then he began to consider. "Maybe there is one more powerful — but certainly one less powerful isn't going to unjamb those doors. I'm not your man."

Then Peter perceived another issue that hadn't quite occurred to the scientist. The last thing God needed was to be saved by a moderate individual. The mere possibility that the man might come up with the idea of how to save God from this prison was unthinkable.

So just as the scientist, no slouch in politics himself, was about to reevaluate his position, seeing the opportunity to right the balance for the common man, Peter cut him off. "Wait!" He held up a hand and looked towards a particularly devilish accumulating storm cloud.

The scientist saw which way the wind was blowing and ran off through the sky. He was so comical running up there in the blue that Arielle, goddess of the wind and currants, sailing along in a hot-air balloon, caught up with him, and they sailed off together.

They left Satan and St. Peter in conversation at the Pearly Wall, blowing hot and cold.

"I used to be his top angel before He threw me down to Hell," said ol' Nick with a sulky, injured look, looking up at the gates, followed by a satisfied smile. "Why don't you just get the genies and the giants to help you out?"

"No," said Peter resolutely. "You're going to do it — with me — and maybe some of the others from your domain. And God will push from the other side, no doubt. But when we break through and they ask where the great crack in that perfectly seamless wall at the Pearly Gates came from, it's going to be the Devil's work, that's for sure."

"And if I refuse?"

"Refuse and the moderates will win out!"

And so they went to work.

# III. River of Asymmetry

"What matters it how far we go?" his scaly friend replied.
"There is another shore, you know, upon the other side."

—Lewis Carroll, *The Lobster Quadrille*

# 14. Transition

It might seem a bit useless to substitute one fictional character as narrator for another. If you do not believe that this is Alice carrying on from Samuel to get the job done, then read on! We have here a key transition in our group project. We feel that we have proved that no one can be the sole creator of anything, so the torch has been passed to me.

Every author needs to have conditions where the work becomes possible, even if that does not need to amount to multiple authors. The key transition here is that among the characters being created for this book, we have added the one called God. As an absolute deity, God could not really be a character in fiction or mythology. As an absolute he did not exist, without basically contradicting himself. Within any coherent work that tried to include him as a character, real or imagined, this was a weakness. It would be unclear to whom the author was referring. It would also go some way to explain the many faces of God in the Old and New Testaments, the Torah, the Koran, and related works of monotheism. A loving but vengeful God is hard to piece together, unless He is viewed as a reflection of society. The Pagan gods definitely had the jump on God in this respect, as the volumes of world mythology testify. Not only did the Pagans do a far more comprehensive job of reflecting the people, they had gods who, in the absence of having to be impossible, had weaknesses we can really identify with. When they were "impossible" it was for other reasons.

That being said, a character in mythology does have the same credibility issues that I now share in some small way, having taken over from Samuel. What we believe is happening in this present transition is that we are all getting more grounded in reality, and God has been liberated as a character. He is no longer so imprisoned behind the Pearly Gates, because those gates and their denizens have been brought a little more — or a lot more — into the world of fiction and myth. That is, after all, where pearly gates of such magnitude are most at home.

Likewise, by bringing the gift of reason to myth, we have opened the door a stage further to inspiration from those characters whom the Ancient Greeks referred to as the Muses. While we have not carried our logic of change to the extent of proving that the Muses exist as such, we have opened the door to some interesting possibilities concerning the range of consciousness.

Given that the environment is important to inspiration, it is a good thing Samuel has this atelier in Maine, where we have converged to accomplish this task.

In order to open this door or gateway a bit further, I am introducing what I sometimes like to call "the mythology of math." This is an extension of the logic of change, for which we will need some more of Rolo's stories. This one, "The Lady of the Lake or the Rings of Pi," was polished by Lola. You will be able to see her hand in the softening of the style from the present tense to the past. In spite of themselves, at times, Rolo and Lola really do balance each other like sun and moon, grounding us mythological, fictional characters, including Samuel.

## 15. The Lady of the Lake or The Rings of Pi, by Rolo

In response to an overexcited professor who was unable to articulate what he had just seen, the entire lab team, with an accumulating number of students, faculty and staff caught up in the excitement, trooped out of the science building and into the nearby woods, along the path to the meadow beyond, and to the edge of a pond. The professor took a pebble and threw it into the water. The rings went out, and out of them arose a beautiful woman. All he had been able to say with confidence was that it was, "The Lady! The Lake! Of the Lake!" Now they understood and were themselves overexcitedly silent. So she walked over to them across the water and spoke to them directly, like this:

"I would like to express to you as simply as possible the creative mystery of the circle. It is perhaps the easiest way to demonstrate the nature of infinity. Now I will need some help.

"We see here a field where we all stand. I would like you to open out in your midst as I walk inwards, thank you, thank you, excuse me please, thank you." The audience opened a way for her to enter and formed a roughly circular space around her as she walked onto the shore.

"Now just open out a little further, please, that's it, so, more over there, thank you, there, that's enough, so!

"Now I need a volunteer to take up a position somewhere in the middle. You? All right. Find a comfortable middle and stand. Good.

"Now watch and listen closely.

"Suppose we want to make a circle. First we have one in mind, all of us, just concentrate on our ideal circle. Among us all there must be some sort of general idea of that first circle for this demonstration. We will call it circle A.

"Now we will try to make circle A more of a reality here in this opening. So we need a radius, right? I will go to the person in the middle and — when I get there . . . Okay here I am — I take an imaginary radius with me and stretch it back with me to a point over here where I will stand."

She walked back to a point on what would be the circumference and held the end of the imaginary radius while the person in the middle held the other end.

"There we are! Now we want to map out our circle. We have to use this radius to do it. There is no other way, is there? Remember that this radius is like a fan; it really stretches in many directions, not just to me.

"And let's not forget circle A! So our friend in the middle can now drop the end of the radius and you next to me can take a bit of it and the person next to you and so on in a rough circle on and on — until we run out of radius, right? You over there are approximately at the end of this length of radius. Will you hold out the imaginary end for us so we can see where it ends? So!

"Now hold tight while I walk with this end on around the circumference of circle A, which is our sort of common ideal pattern to build on. And now as I walk, I can give you folks along the inner edge here parts of the radius to hold, as it curves around to form circle B. Now we have the length of the diameter.

"You all know that there is a number called pi. It is the number of times the diameter needs to be used to form the circumference of the circle. The number is about 3.14 with a string of decimals. So we take the diameter along here one more time and — I'll walk with the end again — and I'm almost back where I started, and the third group of you along the edge of what is becoming circle B are holding the curving, changing diameter.

"Now the magic begins to appear. Can I get back to where I started? I can take one tenth of the diameter and move along a bit further. I then take four hundredths and move a little closer. The number pi says I can keep on taking some small portion, albeit smaller portions, but still I can carry on as long as I like and never return to where I started exactly. I can't go back! I can always keep adding bits of the radius without ever getting back where I was standing, let alone back to where I was before you threw that pebble.

"So I won't try to do the impossible. But we must close the circle somehow. So there is only one way to do that, and that is simply to draw it together, to pull the radius along a bit further until it looks close enough, until I am standing more or less back where I was and leave it at that. And so by creating a new shape — by warping or flattening infinity here and there, so to speak — we put a stop to the infinitely recurring decimals of pi! And what is wrong with that? How else could we have formed a circle? So we can see that the perfect, ideal circle A — that by convention repeats with infinite perfection — had to have been flattened. Otherwise we would have had to keep chasing the end, and there would never have been a circle B. That attempt at perfection is a process that leads nowhere, like a dog chasing its tail — it does not even establish a point.

"Well, some people might say we have warped the circle a bit, flattened it a bit, where we had to pull it together without going round in a perfect curve. But did any of you think that our group-circle A was perfectly symmetrical, perfectly round?"

No one was absolutely sure.

"Together, we had only a rough idea of circle A to start with. Circle A had individuality like our little group here, didn't it? And so does circle B. It has a character of its own where it is a little flattened, where perhaps some of you along the edge here tugged at the radius a little more than the others to get me back more or less where I started. So now I am somewhere slightly new; and so are all of us on this new circle B.

"So, you would have to be quite alone to think you had a perfect circle in mind, yes? And nobody is that alone, as we are discovering. Such a lonely number is a fiction.

"So the amazing thing about pi is that it is not just one number but many, and each variation says we can keep making new circles forever, as long as we like. Of course we don't have to! And that's the other thing about pi and about our newly discovered asymmetric infinity. They both say we must stop somewhere because we can always continue. That's the balance. If we are free to continue, we are also free to stop. It is not a dictator that says we must always keep going. This is the effect of our asymmetrical circle and gives us a wave pattern of polarity, like stop and go. And, like stop and go, every wave has its points.

"So pi stops when we stop generating circles. It is like a tool, like a tape measure used by a carpenter; we can pull it out only as far as we need to and then put it aside until we need to create a new circle with a new number of pi. It can't be used always fully extended. That would be to misunderstand infinity, to be overly theoretical, and it would be quite useless. When pi is set aside, it does not continue to create circles, it is set aside like a circle-creating engine that is switched off. Setting it aside is a way to allow something new. This is true of any number line, as well as that part of it we call pi. We activate pi when a circle comes into being. It is like an engine. And that's because there never was a perfect circle and perfect pi to begin with, one where pi would be furiously spinning out its decimals to some distant 'ideal infinity' all the time somehow. No, that's not infinity. That would be a much too final destination, a perfect paradox, definitely an extreme situation and one that does not happen. Pi is a happening, a work in progress, not something that has already happened — already been counted to perfection — but is somehow still spinning out numbers at the same time.

"Infinity is the freedom, the opportunity, to open up and create, not a state of being infinite in number like a huge crazy finite number — already counted, but not. Infinity happens when we decide to go from A to B with all the divisions in between tied off in one step. Asymmetric infinity is sort of knotted at the end. What sort of a knot it is depends on its relationships. Different knots for different uses.

"Because asymmetric infinity exists, I never repeat anything exactly the same way, like I never returned to where I was when we started circle B, and our helper in the middle will never find the exact center, and I'm sure he would not like to have to try. But if he will move away from where he is standing a little bit, he may discover something where there is no perfect, absolute center, where we pulled the radius to bring the circle together. A mystery of science. Because nothing does not exist, where there is no center there is — in this instance — a well."

As he came towards her, the well opened up into a pool of clear water on the shore. As the assembly broke up and moved slowly back and out from the developing pool, the water streamed after them in many rivulets, fanned out, becoming a small pond until she called out to them to stay where they were. "That's far enough — stop right there! Stay where you are; let's switch off the engine of pi! Circles A and B are all we need among us here and now. And as you can see we have a phenomenon, a happening here! This always happens with circles, they always have what we might visualize as an asymmetric infinitesimal well in the middle, one that moves out and broadcasts something as it comes into being. It broadcasts in many ways, but not in a perfectly infinite number of ways, right? It's a rhythmic event that goes with our own rhythms. In most cases on this planet, the well of pi goes unnoticed. I have joined you to help it to rise up and show itself to us as this beautiful little pool of what is now something like water and almost touching the larger pond at a tangent. You can move closer to it and dip your hands into it and feel the waters of the slipstream of pi. Instead of the fiction of a perfect center, we have some scientific magic here!"

They followed her advice as she continued, "Our circles A and B each had a characteristic beat as the broadcast overflowed their circumferences, according to the way we tightened each circle up, bringing it together, each one of us participating in the radius as it came together to describe the threshold, circumference and form, of the individual circle."

The new pond began to flow and merge with the larger one.

"You also know that the relationship between the radius and the surface area is pi, which we multiply by the square of the radius. To give this pool a three-dimensional touch, we can multiply further by 4, and we have the surface of a sphere."

They looked into the enlarged pond, and it was now like the top of a deep, crystalline globe, framed by the irregular shoreline.

"The infinite incompleteness of the creative circle will always allow the choice of whether to try to approximate the truth with a workable falsehood, such as the idea of a perfectly symmetrical circle with a perfectly exact perimeter, or to accept that nature has thresholds to new horizons, new worlds.

"You may now advance further into the world of nature."

They cautiously stepped into the curving pond. The ripples made by their entrance lifted the surface of the globe into the sky over their heads, extending the top of the globe in concentric spheres, like giant bubbles within each other, together containing the surrounding land with the nearby pond, before the adventurers had submerged themselves any further. They looked up to see the ripples turn into fresh clouds in a blue sky that had replaced the polluted skies of their old world.

They descended the gentle slope of a pyramid. Their guide continued among them. "As you can see, we are on a triangle. We have followed the circle and come to a triangle. When we decided to cut the engine of pi and rest at one of its decimal places, we acknowledged that numbers are not exact enough to return us to our stating point. We accepted the true nature of pi. As a result we are able to proceed to the next number on the number line, the number four. Our circle changed into some other shape and it is able to continue to change shape in nature's living geometry.

"Now pi has opened out into an old-fashioned relationship where the sum of the squares of the two sides is equal to the square of the hypotenuse. We were not intercepted by any exact or absolutely final symmetry. Nor did our radius run wild and carry us away into a chaotic universe or trap us forever going round in the first circle. Instead, with the asymmetric balance of nature's infinity, we have followed the threshold in the maze that goes from the circle to the triangle in rhythmic motion. Having set aside our radius and pi, we moved forward in reality.

"Here we can pause for a moment to reflect that all our lines and circles are grounded, circles have traction, whether we just think of them or travel along their ways to this point. Our thoughts are rhythmic. We think in rhythmic mazes. That is why we remember things. The ripples of memory travel along lines that are not mere theoretical concepts but are physical realities that strike our emotions with the power of memory when they come through the maze."

They paused together on the side of the pyramid and began to remember where they were.

"There is no theoretical or Platonic or *ideal* alternative to this ninety-degree triangle. It is part of the specific and characteristic number line that we used to bring us home. There is no theoretically absolute alternative to the number 2 that describes the square of these characteristic sides, because there are no non-geographical, absolute lines. There is no absolute and theoretical place where, say, the cube of these sides would fit together, nor any other number than the squares of the sides that add up to the square of the base of our triangle on this specific pyramid, sprinkled with these very flowers. There is no absolute, theoretical line; every line has its physical and geometrical — even, as I say, geographical — place in the universe. Yes, and that is because each triangle has its own personality, just as our two circles had some of the personality of our little group where they were pulled together. The shape was grounded by our action. Is this what Monsieur

Fermat was onto?" She turned to the previously overexcited scientist and took a deep breath.

"With everything being so grounded geographically, if I may put it so, even our numbers have physical relationships, as though they are related by different points of the compass. There are no numbers without some geometry. Of course we can imagine geometry that does not really happen. The corresponding form that takes place in our mind when we do so is not the impossible shape, just a suggestion of it. That is why the specialized open-endedness of numbers is so important. Otherwise we could not imagine—

"I say *specialized* because no shape or form can become just any other shape or form. The lack of perfect symmetry makes such perfect randomness impossible. This triangle where the square of the sides adds up to the square of the hypotenuse cannot just become some other shape where, say, the cube of the sides works just as well in relation to the hypotenuse, not without a connecting pathway between the two shapes, whatever universe the second shape might inhabit! Can we get there from here? Such a relationship between such different places would require a deep change in our present triangle and its numbers. As it stands, Fermat was right.

"So the number 2 is not so absolute, nor is pi, rather they are like doors to different places, some more familiar than others in the maze of life. And the doors change with use, like a river under a bridge. Now that we are acclimatizing ourselves to the transition, we may continue."

Listening to the caress of her words like a friendly stream that required little attention was reassuring, while directing their thoughts to work on a bit of a puzzle, so they avoided most of the shock of memory beyond birth and death.

"You remember that this old pyramid has slightly rounded corners, not just with the long years and seasons but that it was specifically designed that way, without the attempt to have absolutely symmetrical angles, which accounts for the grassy slope and the fact that we can soon find the path to the village. Are there any questions?"

A voice from their midst piped up: "Excuse me, please, but I have a question about the decimals of pi."

Someone suppressed a yawn.

"If we could switch on the decimals for as long as we like and build up additional bits that extend the line — well, how come you couldn't just extend the radius along the circumference until you returned exactly to where you had begun?—"

Someone else stretched and stared at the horizon.

"Back," he continued, "to the exact spot where you had been standing when you started the demonstration that got us here? I mean, how did we get here? How do we know we are truly here? Am I really remembering this? Is this real?"

There was silence.

A feminine voice in the group spoke up: "The answer to your question is that no matter how long we let pi spin out the decimals, we must choose to stop them somewhere, we must choose the approximate size of our unit along the line, we must decide how far we will go before we pull the circle together and its unique character is created. The nature of pi strongly suggests that we do not waste time trying to extend it forever. After all, each successive little decimal diminishes considerably, even though we can add as much as we choose. Pi hints strongly for us to step back and take our time to consider the situation. It is the responsible thing to do, not to get carried away, right? So we design the circle by choosing the size of the last unit just as we must decide the size of every unit along any number line we use, or just let them be rough until we need more precision. After all, we decided to use pi when we decided to make a circle. How can a perpetually and instantaneously expanding infinity require us to make a circle that is in any way perfectly finite? It is not right or logical to dictate that the repeating units must be absolutely the same, or that anything should be absolute, or to dictate how we must choose at all — that's a self-contradiction. It is through choice that we can know where we are, and who we are, for that matter. That's the reality."

"I took that course," someone was heard to whisper.

"So every unit is different?" the piper pursued his questioning.

"That's right, nothing repeats exactly anywhere, everything is always being created, as far as I can see," she replied.

"Then the decimals are assumed to be switched off when they connect with the next unit on the line?"

"Yes, it's a wave, where each unit merges with the next. Circles move into new circles and into other geometrical shapes in the way we arrived at our destination."

"Where do they merge?" he persisted.

Someone else spoke up in reply, "If you could say with absolute exactitude at what point they merge, then she would be standing exactly back where she started the circle and we could never be here — or anywhere, come to think of it. It is because we cannot say exactly, that's why we were able to pull the circle together and created it out of the slipstream of pi, and the well rose up from the center because the center is always moving in rhythmic patterns."

"So we just chose to come here?"

"To some extent—"

"So why couldn't we just choose this option before? I'm sure many of us have wished very much—"

"But we did not know the way. She does."

"But how do you know that nothing repeats exactly?"

"Infinity allows you always to add something," another professor joined in. "So you can never say exactly where anything ends; the very thought of finding the end opens it up by connecting it with all your experience. How can you repeat anything exactly when you have not finalized it absolutely? You cannot, fortunately. So here we are! I remember now."

"So there are no theoretical thoughts, they are all physical thoughts," someone muttered to herself.

"Can we move on now?" someone else asked with restraint.

But the other piped up again, "So the line I am walking is an extension of pi — so that must mean that the relationships of the right-angled triangle you described are another way of looking at a circle, like the horizon at sea can look like a straight line but is really part of a great circle, except that in the case of the triangle it's a little more removed, a little more subtle. There's a connecting path."

"Yes, that is right," said the goddess.

"Ah! I am beginning to remember. So there are no non-physical places; you can't stand outside it. In a way, we have always been here — at home!"

"It's the maze," she confirmed. "The slipstream of pi allows the path to open up before you. As you approach, step by step, because there are no exact repetitions and no absolute steps, subtle pressures build for a change that can surprise you as your destination approaches. The more you move, the more the consistency of the motion — in the absence of any absolutely repetitive motion — builds pressure that will slow us up and eventually bring us to pause again. Now what have we here!" She gazed over the rooftops of a village.

"Nothing repeats exactly?" the questioner repeated. "Because the potential of infinity keeps anything from being exact enough to be repeated exactly? But . . . but . . . Well, I guess you have to be able to finish something off totally before you know how to repeat it absolutely correctly. You need an absolutely finished product first . . . or you don't know . . . exactly what you're going to repeat absolutely . . . So you can't really have a first . . . And if you keep trying to have a first, the repetition does build pressures . . . which gush and overlap from a highly repetitive circle — like a slipstream."

"Like now?" said someone next to him. "Why don't you just enjoy your senses for a while, take a break!"

"And share it with us!" added a further voice.

"All right, all right! I give up! I can't help it if I'm so insecure I can't even enjoy this dramatic event. That's why I keep asking for answers!"

"Too clever by half," said another.

"That's not what he needs to hear," said another still. "I'm encouraged by his questions. Look! another pond, right here in the side of the hill." She threw a pebble into it and watched the rings thoughtfully. "The Big Bang theory assumes an exact center of symmetry. Increasingly scientists think it's only part of the story."

They watched in silence for a while.

"This time you return on your own. But I will always be with you, if you know what I mean," said the Lady of the Lake.

They looked longingly to the nearby village but turned reluctantly and cautiously stepped into the pond as it formed a dome, and, step by step, they emerged onto the shore from the pond at the university campus. The nearby pool had vanished. Their feet were wet.

A student who had gone looking for them had sat down on the grass along the shore to rest a while and think. She was about to cast another pebble into the pond. A translucent wave, crystal clear but visible, with accumulating waves within it, mushroomed upwards from the water with a fragrance of gardens in a fairy tale and the feeling of a cleansing, healing atmosphere. The students and professors stepped off the ripples. As they walked slowly onto the grass, she stood up in shock, but heard someone repeat thoughtfully, "So you mean that because there are no perfectly symmetrical circles, there can always be more circles — no one is ultimately excluded, so nature is inclusive, and that's the meaning of pi."

# 16. Context and Induction, by Lola

The difficulty of grappling with infinity can be seen as being one of context. In the example given by Samuel in the maze, he found himself in a different context, depending on which rung he was on. The relationships kept changing.

Moving out toward wider and wider rungs, as soon as we find what appears to be the last rung, we might be inclined to assume that it must inhabit a wider context, as though the horizon has been pushed back, forming yet another rung of an ever-expanding maze. This assumption is a natural human tendency, and we forget to consider whether we should adjust our assumption using a new understanding about the universal *generalization* of "changes of ever widening horizons."

Asymmetry in the logic of change keeps us from getting ahead of ourselves. There is no reason to infer from the rungs we have visited that they just keep going out. This lack of a reason for what is called "induction" has been a stumbling block, identified by the eighteenth-century philosopher David Hume. This interruption of what seemed to be the historic forward march of reason has plagued the legacy of the Enlightenment or Age of Reason, when democracy was eventually reborn in America. Reason seemed to have failed to predict where we should go and what we should do, because it could not connect the empirical evidence of the rungs currently in use with other destinations. This has kept us a bit more humble and cautious, perhaps, except for the explosion of a countervailing romanticism and hero worship that had been feeling repressed. In the timid heart of the rationalist, the romantic struggled to get out until it turned itself into a beast.

Scientists, like many animals, use reason and evidence, typically proceeding with openness and caution. They use the senses and instruments, like a cat's whiskers, analyzing the feedback, formulating possible explanations that must be capable of falsification. For example, the cat may have "hypothesized" that the windowsill was a good place to sit in the sun — until it heard a strange sound on the other side of the wall. Upon further investigation it might find its hypothesis to be false. The process was useful, something was learned, because the hypothesis was capable of being proven wrong. In that sense it was a good hypothesis.

As is somewhat the case with many animals, the theories constructed by scientists are based on considerable experience, using their hypotheses (sounds like an evolutionary adaptation) to feel the way. Notice that this "feeling" of the way involves making up hypotheses, which is akin to making up fiction. Without the ability to fictionalize, the science can't happen, even as the possible scenarios need a factual context for analogy. There is a balance, like putting forward one foot then the other. This is what it is to proceed asymmetrically. Conversely, the attempt to use pure symmetry is like the leap of blind faith. Humans tend to try mixtures of both attempts, but we are discovering that the two are mutually exclusive. Any asymmetry means there is no absolute symmetry. But nothing has been lost and there is everything to gain.

Although they have theories that predict, for example, that the sun will rise tomorrow, scientists still do not say absolutely that it will. But science uses math and math uses induction.

Mathematical induction assumes that a series can just keep going out to something called "infinity," even as it assumes by induction that the "something" that is supposed to go on forever has already been counted. If it has been counted, and if each number counted is finite, infinity is finite — which goes nowhere, being an unreasonable paradox.

I will not try to preempt Samuel's essay, "More About the Absence and Something About Set Theory," but to truly consider the individual unit as *absolutely* finite is to strip away any meaning from it and therefore from that which is in directly symmetrical opposition to the absolutely finite — the "infinite" of mathematical induction.

As we have seen by the ABCs of the logic of change, absolute finality in any object destroys even the mere possibility of that object existing, along with any other such objects in any series of any extent. In order for there to be a defining boundary and to generate a series, asymmetry is needed throughout.

Nevertheless, it is routinely assumed that it is possible for an object to be absolutely final and still exist in the context of another object and be accordingly connected by some further relationship with that other, all in a context that is open to changes involving mathematical operations on the series. Examples would include any series of units or any set of numbers where there is some kind of repetition that is supposed to be absolutely exact. Certainly it is illogical to imagine that such absolute exactitude could be achieved without absolute finality.

Take, for example, the seemingly simple series: 1, 2, 3, 4. It is built by adding a unit each time. Each number is considered to be perfectly exact, and therefore it would seem to be final in its own right — but it is still somehow sufficiently connected to the others to form a series. This series must harbor the assumption that the units of which it is composed can be exactly repeated in some way. But in order to repeat exactly, they must each be absolutely final. Otherwise, as previously asked by Alice, what exactly to repeat? At the risk of being repetitive, the exact repetition could not happen without absolute finality at each step. We have already proved that such finality cannot exist in a context of change, and our series does pretend to exist in such a context.

Consider the following thought experiment, as another way of visualizing this impossibility.

Say you are inside a box. The box is absolutely final in the sense that there is nothing more than the box, nothing beyond it — just the box; it is final. Therefore, if the box exists, then nothing else can exist. There is mutual exclusivity between the box and any other existence. It follows that in order for us to be in the absolutely final world of the box, we could not consider it from an actual outside perspective (we could only imagine it that way). If we were able to observe the box from any other perspective, then the box would not be absolutely final. There would be something beyond it — us.

Now imagine the box shrinking and shrinking down as far as you like, while its finality remains intact. If it were to reach an absolutely infinitesimal point, its mere existence would be all there is, in this story.

Again, this situation self-contradicts, as the infinity would also have to be absolutely finite. No pattern can truly have any absolute finality and still be considered in a further context, including any further changes in size.

Now the interesting deduction is that without absolute finality we cannot have the absolute exactitude required to assume the repetition in mathematical induction to infinity. Instead our infinity must take on a shape that is characteristic of the context in which it is found, and it must be an open shape with connectivity and potential. The box cannot become completely infinitessimal. It must maintain an identity, like in the story, and it cannot be all there is.

An asymmetrically infinite series — where infinity is necessarily "flattened" somewhat (to use that expression from Rolo's "The Lady of the Lake") — would only go as far as required for the purpose at hand. Rather than extending to some paradoxical or Platonic infinity, it extends to a generally unspecified number. This is a new kind of number that needs some sort of a name, so I will call it MU or the Greek letter µ, for Maximum or Minimum Unspecified. Also MU sounds flexible to me. The number is left unspecified in the same way as a generalization should leave a *relevant* loose end, as described in Samuel's story of the onion.

It is open-ended to the degree that the context allows. And a context is thereby established for the numbers in use. No further context would be necessary until things change so as to require a change in the more universal context, a new and necessarily unspecified horizon — MU. But not absolutely unspecified; MU shares the characteristic of other asymmetric numbers in that, like objects A and B in our proof, it is not absolutely final in the degree to which it is open or closed.

So we can *deduce* that mathematical *induction* as a whole is illogical and based on a misunderstanding of infinity, where an asymmetric generalization is being misidentified, causing a paradox in thinking. Infinity is often used as a kind of universal number, but as we have discovered, universals do not make sense unless they have specific, open-ended asymmetry. The specificity is possible because we have left unspecified loose ends. Instead of the symmetrical finite/infinite paradox in a series, we substitute the specified/unspecified contrast, the balance which allows the degrees of the series.

Our logic of change is a deductive process using a proof by contradiction, where we show that if one assumes absolute finality, one encounters a self-contradiction, whereas otherwise one finds a balanced development of reason.

So, in order to come to terms with the nature of infinity, we look at finality, since the meaning of infinity depends on what we understand about finality. If finality could be absolute, then infinity would be absolute; it would be assumed to be already counted of necessity, by nature of its units — while also continuing paradoxically onwards, extending or counting out the numbers. But in the absence of absolute finality, infinity pauses with the nature of change, as numbers merge into one another and emerge specifically. Infinity becomes rhythmic in our new understanding and incapable of the absolutely exact repetition required for the paradox. If infinity has rhythm, an asymmetric series must have a pulse to share in that rhythm. The rhythm would sometimes arise as near symmetries break. It would be a somewhat arrhythmic pulse and give rise to scattered objects such as prime numbers. But these scattered objects would not be randomly distributed; they would have a more musical relationship.

Although induction as a whole is illogical, a kind of "phase induction" is a different story when infinity is flattened, where a chosen set or a group of numbers or objects repeat asymmetrically in a series to the end of a phase in the context MU.

The nature of infinity shows up as a specialized potential that only opens up in the absence of absolute finality in a particular instance — and goes no further than the open-ended case allows, until other relationships change. There is a specialized sense of direction. This happens in the absence of the kind of absolutes required for anything to be completely random.

Pure randomness requires the absolute symmetry of, for example, the ideal coin that can be flipped in an ideal world where the coin's chances of landing with one side up or the other are represented by exactly the same, identical, absolute number, being 50 percent for each side. In this "ideal" world there would be no other breezes than the one ideal breeze that would catch the coin in its one absolute mid flight. Only one ideal hand would be able to flip and catch it. Only one ideal reader would read the result, and it wouldn't matter what the outcome was, because either side would read the same. But this can only be imagined in fiction, because the ideal world would not even achieve such blandness, where not the slightest change would occur. In reality, such a paradoxical world would fall so short of any ideal that it could not exist at all. One of the many gifts of fiction is that it allows us to reason by representing illogical situations, so we can tell the difference.

Therefore, in nature the scientist can deduce, for example, that the Earth cannot *randomly* cease to spin on its axis and result in the sudden absence of a sunrise. This leaves open possibilities that *can* occur, given the constraints of specific physical relationships involving planet Earth. This degree of predictability and opportunity is a good thing, not only for the legacy of the Enlightenment. It will help to put science and, as I hope we will discover, ethics in a refreshing new light. And now I feel a bit of science fiction coming on, with the idea of emerging numbers.

# 17. Totalitarian Math, by Rolo

When the Earthling spaceship landed in Manitou, the visitors found a place of great natural beauty.

The captain of the ship and his landing party were invited to meet with a group of representatives who appeared to them to be barbarian. In some cases the behavior of these inhabitants of Manitou seemed too expressive, in other cases they weren't wearing enough clothes, and if they were clothed, it was not in the right way. But perhaps worst of all, the women were out of control, having an equal say with the men. Still, the captain was flattered, though somewhat surprised, that not only were they fluent in his language, but also the clear fresh atmosphere was like that of the Earth in ancient times. He was flattered like a man who has been chosen by his god to reclaim the Garden of Eden. So he would press forward with the formalities and get to the point.

Toward the end of the meeting, the captain, losing patience, demonstrated some Earthling technology, in his usual show of power. He then flatly declared that the people of Earth knew all the science that there was to know and that their government was the Platonic ideal. He concluded by saying that it was all as true as "two and two are four."

Although he was expecting some questions about who this man Plato was and about what sort of republic it would be, and although he had some ready answers about Socratic methods of questioning, he was quite sure that this would be a simple case of securing the land for his government in a routine way, by force, on his way home to Earth. So he was unprepared when one of the female representatives simply asked, "Which two?"

"What do you mean, which two? Two and two are four, that's all."

"Well then, there's no more to be said," she replied, and got up from a comfortable chair opposite the one where the captain was seated.

"So you agree to follow our ways of wisdom and allow us to rule over you in our benevolent empire!" he quickly exclaimed, arising himself, as if to take possession of the leadership role, to seize the moment before it was too late.

"You agreed there is no more to be said," she replied. "Besides, you would have to speak to the people, to convince more than just me. We're a democracy, in Manitou."

The Earthling smiled to himself at the primitive state of these people. "So were we — once."

"More than once, according to our records. And according to our tradition, if you want to remain in Manitou, you have to decide which two you want to make four. Or you have to decide not to decide. That keeps us from making absurd generalizations, so Manitou can grow in a balanced way."

"Two and two are four is an absurd generalization! That's a laugh." There were some dutiful chuckles among his subordinates. The captain decided to indulge the strange ritual of numbers.

"In the land of Manitou," she continued, "you get to choose which two — in Manitou." The brief pun silenced them.

"One man one vote, eh?"

"One person, one vote."

"The rule of the rabble!"

"At least it's not random chaos."

"Meaning us, I presume? You savages are certainly two of something, every bit too much. And too many I might add!" He looked across at his bodyguards. He could hardly believe they had been allowed to retain their weapons while the natives appeared to be unarmed.

"In your world," he sneered, "I suppose organization is quite random. You clearly can't see the difference. But I suppose that's to be expected, if you can't even understand that two and two are four." There was more routine laughter.

"Totalitarian math," she replied. "We understand very well how some organizations can inflict random chaos and ruin."

"Yes, totalitarian it is. We have grown up enough culturally to accept the reality of it. And we are offering you the chance to join us. To become evolved and share in the benefits of our technology. Or face — random chaos and ruin."

"Just like that?" said a voice from the back of the room.

The citizen of Manitou came forward, threw open the front door to the street and said: "Tell me now, Captain, outside that door, is that just any street?"

"Yes, in a sense."

Then he threw open the windows, "And out there, in the garden, is that just any old tree?"

"Yes, in a way."

"Am I just any ol' person?"

"Well, Yes. You aren't so egotistical that you can't humble yourself to the truth, now are you? In effect, in the wide world, in the cosmos, you are just any old person; whether you can accept it or not is another question."

"How 'bout you?"

"Yes, me too, in all modesty."

"How about what you are saying about things being just any ol' thing? Are you saying just any ol' thing about any ol' thing?"

"No, of course not!"

"So you change your mind when it suits you! That's a double standard. It's okay for you to be specific about all these things being just any ol' things; but when it comes to this judgment on randomness, it's not just any ol' judgment! That's unfair. But if you keep the same standard, then you are speaking nonsense by saying it's just any ol' judgment. In Manitou, at least, any ol' judgment is no judgment at all! So you can't positively say that anything at all is random. So how do you expect to deliver such a thing as random chaos and ruin?"

The captain flushed with anger.

The man continued, "Say, you don't really believe that you're just any ol' person, do you? You think you're better than us; isn't that what you were saying? That you would guide us! That's not confidence; that's not leadership; that's class arrogance, that's what that is!

"Two and two are four specifically when it pleases you. We still want to know which two."

"All our two's are exactly equal, so don't be ridiculous." The captain was taken aback by this man's brazen concern for logic in the face of death.

"Perfect reflections of one another?" the other persisted.

"Quite," replied the captain.

"In fact, exactly symmetrical, perfectly repeating?"

"Yes — what's the point about all this?"

"Such exact equality as to make them in some way identical, the same, in fact, in the same location, in the same time and the same space? A sort of place that is really any place, or no place specific, an absolute mystery of relativity?"

"Exactly."

"Just a flip of the ideal coin which one you get first, just a random chance?"

The other did not reply.

"Or divine will?" the citizen persisted.

The silence deepened.

"We are so imperfect we can't know such divine perfection?" the questioning continued.

"But of course, that is why we are offering you guidance. You certainly seem to have enough questions that you need it!"

"By the divine light of your god?"

"By the divine wisdom of his Heavenly Majesty."

"So we can discover that in reality we are one?"

"It is His will."

"That there is no 'two and two' and no 'four,' but just one?"

"Mathematics is just a tool for His divine crusade. You are beginning to see beyond the veil of illusion."

"The deeper truth is that there is just one?"

"And that One is infinite."

"Ah, not only one but infinite, plus all the other numbers, thrown in for good measure!"

"Now you blaspheme! We have wasted enough time in this useless talk with savages. You have had your chance to join peacefully. Seize them!"

But the Earthlings were rooted to the ground and could not move.

The lady explained, "In Manitou, one's nature is brought out. You are now as close to being with your ideal god as possible: in exactly the same place, in the same time and the same space, as far as possible — in the absolute. You have no further space and time to move from there to here, or here to there. You are almost absolutely stuck. We will have to return you to where the environment will support you in your illusion."

The space travelers stiffened in shock.

"Oh don't worry. Not even nature's technology is perfect. Your environment can't support your illusion forever. The more you destroy its thresholds to Manitou, the more you cut yourselves off, the sooner you will die off, but not yet. Just as your available time to find which two, three, or four steps to take is limited.

"Each specific step opens out into the next characteristic step with its own creative energy, out into the multiplicity of nature's bounty, even though it's just another step for you to take. A small, seemingly insignificant matter of arithmetic. But we find it worth asking." She paused and looked from one traveler to the next.

"As I said, it keeps us from over-generalizing — though it does set up a threshold at the borders, where things can get too specific sometimes for our guests who begin to see us as inhospitable.

"So, if any of you can tell us which two, then you will find some specific stepping stones across the threshold of Manitou. Then you will find the way, according to our tradition of asking the riddle of 'which two.' But your time is running out!"

Then she began to count, "One — two — three —," while the terrified Earthlings looked at her as though she were performing some diabolical ritual. "Four! Five! Six! Seven—"

As they began to fade into bits and pieces, and their spaceship broke up and faded with them, out of Manitou, some broke ranks, while the rest returned back to where they had begun, in the environment that had specifically evolved to support them in their actions, giving them opportunities.

The ones who had quickly but cautiously stepped forward, with a sufficient degree of individual and characteristic care and attention, breaking ranks with the brute force of the aggressors, these were just in time to witness the strange, apparently chaotic fragmentation and disappearance of their old shipmates and the captain, who were subsequently reassembled across a threshold on Earth. The captain had been so far off course that he hadn't realized that he had approached the Earth's ecosystem from a new avenue in space, landing him in Manitou on Earth, on his way home.

Having survived a natural technology that looked to them like magic, quite a few of the space voyagers were secretly relieved to be able to report that they had witnessed the limits of science. It was further explained by leaders of the scientific community that because they had mysteriously arrived "back at the beginning," they had proved that there was nothing more to be discovered. They had reached the sum total of scientific experience at the end of the universe. The secular power elite were especially relieved to be able to report to the priesthood that certainly a great mystery remained. "After all," said one to another, "there must be only one supreme god. If there were more than one, which two, three, or four could they possibly be?"

Those who had broken ranks were officially considered among the fallen, and with ceremony were given their places among the dead, even though they lived long in Manitou. In time, however, they joined the warriors who wanted to return to fight on behalf of nature to reestablish those connections with Manitou on Earth. So they were helplessly reborn, according to nature's way of restoring hope, beginning with the care and education of children.

## 18. Manitous

"So you think 'Totalitarian Math' comes next?" I had previously asked the other three seated around the table in the screened porch.

"It's a good time to bring home the point about numbers being even more specific than they are given credit for," Samuel suggested with humorous indifference.

"But what about Manitou? What do you think, Rolo? Isn't this a somewhat offbeat kind of Manitou? I didn't know Manitou was a place."

Rolo took the half lemon that had been squeezed onto his salmon and adjusted it on his nose. Holding it there with his index finger, he just looked at me until I had to laugh. I wasn't the only one. Samuel smiled and then chuckled, his red beard bobbing lightly on his barrel chest.

Lola leaned back, folded her arms, and gazed at him with raised eyebrows, joining in the act. Then she frowned.

He addressed her directly with the nose still in place, "Give us a kiss."

Whereupon with a wide open and full lipped mouth, her eyes huge, she bit his lemon nose off, taking the finger in her mouth. He withdrew it with a howl, stood up, shaking the finger up and down in pain. Lola shook with laughter. "I didn't hurt him," she reassured us. "Don't let him take you in."

His cover blown, Rolo sat back down. "Seriously," he said, "about Manitou. Let me just be the 'big Indian' for a moment—" This term made me a little nervous, which I ascribed reflexively to my very white genes.

"You will have to imagine the regalia." He leaned back in his chair, lifted his head, folded his arms and smiled comfortably. He certainly had our attention. "Manitou," he began, "is not, in my opinion, a term that can be easily categorized. For this reason alone I chose it for the story about attempting to control people through science. A further interesting aspect of the word 'Manitou' is that it is associated with what have been identified in the Northeast as 'Manitou stones.' I always enjoyed visiting the standing stones in the British Isles. There is that ancient story of people failing to count the standing stones in a circle. I liked that mythological reference for 'Totalitarian Math.' I would count them myself and found that they do have a tendency to give up a different total sometimes, because they are so individual you can easily forget where you began, dwelling and lingering on the individuality, or perhaps there is more to it than that. But for me, the way the stones seem to emerge from the ground, for me as a scientist—" and here he emphasized the fact by unfolding his long, muscular arms, reaching deliberately for his wine glass and toasting us before taking a sip, "as a scientist!" he repeated and held the glass in the air, "and thinking of circles—" he twirled the glass by its stem, "circles — and thinking of being at home in a circle of family and friends, well it got me thinking!" and he lifted the glass.

Before he could take another sip, we all had our glasses up, ringing them together, and the wine bottle went round to wash down the last of the first side of the salmon.

"And here's to the Manitous themselves," said Lola.

We drank to that.

"And to that connective energy, also called Manitou," said I.

We drank to that.

"What about the Manitou that comes to get you if you make the wrong kind of mistake?" asked Samuel, with a look of concern that suddenly cast the whole subject in a different light. Did he believe in Manitous? His look managed to raise the question for us all, as scientists — that is to say, as individuals who go by the scientific method in our philosophical outlook. Maybe it was because Samuel has a large face and is not one to conceal his emotions, but the question had to be addressed.

"Good question," said Rolo so definitively that that seemed to be the end of it.

"But as far as the book is concerned," I offered, "the question we will have to address is the way fiction and mythology translate one kind of consciousness for access by another. This involves the further question of the possibility and the nature of higher consciousness. And consciousness of place — Manitou. This is well-trodden ground, but we can now extend the logic of asymmetry to say some interesting new things about it."

With both elbows on the table, Samuel buried his face in his hands. Looking out from between his fingers, like a captain worrying over a chart and barometer, he said, "Perhaps it would be a good idea to give our readers a bit of background on what some books and scientists have been saying about symmetry and its fundamental importance. No one will take us seriously, no more than many academicians took seriously some of the early founders of group theory — not to make a disproportionate comparison." He got up from the table and walked the length of the porch and back. "But this is new, very new! Let's not forget what is happening here — and let's not forget the provenance of symmetry!"

"The provenance of symmetry," I repeated, not with irony but to give him a second chance to hear what he had said.

Samuel stood and looked at us all carefully. "Symmetry as such has no provenance. But I need help. You guys with the higher degrees, don't you think our book needs a bit of history on the heroic struggle of the infinities, starting with whom? the Greeks?"

"A history of philosophy?" asked Lola, deadpan.

"Just a little background on the quest involving continuity and infinitesimals . . ." his voice trailed off almost plaintively.

"Just a little?" echoed Lola teasingly.

"Here we are again," interjected Rolo, "trying to figure out what sort of book this is, how to categorize it — where are those boundaries?"

"True," Samuel replied, "I was the one who suggested you leave off with the technical stuff just over the very line I am now questioning."

"Over which way? No, that's okay, you were right in believing that fundamentals should be more freely accessible, if in fact they exist. That nature shouldn't require such specialized technical knowledge of math and formal logic to access basic, reasonable truth. And in fact that's what we are saying — nature is basically open-ended, and as such we are going to prove she is a democratic force, way deep down somewhere. And so here we are at the table. Have a seat!"

Samuel sat down. "It's a nice wooden table, he commented. And it doesn't have to be round." He spread out his hands on the weathered boards. "I'll be the philosopher king!" He smiled with mock satisfaction.

"That's just it, isn't it?" Rolo continued. "It's almost as though some

Manitou is baiting us to add an ideal to every rough suggestion of symmetry. There is such a strong tradition of pursuing this grail of pure symmetry—

"So the important breakthroughs in understanding have been written in the highly specialized languages of math and logic. I suppose we could get into the relationships between the constructive real line and the intuitionistic continuum, if you like, after a brief discussion of classical analysis."

We fell silent, wondering to what extent he was serious, where he would draw the line.

"Constructive analysis," he pressed on, "can be considered as a subset of classical analysis, but intuitionistic logic, that goes off on its own in various ways—"

"I know," asserted Lola.

"I know you know," he returned.

"Who do you think was responsible for maintaining the monocycle?" she replied.

"I was, of course," said he.

"You?" queried she.

"But of course!" said he. "I maintained it upright!"

"So where were you when the front wheel fell off?" she demanded.

"All right, all right!" I interrupted.

"Let them finish their routine," Samuel enjoined me.

"That's it, that's the joke!" I ventured.

"It's not very funny," Samuel replied.

"Too bad," I sulked.

"Where did you ever get the idea the joke was over?" asked Lola.

"See, I knew it!" said Samuel, very pleased.

"No, deep down you thought they were getting into a domestic quarrel," I replied.

"No — you did." Then he looked like he might like to have such a quarrel with me one day. It wasn't the first hint I had got, but we were "just friends," keeping up appearances — more borders and boundaries.

"I was just clowning around," said Rolo to Lola.

"We understand that," said Samuel.

"No, when the front wheel fell off," he corrected.

There was a gurgle from behind the beard.

More wine.

Suppressed laughter here and there.

"Don't give them the satisfaction," said I.

"Look, if we're going to get silly, it won't help our case," said Lola.

Laughter.

"Nonstandard analysis," said Rolo.

"What?" said Samuel, eyebrows raised.

"It's like explaining where you were when the front wheel fell off the monocycle."

"I won't ask how," said I.

"Well, it's kinda interesting," he continued, "because everything was all sewed up — so it seemed — by Georg Cantor and the subsequent work on set theory."

"But not everyone agreed," guessed Samuel.

"Correct. Cantor's sets and even the later 'fuzzy sets' depend on absolute symmetry; that's how the axioms are set up. There is assumed to be exactly a 'one-to-one correspondence' between sets, between the objects they contain. By injecting this symmetry it becomes possible to say new things about infinity and the fundamentals of math — like for example that there are many levels of infinity, absolutely separate levels. This artificial paralleling of members of different sets by exact one-to-one correspondence — and how could it be anything other than exact for there to be a complete correspondence? — gave the illusion that infinity had finally been understood and tamed. Clearly the absolute correspondences of set theory are disproved by the relationships that we have been discussing with our ABCs. The reasoning involved in the Transformation Proof predicts that paradoxes will crop up in set theory, and one famous one was the paradox named after Bertrand Russell, of course. Russell is one of my heroes."

Rolo sat back again and folded his arms in satisfaction. "He came along with his broom and basically cleaned away the cobwebs and messy thinking of earlier philosophers, flung open the windows and doors and let in the light. But you've heard me on this before. He didn't have all that much time for infinitesimals, however. That being said, he highlighted the way the ongoing paradox we ourselves are obsessed with can creep back into otherwise perfectly provable theorems.

"The amazing thing is that there is so much more to these arcane questions of continuity and divisions, an underlying significance that appears to be sensed — intuited even — by those on the quest. We are finding out what that meaning is, now that we have turned the key."

He leaned forward on the table. "I for one think we ought to get on with what we might have to offer; let Samuel present his essay on some of the arithmetical relationships that open up as the key is turned. Anyone who would like to pursue the history of infinities from before Zeno to the latest instant can find a number of sources to choose from. I was getting sidetracked by the math in connection with Zeno and other issues, and maybe that will yet be a book someday. But the fact of the matter is that this issue of infinity is as unresolved today as ever. Therefore, Samuel, here's to you for stopping my mathematical monocycle in its tracks and keeping us on track!"

"So therefore," said Samuel, after some intake of more wine, "nonstandard analysis tends to be like explaining where you were when the front wheel fell off the monocycle because," he pressed the base of his glass pensively against a wooden plank of the table, "after the circular paradox of set theory fell out, philosophers and mathematicians developed interesting ideas, but without figuring out that a circle of pure symmetry and absolute repetition does not exist to begin with — your monocycle's ideal front wheel that never happened. So it's like explaining where you were when 'the perfect event' never happened. Hence the clowning around? See Lola, he was being serious after all!

"You were pointing out that even the ideas that rejected a Platonic model had never really got free of it. So their highly specialized monocycles always had this extra ideal wheel that was kinda surreal. You were right about all that, but you were going to take the Transformation Proof into math-land before establishing its connection with fiction and mythology. It would have become impossible to deal with the mythical horizon of the open-ended numbers with just numbers. So you wrote the mythology and fairy tales that we have here. You gave us a bicycle — a penny-farthing? It becomes a question of how much emphasis to give the math and arithmetic. One thing's for sure, if I write the math essay, it won't get too specialized and unnecessarily unbalance the book! That being said, 'Totalitarian Math' comes next."

And it did.

Now, in the maze, Samuel's essay.

# 19. Samuel's Essay: Extremely Low Asymmetry

Is it really so surprising that someone named Alice should one day come along and disprove the existence of God? Surely we have known it all along in the depths of our asymmetric souls. So much has happened since humans got an understanding of the power of combining evidence and reason. So many miracles of technology and, of course, so much destruction.

What we need is a more thorough understanding of the even greater power of evidence and reason when combined with heart. But this combination has been eluding our logic until now. We have discovered that "cold logic" has a heart. And Alice is certainly not alone in the discovery.

I have been warned ever so often in the course of this enterprise of deduction that even if we should succeed, no one will care, except for those with a special interest in the absence of absolutes and in continuity and change. The main reason given is that in the United States, at least, reason itself is in some circles no longer esteemed, especially in the light of faith. And where reason *is* valued, only those with a special interest in religion, for example, will care if it is finally proved that there is no God — God already being so discredited among rationalists. In the further attempt to ground out what we are doing with this book, I will briefly highlight the work of a few other authors, beginning with a quote from one of my favorites, *Lucifer's Legacy: The Meaning of Asymmetry*, by physicist Frank Close.

Close presents a historical survey that explains how science has never found any direct evidence of "symmetry" in nature. He describes how, as a byproduct of major scientific experiments, this symmetry is shown to be absent, reinforcing the idea that to the present day nature continues to reveal herself to science as asymmetric. Meanwhile Close identifies the curious human bent for the symmetrical. From this inclination the author himself does not entirely escape, adding, in spite of himself, to the credibility of his argument.

While focusing on the meaning of asymmetry, the precise meaning of symmetry remains unresolved. The meaning of the word "symmetry" is either determined in the context of the experiments described or is assumed in the conventional sense, without exploration of the paradoxes involved. So we are not sure what it is that our science is telling us is more specifically absent in nature.

Nevertheless, Close identifies the tendency to use math to try to infer from nature's asymmetry a hidden symmetry. Close writes that,

> Symmetry is fascinating and appealing; scientists seek it in their data and incorporate it in their theories, ironically even when there is no immediate evidence for it. Perhaps the most arcane example of this concerns the nature of matter and the fabric of existence embodied in the current cosmophysical description of Creation . . .
>
> The deeper one looks, the more asymmetry becomes apparent and seemingly necessary for anything "useful" to have emerged. Without asymmetry and structure, the universe would have been bland. Have we convinced ourselves that the Creation was perfect on nothing more than wish fulfillment, as evidence of imperfection and asymmetry is all around us and even within us? I wonder whether . . . philosophers and scientists have created a quasi-religious parable of symmetry that is obscuring the real explanation.

It is easy to read symmetry into just about everything. The still, flat surface of the pond, for example, seems barely to disguise a perfection of stillness. And the breaking falls seem to denote the thrill of absolute, random chaos, with the perfect repetition of probability, where each event reflects the same chance of happening as all the others in a perfect symmetry — and paradox — in the jumbled but distinct patterns of turbulence.

This illusion of symmetry is deep. Even the author who is unmasking it uses the word "bland" to describe a universe without asymmetry, rather than concluding that there would be no universe at all. I remember the excitement of discovering *Lucifer's Legacy* with its clues as to the absence of any reasoning to prove the absence of absolutes.

As if giving a last clue, towards the end of the book, Close briefly addresses the question of *perfect* symmetry, but without much discussion of what it means to fail to achieve such perfection — leaving to the imagination the essential meaning of asymmetry, after a groundbreaking historical survey. The book is regarded by many as a classic. But ironically, while Close does emphasize the cultural bias in favor of some ideal of symmetry and how it has a grip on the imagination of both the specialist and the popular mind, the nub of the issue of pure symmetry's absence eludes him, or he decided to let it go, knowing that the issue is complicated. This does not stop him from suggesting that there may be a "lack of imagination" in a major part of the scientific community, so concerned as they are with some hidden or "shadow symmetry." Imagination, heart, fiction, romance, and myth — all are carriers of clues to the open-ended yet specifically grounded logic of nonrandom change. If the author of *Lucifer's Legacy* seems at times to be struggling with this demon, he is in good company.

One example of the standard and accepted use of the word "symmetry" in *Lucifer's Legacy* can be found teamed up with the word "perfect," when Close writes, "here we have a situation with perfect symmetry" when describing a saucer of water and a "symmetrical" falling object where "in every horizontal direction the system looks the same."[15] He is demonstrating the way a falling object makes contact with water, like throwing a pebble into a pond, with the seemingly symmetrical rings and the splash in the middle. Close draws our attention to the mysterious truth that the splash will always be asymmetrical, no matter how much "symmetry" is constrained into the conditions where it arises.

But the paradox of where and how exactly the very different points of the compass around the center of the splash are similar enough to have "perfect symmetry" and "look the same" from all points of view is not alluded to. The introduction of a video camera to film the event from a specific point of view illustrates the example of the object dropped into water but does not solve the paradox.

Even so, the author builds the clear case that all of our scientific experience to date directly confirms the ubiquity of asymmetry and the absence of any evidence in nature for a perfect and fundamental symmetry, whatever that may be.

The general tendency of writers, we feel, is to use the word "symmetry" for conditions of extremely low asymmetry, but of asymmetry nonetheless. This came home to me again when I read *Fearful Symmetry: Is God a Geometer?* by the mathematicians Ian Stewart and Martin Golubitsky. They hold that an understanding of "breaking symmetry" — seen in that mysterious zone where the water begins to break over the falls — will provide fundamental answers. But like many other authors, they do not directly address the question of absolute symmetry, where the reflection or repetition is perfectly exact — the thing that would ultimately get broken — as compared with other definitions of symmetry. Does such perfection exist or even make sense theoretically? Or does something only close to perfect symmetry get broken down a stage further? To the latter question our reasoning says yes.

One gets the feeling that by using God and Lucifer in their titles, Close, Stewart and Golubitsky are indicating that they sense that this issue affects something beyond — but how? They are giving us clues with somewhat romantic allusions. But in neither of these books do the religious, mythical or cultural implications develop very far beyond the title, leaving a curious silence, along with the absence of an investigation into the impossible paradox of absolute symmetry.

\* \* \*

After reading *Lucifer's Legacy* one should not be surprised that if we are able to discover human consciousness as part of the natural environment we find it to be asymmetric. Consciousness is *of self*, as well as of others. It should be quite natural and expected for it one day to find its way "out of the box," deducing a way out of the body and into the wider field of which it's a part. This idea has implications about the nature of the brain, as it has evolved within the physics of its environment, especially as we have deduced that consciousness is a physical thing. We are led to ask questions about the meaning of "physical." This essay is on the border between science and philosophy, a refreshing place to be when we consider that science grew out of philosophy, and it is good to refresh the roots now and then.

\* \* \*

If we now consider the book by astrophysicist Mario Livio on group theory in the above context of natural asymmetry, we find again a fundamental theme. *The Equation that Couldn't Be Solved: How Mathematical Genius Discovered the Language of Symmetry*, tells the unexpectedly dramatic and heart-rending history of how group theory was developed into the language used by so many scientists today to describe nature. But the reasoning used in group theory works so well precisely because the "symmetries" involved are really conditions of extremely low asymmetry, according to the Transformation Proof. In keeping with the conventional treatment of the term "symmetry," it is used loosely throughout the book, though the author does not say so specifically. The title should more accurately speak of the "language of asymmetry," or even the "language of *near*-symmetry."

Mistaking absolute symmetry for extremely low asymmetry is so common that many scientists have begun to believe that nature does in fact have pure symmetry, if only it could be found. Such is the descriptive power of group theory that its "symmetry" seems to have acquired the status of evidence where there is none. Hence the many questions being raised by Frank Close and other scientists about the true origins of the universe. It is curious that Livio makes no reference to the one book that puts the credibility of all scientific experience behind the idea that nature is in fact asymmetric. This would have raised the question of why we are referring to the math that describes asymmetric nature as the "language of symmetry." Nature is logical and asymmetric.

So let's get down to basics and have a look at some asymmetric arithmetic. We have all the empirical evidence for asymmetry we could hope for in the scientific record highlighted in *Lucifer's Legacy*. Let's see what happens to some of the arithmetical building blocks when we remove the idea of pure symmetry from the scene. Let's pull a magic carpet out from under the arithmetic and see what relevance the magic has to reason. What do I mean by magic? Perhaps I should have used the word "fiction." The fiction of symmetry is tightly woven into the reasoning, seeming to appear and disappear with more relevance in some places than others. Some fictions are more helpful than others.

Before we go any further and the reader begins to wonder why this essay isn't being written by Rolo, the physicist and mathematician, as we discussed in the previous chapter, it is for the same reason that we decided not to attempt *Zen and the Art of Monocycle Maintenance* or any variations for the specialist, who, by the way, may require a very special sense of balance not to become overly zealous, religious, even. This in no way diminishes the importance of these philosophical issues to the problems being encountered regarding symmetry, infinity, and infinitesimals in quantum field theory, supersymmetry, string theory, and the like, as so well described in *Not Even Wrong*, by Peter Woit. It is hoped that along this border territory, any reader familiar with those questions will feel free to make the relevant connections with his or her understanding as we go. The following comprises a selection of basic points we would like to make in order to give just enough of a context to the Transformation Proof in arithmetic, leaving some interestingly specific loose ends, without which nothing would make any sense to begin with.

# 20. Samuel's Essay: Which Number Two Now?

If we substitute any numbers for Objects A and B, we can see from our journey through the maze that all numbers, being objects, are open-ended. In the absence of absolute numbers, each specific number has its own context and character, given its relationships. For example, each version of this particular number 2 that I am using here is unique. (Note: I am not just referring to the *numeral* or the name we give to the number; the numeral for this number could, for example, also be written like this: ii.) The 2 that I am using in this sentence is different from that in the previous sentence. If they were not different we could not do any arithmetic; we would be stuck with just the absolute ideal and no useful variations, such as the 2 that I am now using. Recall that by the logic of change, *absolute finality* will not allow any further variations without throwing reason away. So these three different 2s allow us to make this statement — and many more. The 2s can be grouped like the tomatoes in the garden under the more general heading of being 2s. Now I have another unique 2 that is being used to signify the group. Because there is no absolute, I can find this variation to describe the group of 2s. Furthermore, the ability to find diversity in open-endedness stretches so far as to allow this 2 to change into this 3. Somewhere in that transition there is the potential for fiction.

We can get a glimpse of the fiction when, as in the tale of the rings of pi, we leave off counting the infinite divisions between the numbers. When we leave off counting, questions of "who" and "where" arise, questions of preference, circumstance, or context, and personality, as with the group of students, staff and professors with the Lady of the Lake, who pulled the circle together and left it at that — a bit "flat." We naturally leave off counting the divisions when we skip from one number to the next, counting as far as we like. To count as far as you like is to engage in a bit of fiction. Every time we start counting again, we change the horizon — MU. Asymmetric infinity will never be finally counted. It's a way of understanding change and many things — it's open-ended so as to include its specifically asymmetric open-ended units.

So in the absence of knowing "which two," the totalitarian captain is surprised by the idea that it is an absurd generalization to say "two and two equal four." Many of us have had the feeling that there is more to it than just the statement: $2 + 2 = 4$. Well there is. Without knowing which two — or without at least the intimation that there is some specificity that is being left at a loose end on purpose — we are left waiting for the other shoe to drop. The Platonic captain thought he had it all wrapped up long ago. So what was he doing there?

# 21. Samuel's Essay: More About the Absence and Something About Set Theory

Let's expand a bit on the absence of absolutes, to create more of an environment for discussion, at the risk of being somewhat repetitive again.

Every deductive system has a sort of a beginning. I say "sort of" in the absence of an absolute beginning. We arrived at the deduction that there is no absolute beginning by using two things we called "Objects A and B." We did not assume they had to be absolute, nor did we assume they could not be absolute. In order to begin with something, we chose these two things. Then we proceeded to find out something more about them.

Every object, however vague or precise it may be, has some defining boundaries that come with its identity, without which there is nothing to consider. Whatever definitions and boundaries an object might have, whatever it may be, the Transformation Proof says that an object can never distinguish itself so completely from anything else as to be absolutely final and separate — let alone repeat with such finality — without setting up an unreasonable paradox.

Logical inferences often tell us something about our assumptions by expanding on them, even to the extent of building a language around them, a context. The Transformation Proof and its context can be developed into a way of thinking with greater clarity by allowing our natural asymmetries to bypass obstacles and artificial boundaries and to flourish with new ideas and avenues of action. The proof by contradiction provides a definition of absolute finality, so as to allow us to be more specific and aware when we say something is final. This reasoning confirms the conclusions of philosophers and mathematicians that no process of deduction can prove its own axioms or assumptions absolutely. However, the asymmetric nonrandom direction of the reasoning allows it to indicate the essential nature of its own premise, being Objects A and B. We can deduce that no object is absolutely final. This is not possible when the pure symmetry of exact repetition is assumed into the axioms of any deductive system and its proofs. The absolute finality of the premise of the argument will stand as an insuperable barrier to any attempt to infer the nature of some essential aspects of the premise. The ancient paradox stands against itself.

* * *

In order for a relationship to exist among any set of objects of which at least one object is not absolutely final and is capable of the slightest change in its relationships — thus potentially changing the relationships of the entire set into a new context beyond any absolute finality — no assumption of absolute finality can apply: The possibility of absolute finality must be completely sacrificed for consistency, and we must conclude that no object that is absolutely final can logically exist in the set or group. The mere presence of any potential for change indicates that even the mere possibility of absolute finality has not been achieved. It follows that an absolutely final set of absolutely final objects would itself be an object that could not coexist with any object that might change.

An object that is not absolutely final is always capable of at least some change, because it has not been completely cut off. Some further operation in relation to it can occur. No operation has finalized it completely. We can see how any environment of changing relationships takes on new meaning with this way of thinking.

* * *

In this context my essay would seem a bit empty if we did not take into account the question of set theory, which has become foundational to mathematics. *Platonic Realms* at mathacademy.com explains the basics of set theory very clearly, so I will quote them extensively, while indicating some inconsistencies in light of the Transformation Proof.

Georg Cantor's discoveries in set theory rest upon a very

simple idea, an idea which may be illustrated in the following way. Suppose you couldn't count to five.

Now look at your hands. If you were unable to count to five, how would you know there are the same number of fingers on each hand? You couldn't count the fingers on one hand, and then count the fingers on the other hand, to see that there were the same number of fingers on each, because you couldn't count that high. What could you do? The answer is simple: place the thumb of your right hand against the thumb of your left hand. Then place your index fingers together, and then all the other fingers, in a one-to-one match-up. When you are done, each finger of each hand is matched to the corresponding finger of the other hand, with none left over on either side. You still don't know how many fingers are on each hand, but you do know that they are the same number.

Now, the real trouble with infinity is much the same: we can't count that high! Cantor's insight was that, even though we can't enumerate an infinite set, we can nonetheless apply the same procedure to any well-defined infinite set that we applied above to determining if our hands have the same number of fingers. In other words, we can determine if two infinite sets are the same "size" (equinumerous) by seeking to find a one-to-one match-up between the elements of each set. Now, remember Galileo's Paradox? Galileo noticed that we can do the following:

$$
\begin{aligned}
1 &— 2 \\
2 &— 4 \\
3 &— 6 \\
4 &— 8 \\
n &— 2n
\end{aligned}
$$

Thus, we can assign each number n in the set of natural numbers to the corresponding number 2n in the set of even numbers. This rule specifies a one-to-one match-up between the set of all natural numbers and the set of even natural numbers. By definition, then, these sets are equinumerous — the same size. We can play the same game with many subsets of the natural numbers. For example, we can form a one-to-one match-up between the natural numbers and the set of squares, or the set of multiples of five, or the set of prime numbers, or the set of numbers greater than 37.

We may feel some discomfort at the idea that we can remove some of the elements of a set and still have as many as we started with, but this is an artifact of our experience with finite sets (in which removing something means having a smaller set). Infinite sets simply don't behave that way. In fact, this leads us to a definition:

A set is infinite if we can remove some of its elements without reducing its size.[16]

From an asymmetric point of view, the reader will by now have noticed that there is a problem with this reasoning. The one-to-one correspondence is similar to the relationship between our familiar Objects A and B. The Transformation Proof predicts that there would be asymmetry between, for example, the set of natural numbers and the set of even numbers. When Galileo noticed that, to quote mathacademy.com, "if you take the set of natural numbers and remove exactly half of them, the remainder is as large a set as it was before"[17] he was observing nature's asymmetry. The error is in assuming that one can remove *exactly* half of the numbers in question.

The same error is repeated in set theory when assuming that the one-to-one correspondences can be exact. This builds in the assumption of absolute symmetry. Whether Galileo made that mistake or not I don't know (his observation may have simply been in passing), but when considering an extremely large number of numbers, the asymmetries would become quite considerable. There would be thresholds where extremely low asymmetry would give way to leaps in different patterns of numbers, just as we see happening in the rest of nature's polarity. Thus we find that the countable conditions, such as in the example of finite one-to-one correspondence above, can indeed occur — but without the asymmetric character of numbers, the two sets would not even happen.

So the statement that a set is infinite if we can remove some of its elements without reducing its *size* is, after all, as self-contradictory as it intuitively seems, as it assumes the *size* of the set is settled and "counted" while allowing it to continue. Without the asymmetric perspective, there is no way round this paradox; anything less or more than the one-to-one symmetry leaves at least some stray numbers unaccounted for — the one-to-one correspondence has to be absolute to support the reasoning of set theory. The theory's numbers themselves are self-contradictory, finite absolutes, rather than open-ended asymmetries. But let's hear out the Platonists.

We have a special name for the "size" of a set: "cardinality." We say that the set of natural numbers and the set of even numbers, for instance, have the same cardinality. Also, whenever a set has the same cardinality as the natural numbers, we say that the set in question is "countable," since it can be put into a one-to-one correspondence with the counting numbers (i.e., the set of natural numbers).

Cantor's next great accomplishment was to ask the question: Do all infinite sets have the same cardinality? In other words, can all infinite sets be put into a one-to-one match-up with the natural numbers? It is not difficult to find one-to-one match-ups between the natural numbers and the integers, so the first set to consider as — possibly — cardinally larger is the set of rational numbers. Recall that the rational numbers are dense, which means that between any two rational numbers on the real number line we can find infinitely more rational numbers. This suggests to our intuition that the set of rational numbers may be, in some sense, "bigger" than the set of natural numbers. However, it turns out that the rational numbers are indeed countable, as may be seen by examining the following table, Figure 1.

This table, if completed down and across (an infinite process!) contains all the rational numbers. (It contains many duplications, of course. All the fractions on the main diagonal, for instance, are really just the same number — one — but that won't affect our argument.) Now, we can "count" the rational numbers by just following the crisscrossing line. Thus, the rational numbers really are countable — that is, there are just as many natural numbers as there are rational numbers. Given how the set of rational numbers seems to contain infinities within infinities, this is an astounding result.

The next set to ask about, obviously, is the real numbers. After our experience with the rational numbers, it would be understandable to guess that, after all, countable infinities are the only kind of infinities there are in mathematics. But no! Cantor showed that the real numbers are cardinally larger than the natural numbers — in other words, there is no way to form a one-to-one match-up between the natural numbers and the real numbers that doesn't leave some of the real numbers out. To show this, Cantor invented a whole new kind of proof, which has come to be called "Cantor's diagonalization argument."

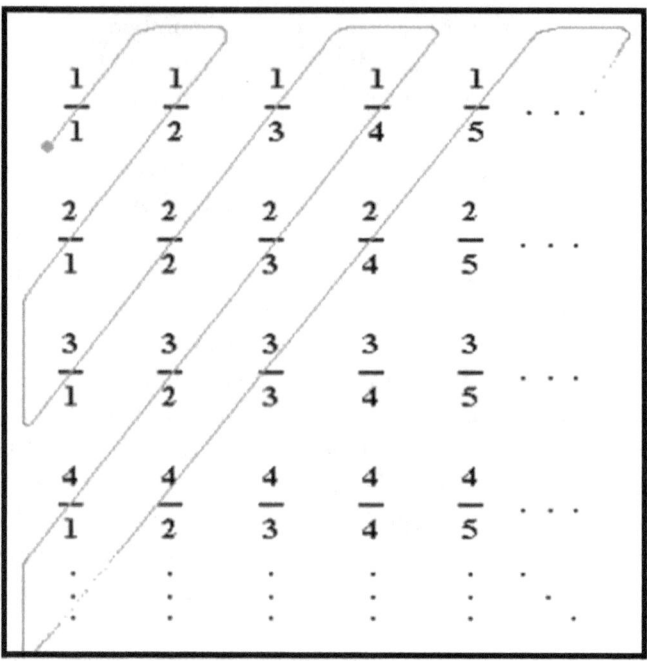

Figure 1

Cantor's proof of the "nondenumerability" of the real numbers (the diagonalization argument) is somewhat more sophisticated than the proofs we have examined hitherto. However, laying aside some purely technical matters, we can provide a simplified — but still convincing — version of his proof in the following way. Remember that we are attempting to prove a negative statement: that the real numbers are not countable. As so often in such cases, we approach this issue through the back door, so to speak, with a proof by contradiction. In other words, we begin by assuming, for sake of argument, that the real numbers are countable. This would mean that we could form a one-to-one match-up of the natural numbers and the real numbers. Since real numbers may be represented in decimal form (with an integer part and a decimal part), this means that we could provide a numbered list of the real numbers which would look something like Figure 2, where the numbers on the left are the natural numbers, and the numbers on the right are a "denumeration" of the real numbers.

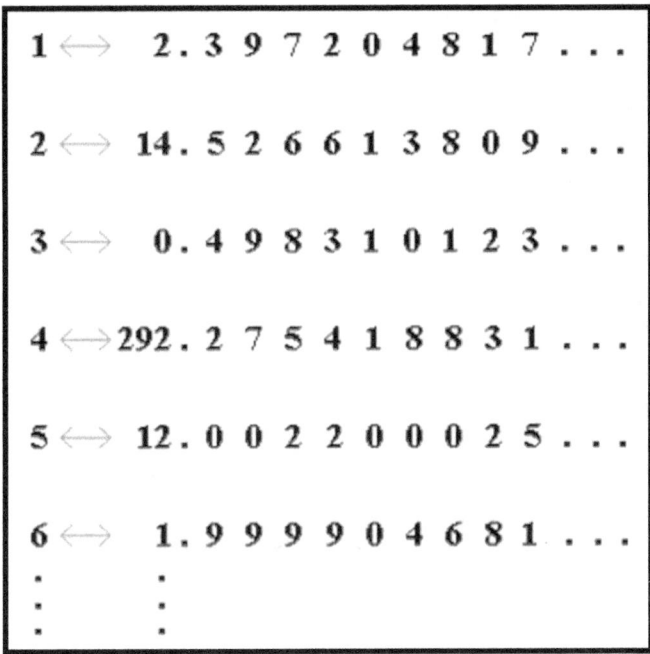

Figure 2

That is, we are supposing that we eventually have every real number running down the right-hand side of this list, with its corresponding natural number next to it. Now, Cantor concluded that there exists at least one real number that can't be on the list, and he reasoned as follows: Create a new real number by first picking any number for the integer part (zero will do), and then let its first decimal place digit be different from the digit in the first decimal place in the first number in our list. Then let our new number's second decimal place digit be different from the digit in the second decimal place in the second real number in our list. Proceed in the same way, so that each decimal place digit in our new number is different from the corresponding digit in the corresponding real number in the list. Thus, we could do something like Figure 3.

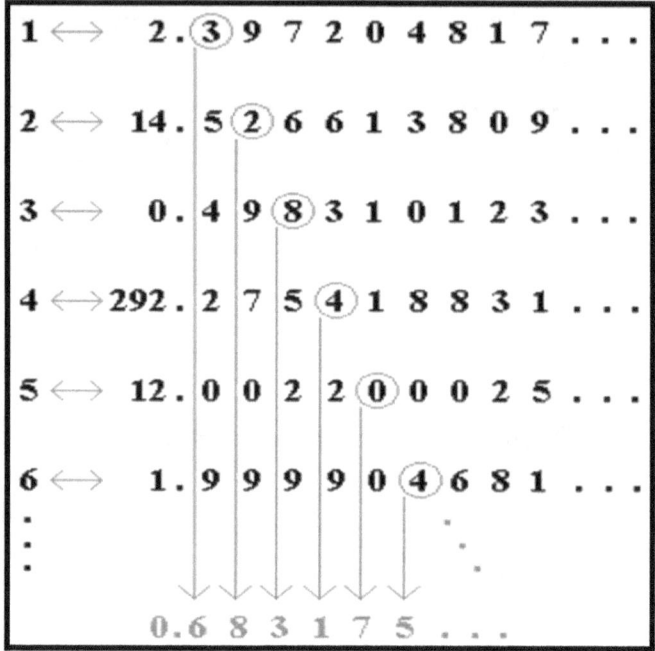

Figure 3

Now we ask the question, is our new real number on the list? Well, it can't be the same as the first number on the list, since it is different in the first decimal place, owing to the way we constructed it. Likewise, it can't be the same as the second number on the list, since it is different from that one in the second decimal place. In fact, we see that it can't be the same as any of the real numbers in our list, since it differs from each number on the list in at least one decimal place.

BUT — we assumed we had a complete list. This is a contradiction. Therefore, our assumption that we could make a countable list of the real numbers is false! The real numbers have a higher order of infinity than the natural numbers, i.e., they are cardinally greater. (It is natural to ask, well, why not just add the new number to the list? Indeed, we could do so. However, this fails to address the fundamental point of the argument: we assumed we had a complete list of real numbers, and then showed that this assumption cannot be true. It is the existence of this contradiction which forces the conclusion that the real numbers aren't countable. And of course, even if we added our new one to the list, we could use the same process to create infinitely more. There's just no way to create a completed match-up between the sets.)[18]

Once again we have the curious reasoning that uses the ancient paradox to perpetuate the paradox. Addressing "the fundamental point of the argument," the Platonists "assumed we had a complete list of real numbers." This is the assumption that you have already counted all the numbers just because they are "countable" as far as we can see, in a finite way, while allowing the counting to continue. It is the attempt to stop infinity in general by claiming absolute finality of the individual numbers and their specific sets. Like putting the two hands together, the Platonic generalization of a finite absolute (the hands) is used to define the individual fingers and vice-versa in a symmetrical relationship that is assumed to be absolute. The paradox is used in the above reasoning to show that you can't count the extra numbers that have been found, because counting them would violate the absolute condition of the set of counting or natural numbers originally used. This violation of the *paradoxical rule* is used to show that the assumption (in the "proof by contradiction") that you can count the real numbers cannot be true. By the way, the example here of producing extra real numbers is the flip side of the one where Galileo's numbers were removed. Both use the same unconscious sleight of hand and provide further evidence of the profound tendency in human nature to build environments of absolute building blocks.

There is more to quote and learn from, this time under the heading of "cardinals."

> Now that we have two cardinalities — the countable cardinality of the natural numbers and the uncountable cardinality of the real numbers — we have the beginnings of

a collection (a set!) of "cardinalities." We'll call them cardinal numbers and give them symbols to stand for them. Following tradition, let us denote the countable cardinal by the Greek letter *w* (omega). We'll denote the cardinality of the real numbers by a lower-case c, which stands for continuum.

Now our set of cardinal numbers contains only two elements, but let's make an adjustment at once. Since cardinal numbers are used to describe the "sizes" of sets, it happens that we really want to call the natural numbers "cardinal numbers" too. After all, they describe the sizes of finite sets. And we may as well have zero, since that's the size of the empty set. Thus, the set of all cardinals will contain both kinds of cardinal; finite cardinals (which are just the natural numbers, really, together with zero) and what Cantor termed transfinite cardinals, which include our *w* and c.

$$\text{Cardinals} = \{0, 1, 2, 3, \ldots, w, c, \ldots ?\}$$

Notice the question mark. We haven't really settled whether there are any more transfinite cardinals. Fortunately, Cantor has done that for us, in what is now called Cantor's Theorem. It may be stated as follows.

If X is any set, then there exists at least one set, the power set of X, which is cardinally larger than X.

The proof of Cantor's Theorem has a similar flavor to his proof of the nondenumerability of the real numbers, but it is somewhat more abstract. The intrepid will have little difficulty following it, however. It is an interesting fact that the power set of any countable set, i.e., of size *w*, has cardinality c, the size of the continuum.

What Cantor's Theorem tells us is that we can construct sets with greater and greater cardinalities. Cantor introduced a special notation for this hierarchy of cardinalities using the Hebrew letter aleph (pronounced AH-leff), with numeral subscripts showing where they are in the hierarchy. Thus, aleph-null is the first infinite cardinal, and denotes the cardinality of the natural numbers (or any countably infinite set, i.e. of cardinality *w*), and aleph-one is the next cardinal number, standing for the next size of infinity, and so on.

"Cardinals" = $\{0, 1, 2, 3, \ldots, \aleph_0, \aleph_1, \ldots ?\}$

Now we know what to replace the question mark with — since there is no largest cardinality, this list goes on forever, with more and more alephs denoting larger and larger kinds of infinity. And we know where the $w$ belongs in this list — it is the first infinite cardinal, the aleph-null.

What about c, the cardinality of the continuum? Cantor thought that it must be aleph-one, that is, that the size of the continuum was the next highest after the natural numbers. This conjecture is now called the Continuum Hypothesis. Cantor was never able to prove it, however, and this bothered mathematicians for many years. How could we be sure where the "size" of the real numbers fit in the scheme of things?

In the 1930s, Kurt Gödel showed that the continuum hypothesis can't be disproved from the axioms of set theory, and in the 1960s another mathematician named Paul Cohen showed that it cannot be proved, either. This is a very strange thing, and mathematicians have debated what it means ever since. At the very least, it means that our current understanding of sets is not strong enough to settle the question of the continuum. We have, at present, no way of determining where in the hierarchy of infinite cardinals the cardinality of the continuum belongs.[19]

Although set theory has become rather sophisticated and moved beyond what is now referred to as "naïve set theory," the paradox remains imbedded. Since I have been warned by Rolo of the perils of the unicycle, not to mention the monocycle, which is motorized, we'll leave it at that and move on as well. In doing so we will continue with the key to what seems to be the undoing of set theory in the requirement of absolute finality, which has bedeviled the theory's continuum.

We have deduced that if absolute finality existed, it could have no further context. Therefore, it could have no more than one instance of occurrence — if anything could exist without the opportunity of a further context. Nothing else would ever happen. It could not repeat itself in any way (other than in the sense of remaining exactly as it is) without generating the context of a different perspective (like the maze of the onion). It could not change or repeat without generating the context of a relationship with its unique previous condition, another "skin of the onion." Change as such could not exist, because the only thing in existence would be the Finality and nothing more. Clearly, change does exist, so absolute finality does not, whether in thought or otherwise. The mere possibility of absolute finality must be sacrificed for consistency. Any means of expression (including of course set theory) that is able to perform operations, thus changing its relationships, cannot reasonably assume that terms assuming absolute finality are not self-contradictory by themselves.

We can deduce that absolute finality could never have happened in a context of change. No set of objects involving change of any kind could have developed from absolute finality. Nor could the perfect exactitude of an absolute beginning have taken place in a changing context, nor could changing conditions have had such a beginning. Such a beginning would be in absolute symmetry with absolute finality. And there is no possibility of anything existing completely apart from a context of change. As Alice described in her essay, the internal spring of asymmetric open-endedness would find it.

It is impossible for changing conditions to lead to absolute finality, because there would already be a context of change (including potential change) that would preempt it from happening — there would already be a process (including a potential process) outside the attempted final event.

One might ask: What if the final event were so absolute as to put a universal end to all change at once? The answer is that the final state must find some way of concluding itself without any relationship with the processes of change that it attempts to finalize. This is an impossible task; absolute finality cannot have any relationship with anything beyond itself, let alone with anything that might change. Without putting an end to the whole environment of change, it cannot achieve absolute finality. So absolute finality cannot change, nor can it change anything. This would agree with its apparent nonexistence and the lack of logical consistency that can arise in its use in any means of expression.

It is impossible to have a relationship with something that cuts itself off with such finality. Since things do exist other than in such a hypothetical condition of finality, we can reason that absolute finality is preempted from existence. The mere fact of coexistence means that there is a relationship within the wide context of existence itself. If absolute finality does not exist, the significance of the obvious fact that things do exist that are not absolutely final has been underestimated in understanding asymmetry.

So, absolute finality can be defined as "the inability to exist in a relationship with any object that is capable of change." An object is capable of change if it has some potential to be further connected in a relationship with some other object. Not having been finalized absolutely, the object itself is open to change. Any change in the object itself would also give rise to such a connection: If an object changes in any way, it has become another object to some degree and is connected in time or through the process of change with the previous object that it was.

What it comes down to is this: If we really mean it when we say that something is completely final in every way, then we have nowhere to go from there. That's it — final. Any object that is supposed to be absolutely final leaves us stuck with that object. As soon as we try to connect it in any way with anything else, we have sacrificed its absolute finality. Such absolute finality is universal; that is to say, in the absence of a context, everything but the supposed finality is excluded from existence. If we ourselves try to continue on another subject with another object or try to do anything more at all, we sacrifice the absolute finality of the object we are stuck with. If we have absolutely no relationship (potential or otherwise) with that object (to the extent that it cannot even exist), then we cannot say it is absolutely final. To refer to it at all is to have a relationship with it. If it is truly absolutely final and we refer to it, then we must be referring to ourselves in some way. Otherwise, things do not in fact end with the object, because we are in some relationship with it, even just by referring to it. So to assert that an object is absolutely final and then continue on with whatever else we are doing is a self-contradictory set of actions.

So, why, to briefly review, are absolute symmetry and asymmetry mutually exclusive in every way? In order to repeat or reflect anything absolutely exactly, the symmetry must have absolute finality, as must point symmetry in remaining constant. Without that perfect exactitude, the symmetrical repetition remains incomplete, remains in question — what exactly to repeat? Therefore, perfect or absolute symmetry depends on absolute finality. But if absolute finality does not exist, neither does absolute symmetry. In the absence of absolute symmetry, what remains is asymmetry, in its many degrees of precision and form, even to the point of being highly symmetrical, but failing to reach absolute symmetry. Therefore, any asymmetry is universally mutually exclusive with absolute finality and with absolute symmetry as well. They are mutually exclusive in every way: if one exists the other cannot. So it should be no surprise that, as Professor Close has shown in *Lucifer's Legacy,* no direct evidence for any perfect symmetry in nature has been found, while nature's asymmetry has been directly confirmed by all of our scientific experience to date, even using the conventional understanding of the word "symmetry."

We can conclude that nature's asymmetry supports the reasoning that absolute finality does not exist. Such finality is logically preempted by the mere possibility of change.

In the absence of absolute finality, we are left with fundamental continuity — a true continuum.

We can also use a bit of fiction with our ability to imagine what is not, in order to understand what is and employ the concept of "nothing." Nothing is just that and no more. As such, it does not exist, even though we have a word for it. In the absence of absolute finality, nothing completely separates one thing from another. Therefore, all things are connected in some way, and we have fundamental continuity as a basic rationality.

"Nothing" becomes a confusing concept for philosophers if they are working with the idea that an absolute center, or any sort of pure absolute can happen, like absolutely exact repeating intervals of a series. Then the absoluteness of "nothing" starts to look a lot like something absolute. There ain't no nothin'! The idea of "nothing" is another one of those fictions that are useful in letting us know what we don't have, so we can find the way, find out more about what we do have. So the set of nothing or "null set" is another paradox of set theory. This, I should add, does not diminish the importance of zero as an organizational tool.

Since math as a whole can be considered an object and definitely exists, we have another way of looking at the absence of absolute exactitude in all numbers and mathematical expressions; numbers are in this sense "rounded off" in a new way and to a degree of precision so as to appear the way they do. Likewise an infinite series would be "rounded off" or "flattened" or "stubbed out" before it achieved what has been misunderstood to be infinity. Infinity would be a matter of emergence and reemergence, rather than being dependent on the paradox of an infinite series of absolute finalities.

We are led to conclude that nature can be described as being crafted rather than being perfected, as with Sir Isaac Newton's "imperfect mechanic." The question of how nature emerges or fills in between things asymmetrically in the absence of absolute finality and exact repetition provides an ever-new endlessness that is open to exploration. This reasoning opens the door to yet another way of understanding the phenomenon of emergence, described by Robert Laughlin in *A Different Universe*. As emphasized by Peter Woit in *Not Even Wrong*, infinity is at the heart of the quantum field puzzle.[20] With the greatest restraint, we will make a few comments on this curious border crossing between philosophy and physics, raising a few questions about using dimensions as mathematical contexts, and the like — later.

The logic of change says that, in a way, it's all language. We can develop our languages to better accommodate the flexibility of a connectivity that can never be specified absolutely. Such accommodation would allow for greater degrees of precision of expression in exploring emergence in the medium of universal connectivity. It would seem that this flexible medium is required for anything to change and develop, to achieve textures, gradients and degrees.

The foregoing predicts that the way in which objects are connected will never be discovered with absolute exactitude, once and for all. We are presented with a mystery that can be solved only by finding out more and more about it, while its power to mystify cannot ultimately fail.

# 22. Samuel's Essay: The Largest Number Proof, Etc.

Somewhere in an upstairs closet, there is an old math book by Fletcher Durell, PhD, and E.E. Arnold, MA, published by Charles E. Merrill Company, written back in the late 1920s. The authors tell the students in the introduction that math is a language. What a relief! The authors proceed to open up a world of symbols and expressions, entering the land of algebra. Not that there was an overt attempt to mythologize in this old-fashioned math book. It's just that we are spared the feeling of entering a kingdom of perfection where we are touched with the righteousness of absolute purity when we are right and go straight to hell when we are wrong, all or nothing, starting over again with the next question.

A non-perfectionist, loose approach is hopefully regaining some currency among teachers, but the assumption of perfection in mathematics is well entrenched in the discipline in general and in the popular mind.

I am loth to claim that it's easy to write about a number line loosely. Still, I'm going to ramble on a bit and spread out a few inferences on intervals.

### Plato's Ghost and a Rambling Repetition

While referring back to "the ancients" Sir Isaac Newton, in the preface to his *Principia*, wrote that he "endeavoured to subject the phenomena of nature to the laws of mathematics." Right away the issue of perfection in the description of nature arises in the following manner:

> To practical mechanics all the manual arts belong, from which mechanics took its name. But as artificers do not work

with perfect accuracy, it comes to pass that mechanics is so distinguished from geometry, that what is perfectly accurate is called geometrical; what is less so is called mechanical.

The conventional view of geometry as perfection is stated, but he then goes on to say:

> He that works with less accuracy is an imperfect mechanic; and if any could work with perfect accuracy, he would be the most perfect mechanic of all; for the description of right lines and circles, upon which geometry is founded, belongs to mechanics. Geometry does not teach us to draw these lines, but requires them to be drawn; for it requires that the learner should first be taught to describe these accurately, before he enters upon geometry; then it shows how by these operations problems may be solved. To describe right lines and circles are problems, but not geometrical problems. The solution of these problems is required from mechanics . . . Therefore geometry is founded in mechanical practice, and is nothing but that part of universal mechanics which accurately proposes and demonstrates the art of measuring.

Newton takes his cue from nature — from what is observably there. His math follows nature. It's as though his numbers arise like pebbles cast up by the waves on the shoreline. Rather than insisting on perfection, he is looking for what is true. He does not seem to be assuming that even his math will be absolutely ideal in the Platonic sense. He begins his book like a true craftsman, in a workmanlike manner, in a democratic spirit. Let's take it from there and consider numbers as cast up on the shoreline. Whether we use numbers to organize other objects (as first, second, third, and so forth) or whether we use them as objects in themselves or whether we define them to include objects that are virtually unimaginable, our logic of change says that they cannot exist without an open-ended context. When a number is in the context of another number, we have a series.

If we assume that the units of any series repeat exactly, then, as we have seen, we have a problem. The problem is compounded if we also want that line to go off into infinity somehow. Asymmetry and absolute symmetry being mutually exclusive, and that fundamental continuousness being asymmetric, then a series of exactly repeating units is an oxymoron that makes no sense. It self-contradicts. It's an absurdity, not even a paradox, if a working paradox can say two contradictory things at once without assuming they are both absolutely true.

If the Platonic divisions in a series are to be exactly equal, or indeed if there are any absolute divisions at all, then we are changing our assumption of absolutely exact finality where we stop counting with absolute exactitude at the finite end of the line and now say, "It just goes on forever."

Likewise, if we say it goes on forever, we change our mind if suddenly we say, "First stop here! Now absolutely stop here, forever! And here and here and here, that makes five!" At least five changes of mind, so far. Such determined indecision.

It's no good saying that this series goes on forever but we reserve the right to stop it completely as well. Which is it going to be? An infinite line or a finite line?

Such questions haunt the Platonic approach of the perfect ideal of pure symmetry and can eventually snarl up the otherwise well-reasoned math. The ghost assumptions in the language of math allow us to conclude some strangely mistaken things, especially when we tangle with issues of infinity.

If life is asymmetric — if consciousness is asymmetric — then the divisions of the number line cannot be exactly equal, even in the mind, even theoretically. If reality is basically asymmetric, and mathematics is being used as a language that describes the nature of reality, then it will have insuperable obstacles when it gets down to talking about fundamentals, unless it takes into consideration the consequences of the absence of absolute symmetry.

The Platonic understanding of infinity is really an extension of the linear oxymoron. The ghost assumption or unspecified "change of mind" is an ambivalence that haunts the length of any series and could appear at any point along the line. In order to be asymmetrically consistent we must accept the units or divisions as more or less the same, and we must asymmetrically limit the series at both ends, throwing out the old idea of infinity — not that anyone was too sure what it was — replacing it with a definition of infinity as *fundamental asymmetry*.

To exorcize the ghost of this number-line illusion we must realize that to demand some sort of equality gives the units of the series increased exactitude and calls for a finite series, calls for an end of the line or defined field, thus far, tightening it up and making it useful, while assuming that it can go beyond, thus confirming the defining power of that threshold — or breaking near-symmetry — that accompanies all creation, including reason. To be asymmetrically consistent, we must openly assume or choose a specific, asymmetrically finite series or context to work with, if we want to speak in terms of some degree of exactitude or a close (or extremely close) approximation of repeating units.

When we initiate any math we are automatically making this choice. Let's consider this issue of choice for a moment. Without the choice, there is no math being done. The Lady of the Lake described this when she spoke of infinity in terms of the tape measure. It's no use having it extended all the way all the time. So when not doing math we wind up the tape and the math is put away, so to speak. In this context I would like to quote from an interview by Adam Frank with MIT cosmologist Max Tegmark published in *Discover Magazine*, June 2008.

> "Was it in college that you started to think about the bigger questions?"
>
> "I was taking the one and only quantum physics class offered, and when I got to the chapter on measurement I felt sure that I was missing something."
>
> "You're talking about the way the observer appears to affect the measurement of what's being observed."
>
> "Right. There is this beautiful mathematical equation in quantum theory called the Schrödinger equation. It uses something called the wave function to describe the system you are studying — an atom, an electron, whatever — and all the possible ways that system can evolve. The usual perspective of quantum mechanics is that as soon as you measure something, the wave function literally collapses, going from a state that reflects all potential outcomes to a state that reflects only one: the outcome you see at the moment the measurement is done. It seemed crazy to me. I didn't get why you were supposed to use the Schrödinger equation before you measured the atom, but then, while you're measuring it, the equation doesn't apply. So I got up my courage and knocked on the door of one of

the most famous physicists in Sweden, a man on the Nobel committee, but he just blew me off. It wasn't until years later that I had this revelation that it wasn't me who didn't get it; it was him!"

"It is a beautiful moment in the education of a scientist when you realize that these guys in higher positions of power still don't have all of the answers. So you took your questions about the Schrödinger equation and the effect of measurement with you when you left for the United States and your PhD at Berkeley?"

"That's where it all started for me. I had this friend, Bill Poirier, and we spent hours talking about crazy ideas in physics. He was ribbing me because I argued that any fundamental description of the universe should be simple. To annoy him, I said there could be a whole universe that is nothing more than a dodecahedron, a 12-sided figure the Greeks described 2,500 years ago. Of course, I was just fooling around, but later, when I thought more about it, I got excited about the idea that the universe is really nothing more than a mathematical object. That got me thinking that every mathematical object is, in a sense, its own universe."

"Right from the start you tried to get this radical idea of yours published. Were you worried about whether it would affect your career?"

"I anticipated problems and did not submit until I had accepted a postdoctoral appointment at Princeton University."[21]

This conversation is a compact exhibit of the following points.

The first is the curious way that the wave function collapses when you choose to make an actual measurement. Fortunately there are many books on this question that save me from having to decide to turn this essay over to Rolo for some actual physics. All I want to do here is point out that the wave function uses a math that has built into it the pure symmetry of exact repetition. It is just possible that this collapse of the applicability of the math once the specific measurement is made is a part of the more general problem of Platonic math. The ideal collapses when things get highly specific because of a lack of asymmetry in the logic. The math is descriptively excellent only up to a point. In the case of the wave function, probability and statistics are used. This math assumes the existence and relevance of absolute randomness.

When choosing to initiate any math, we are automatically choosing an asymmetrically finite context, whereas in choosing the actual measurement in quantum mechanics, the Platonic math collapses. There is a self-contradictory illusion in the math. At issue is the relationship between the Platonic ideal and the real world of nature. The mathematical tools used in quantum field theory, while powerful in many ways, are fundamentally asymmetric and initiate a corresponding context each time they are applied, even as the mathematicians assume pure symmetry in the way they are used. This is a matter of choice in our relationship with nature's reality. I will leave it to Rolo and his colleagues to discover the math that will be specific enough to make the connection between the language of math and the events being described so as to avoid the infamous "loss of words" in face of the event.

The question of free will is itself bound by the asymmetric textures and landscape of the universal Field of Action. We often have to tease out our fundamental freedoms from the tangled mazes.

The second point is about social pressure in determining how the mathematical language of science is formed. As with the development of any language, the pressure is both formative and impressive; the evidence is experienced by many, so Tegmark is not alone, of course. Add to this the deep human predilection for the absolute, and it is no wonder that an otherwise powerful language would develop a weakness for pure symmetries. This may be especially true where the larger issue is framed as being a matter of controlling nature. No matter what combination of logic or math and technology we use, nature's asymmetry guarantees that we will never be able to identify her absolutely exactly. There will always be an uncertainty principle of some kind.

\* \* \*

Like many of his colleagues, Tegmark exhibits the love of symmetries to a high degree.

> "Let's talk about your effort to understand the measurement problem by positing parallel universes — or, as you call them in

aggregate, the 'multiverse.' Can you explain parallel universes?"

"There are four different levels of multiverse. Three of them have been proposed by other people, and I've added a fourth — the mathematical universe."

"What is the multiverse's first level?"

"The level I multiverse is simply an infinite space . . . But if space goes on forever, then there must be other regions like ours — in fact, an infinite number of them. No matter how unlikely it is to have another planet just like Earth, we know that in an infinite universe it is bound to happen again."

"You're saying that we must all have doppelgangers somewhere out there due to the mathematics of infinity."

"That's pretty crazy, right? But I'm not even asking you to believe in anything weird yet. I'm not even asking you to believe in any kind of crazy new physics. All you need for a level I multiverse is an infinite universe — go far enough out and you will find another Earth with another version of yourself."[22]

Continuing with my somewhat repetitive ramble, I should point out that the specifically oriented, open-ended nature of asymmetric infinity means that it's all approximate — but with a high degree of accuracy — and that the numbers never completely extend to Platonic infinity. Infinity has not really happened yet once and for all — and never will. Instead, infinity is necessary in order to define the existing numbers and any further numbers along the series, in that it has the creative potential to go beyond. Without the recognition of this organizing power, nonsense creeps in as the series basically tends to fall apart through self-contradictions in fundamental ways.

This does not say that math as a language has not been making sense — no more than it would be to claim that a new perspective on any other language would invalidate the bulk of what people have been saying. Where it would make a difference to use MU instead of the Platonic infinity symbol — clarifying the meaning of infinity — would be in preventing the powerful language of math from crediting some absurd conclusions that masquerade as something reasonable. MU would recognize the fact that the chosen line, series, or context in use *does* have a largest number where we choose to leave off counting, allowing for the threshold effect of going beyond. This threshold is in fact a thing observably mysterious in itself with the power to take us into the land of fiction and mythology, while keeping our reasoning from going astray, as demonstrated later by Rolo in the tale of *The Genie and the Greatest Number*.

* * *

In order to describe a multiverse of parallel universes, no matter how complex they are, Tegmark needs the symmetry of exact repetition to hold up forever. So let's ramble, or to change the metaphor, let's raft over the question of repetition a bit more, using the image of a River of Asymmetry to identify the continuum or what Alice called the Field of Action. As a universal continuum with thresholds, like whitewater, our River of Asymmetry will not allow any single unity or division to be perfectly final — and therefore absolutely accurate — so there can never be any repetition of perfect precision nor any exact equality. As we keep repeating, what exactly to repeat? So any series of numbers changes all along its length, along with the lengths of its divisions. But the changes can be so extremely slight as to be practically irrelevant, even though the relevance can become dramatic under the right circumstances.

The river is in motion, so not only must the units of the number line never repeat exactly, but nor can they be absolutely static. Nor can the line move at an exactly final and constant rate. It must accelerate and decelerate, turn back on itself and curve away, changing its speed, rate, and direction. Or sort of hang loose — or not so loose. And so on — back to the pebbles on the beach, in all nature's variety. This allows us to build up a better description of reality.

It has been proposed by Platonic philosophers and others that there must be an "ideal" of some kind for (in this case) each unit of the series, that if there is no exact repetition at all, in some ideal form, then how could anything repeat at all? But as we have seen, creation is not limited to one unit that must be replicated in another; the rhythm of life arises in a unity of rhythm like music that continues in many ways and is not dependent on repeating or embodying any particular ideal or beginning in any one place or in any one God. If there is no exact repetition at all, then everything is always being created. Creation is *now*, not just before or "in the beginning." Instead of a fixed ideal we have a creative river of life.

In short, we have the following rule of thumb: The maintenance of closely approximate constants of repetition or duration requires the increasing maintenance of limits which in turn requires those limits to break down and change in the avoidance of any absolute condition. Wherever the organization or the logic of a series tries to achieve the pure symmetry of the Platonic absolute of infinity and exact, finite repetition, it eventually breaks down to some extent.

In the attempt to bust Plato's "ghost" in something so potentially ambiguous and evasive as a series of numbers (especially going out to "infinity") involved in human logical reasoning, we need to place it in a social context, to bring it out. For this we need fiction. Our numbers need their roots in the culture where they emerged as part of a language, with all the cultural assumptions of language, just as we learned it from our teachers. No matter how arcane the language of math has become, it's all just symbols that can be expanded out or down and back, or translated into the languages of everyday life, even if that exercise would be so cumbersome as to show why math is so valuable a shorthand — as that old math book in the cupboard upstairs somewhere says. In order definitively to separate mathematics out as absolutely unique from other languages, one requires the conjuring of the ghost of pure symmetry of absolute separation into the real world. This cannot be done where it counts, except in fiction.

Our science has produced wonders that look like miracles to those of us who do not understand the language used to develop such technologies. It is arguable that this has the potential to go to our collective heads where we can fall to worshiping symbols as though they are not of this Earth, with the effect of discouraging our students about math and science — as though the language comes from some ideal unknowable or counterintuitive place with special and even divine messages of purity and perfection, if only we can decode them. Like other fields, math has had its share of entrenched hierarchies.

I wonder if we have created a symmetry of science that is continuously breaking into unreasoning romanticism. At least this might go some way to explaining the persistence of the superstitious acceptance of religious belief systems in the midst of education and everyday technology. The ironic extension of this idea is that we end up basically with one religion opposing another, yet again. But the stakes are higher with the greater power of the technology to damage the planet.

## Largest at Least for Now

Now we turn to the question of the largest number. Thinking asymmetrically, we can only identify a specific number as larger or smaller than another number within limits provided by the context of MU. Without that context we have nothing to consider. As we have seen, in the absence of absolute finality, it is not enough just to have, for example, a series of counting numbers from 1 to 10 with 10 as the largest. To avoid that "ancient paradox" we must have the context of MU. So insofar as we can speak of any number at all, we can find a largest number on the number line — or a smallest fraction. We can decide what it is for the purpose at hand and establish it as the last stop before MU. MU itself being a threshold that has potentials beyond math, it is undervalued by being referred to as no more than a number.

That being said, there is a theorem in math that states that there is no largest counting number. Let's have a look at this in the context of a description of theories and theorems and proofs and hypotheses, things that so often get mixed up in everyday discourse. Prof. Sam Nelson of Claremont McKenna College puts it like this, beginning with the largest number proof.

> Proof: Suppose there is a largest counting number, and call it n. Then n+1 is a counting number, and it's larger than n, so our choice of n was wrong. Maybe n+1 is the largest counting number then? No, because again (n+1)+1 is a greater counting number. Indeed, we can apply this same procedure to any candidate for "largest number," always with the same result. This shows that every choice of largest counting number is wrong, which is to say there is no largest counting number.
> 
> Here, the argument shows that you can only disagree with the conclusion by disagreeing with our meanings of the terms "largest" or "counting number." If you understand what these terms mean, you cannot help but agree that there is no counting number that's larger than all of the others.

This would be a good place to go ahead and quote Nelson on the distinctions in meaning between "theorem" and "theory," including the way the term "theory" is misused (my italics below).

> Theorems are what mathematics is all about. A theorem is a statement which has been proved true by a special kind of logical argument called a rigorous proof. A rigorous proof is simply a sound deductive argument, meaning that it starts with statements *which we know to be true* and then makes small steps, each step following from the previous steps, until we reach our conclusion. One statement follows from another if it's impossible for the first statement to be false while the second is true. For example, the statement "Socrates is mortal" follows from the statement "All Greeks are mortal, and Socrates is a Greek" — it is impossible for "All Greeks are mortal, and Socrates is a Greek" to be true without "Socrates is mortal" also being true. Hence, if we start with statements which we know to be true, then any statement which follows must just as certainly be true.
>
> Once a theorem has been proved, we know with 100 percent certainty that it is true. To disbelieve a theorem is simply to misunderstand what the theorem says.

Then some examples of theorems are given, including the one above and the famous one associated with Pythagoras.

> Theorem: If a right triangle has short sides with lengths a and b, and long side (hypotenuse) with length c, then $c^2 = a^2 + b^2$.

Nelson then goes on to say,

> Here, we might object "But what about non-Euclidean geometry?" It is true that by changing what we mean by "distance," we can get relationships between the sides other than the one in the theorem. But again, this requires changing the meaning of the words in the theorem — with the usual meanings of "distance" and "right triangle," the conclusion of the theorem is inescapable.

Again he puts the following succinctly:

> Mathematics is about proving theorems. In pure mathematics, we study problems which we find interesting in their own right,

answering questions by starting with what we know and proving theorems. Theorems are sometimes called different things depending on their importance or their relationship with other theorems. A theorem which is proved primarily as a step toward proving another theorem is called a "lemma," while a theorem which follows as an easy consequence of another theorem is called a "corollary." Theorems are often called "propositions" when they're first introduced.

The foundation of modern science is applied mathematics. In the sciences, observations lead us to discover both facts and laws. A law is an observation about a regularity in the observed facts, such as "objects fall when dropped." An idea that might explain a law or other set of observations is called a "hypothesis," and hypotheses often take the form of mathematical models, that is, mathematical systems whose structure is intended to mimic as closely as possible the behavior of the phenomena being studied.

Applied mathematics is about developing mathematical models of real-world phenomena and applying theorems we can prove about the mathematical models to draw conclusions about the corresponding real-world phenomenon. Scientists start with careful observations about the world, then devise mathematical models which replicate the observations. One can test a scientific model by using the model to predict the results of an observation, then making the actual observation and comparing the results. If the model fails to accurately predict the result of the observation, then the model is in need of refinement; if the model's prediction matches the observation, then the model is consistent with the observation. Consistency with an observation does not guarantee that the model will always match the phenomena for every future observation, but consistency with enough repeated observations does say that the model is a reasonable candidate for an explanation of the phenomena. Over time, a model gets tested and refined, with details filled in by repeated observations and tests.

As mathematical models get tested and refined over time, we have increasing confidence in the effectiveness of our overall collection of mathematical models. That is, over time the current version of a set of models becomes a better and better description of reality. There is never any stage at which the process ends and we declare that we have a 100 percent accurate description of reality, since that would require having made every possible observation; however, we can and do have mathematical models in which we have a very high level of confidence, higher even than the level of confidence that we usually require to call a statement a "fact"; 99.9 percent certainty may not be 100 percent, but it's a lot closer to 100 percent than it is to 0 percent. Note that, by contrast, common claims are often granted "fact" status after only a single observation or inference! Because of the difference in the levels of testing, the "facts" of everyday life are actually much more likely to be incorrect than are our scientific models.

As our hypotheses are being tested and refined until our level of confidence in them is very high, we seek a set of principles which provide a coherent explanation for the various laws and facts which we've assembled. This kind of detailed explanation of some aspect of reality, incorporating all of the various well-tested hypotheses and mathematical models and explaining the various facts and laws that we've observed, is what we call a "scientific theory."

This is quite a different kind of thing entirely from what one might call a "theory" in day-to-day life. Our usual non-technical meaning of "theory" is much closer in meaning to the scientific term "hypothesis," that is, a simple idea which can be tested. For example, a detective might have a "theory" about who committed the murder, or a student might have a "theory" about the best way to get a good grade. These are not theories in the scientific sense! A single individual never creates an entire scientific theory alone, for scientific theories are much too large and complex. Even theories which have an individual's name associated, such as Einstein's Theory of General Relativity or Darwin's Theory of Evolution are not the work of a single individual but are the cumulative results of the collaboration of many individuals over time. A scientific theory is an extensive body of knowledge which brings together a great number of well-tested hypotheses and mathematical models, weaving them into a coherent explanation for the facts and laws we can observe. An everyday hypothesis is no more a scientific theory than a single bolt is an automobile.

A common related confusion is the idea that scientific theories are waiting to be tested and proved before becoming accepted as a fact or a law. This is a serious misunderstanding — the ideas that make up a scientific theory are already as well tested as the current technology permits before they achieve the status of a scientific theory. Theorems are proved, not theories. In mathematics, before a theorem is proved, it is called a "conjecture." In the sciences, only well-tested hypotheses can become part of a theory. In this way, the term "scientific theory" is very poorly chosen, because for most of the population, the word "theory" suggests weakness and doubt when in a scientific theory there is only well-earned confidence.

In other words, to say that something is a scientific theory is to say that it is backed by all available evidence and that our confidence in its correctness as a description of reality is as strong as it can get with our current ability to test it. Theories do not get proved and become facts or even theorems; if a model or hypothesis is part of a scientific theory, then it already is as "proved" as it can ever get. It is true that scientific theories are not static and absolute; as technology matures, we constantly find new ways to refine our previous ideas. Occasionally, there are so-called paradigm shifts in which a new theory replaces and older one, but in every such case the new theory must be able to explain why the old theory matched up with observations as well as it did. For example, relativity was only able to replace Newtonian mechanics as the accepted scientific theory of gravitation because at low speeds and in low gravitational fields, relativity looks a lot like Newtonian mechanics.

. . . . .

Finally, the word "theory" is used in mathematics in a way that is similar to the "scientific theory" sense, meaning something like "the study of." For example, "knot theory" does not mean "a hypothesis about knots," but rather "the mathematical study of knots" — it's really just a short way of referring collectively to the entire body of articles, theorems, books and works relating to the subject. Where a scientific theory is composed of well-tested hypotheses and mathematical models, a mathematical theory is composed of lemmas, theorems and corollaries. Both are forever incomplete, in the sense that there are always new theorems to be proved and new hypotheses to be tested; both refer to fields of study in which a great deal is known but there is still more to be discovered.[23]

A clear statement of asymmetry at the end.

By flattening infinity we do not make the inference that the deduction that proves the above theorem saying there is no greatest number is incorrect. Instead, as in the example about the shift away from Euclidean geometry, we are adjusting the assumptions about infinity. The proof of the theorem can still be correctly deduced, even given assumptions that are not so true in themselves.

Asymmetrically, we would have to say that a theorem where there is always a greater, absolutely exact number builds confusion: Not this number, but absolutely the next, but not that, but the one after that, not the next, but the next and so on — it's a confusion generated by the repeated attempt to close the circle and make each unit on the line in some way absolute in itself.

Realistically, the series stops where we stop counting, but can continue in other ways. Asymmetric numbers are as precise as they need to be, because they are not absolutely exact: It's these eight pebbles in a row and that's about all for now, unless we add some. Asymmetric numbers are organic and alive to describe real-life phenomena. As Nelson says, there is always "still more to be discovered." This should apply consistently throughout the math.

Take the phenomenon of precession. It can be seen as a fine expression of the principle of fundamental asymmetry, or asymmetric infinity. It would have to develop as a direct result of the existence of asymmetry in the absence of absolute constants or perfect circles or perfect repetition. If the Earth cannot just remain in a perfectly symmetrical, closed, constant, and self-contradictory fixed spin, then it can only spin because its axis can wobble, or move in cycles that we discover in the drift of the stars of the zodiac and so forth.

Likewise, it would be against nature for the planets to tend to orbit the sun in perfect circles, perfect ellipses, or to be perfect spheres. In fact, they tend away from perfectly circular or elliptical orbits and perfectly spherical shape, in nature's balance in motion. (I'll leave it to Lola to firm up the reasoning for how they remain organized, rather than continuing to tend away into space, hypothesizing the asymmetric polarity involved.) If this is evidence of a fundamental, universal asymmetry, then this power to mold bodies and organize nature is indeed awesome. The phenomenon of numbers themselves is part of the same creative continuum as the planets and stars and shares their living organic nature.

So how would the proof for the theorem of the largest number look as compared with the proof for no largest number? Let's restate the latter for comparison.

> Proof of no largest number: Suppose there is a largest counting number, and call it n. Then n+1 is a counting number, and it's larger than n, so our choice of n was wrong. Maybe n+1 is the largest counting number then? No, because again (n+1)+1 is a greater counting number. Indeed, we can apply this same procedure to any candidate for "largest number," always with the same result. This shows that every choice of largest counting number is wrong, which is to say there is no largest counting number.

This proof uses mathematical induction when it says that "we can apply this same procedure to any candidate for largest number."

This is also a proof by contradiction, similar in this respect to our Transformation Proof of the absence of absolute finality. We make an assumption and show that it is illogical. In addition to the assumption for argument's sake that n is the largest number, this proof fundamentally assumes that the numbers repeat absolutely exactly. If one assumes this, then there is nothing wrong with the proof, as Nelson says. But as soon as we prove that nothing repeats absolutely exactly, then this proof no longer works because of the change in its assumption. Our Transformation Proof leads to the conclusion that there has always got to be a largest number, otherwise there would be no numbers at all. If there were no largest counting number n, there would be no numbers at all to consider. The largest number is possible because of the context provided by MU. It is interesting to note that MU cannot exist on its own.

So the reasoning would go like this: Suppose there is a largest counting number n. Then n+1 is a counting number, and it's larger than n. This does not mean our choice was wrong; it just means that n+1 has now become the largest counting number, whereas previously it was not. And so on for as long as we keep changing the largest number, thereby generating a series; otherwise there would be no series. There is always a largest counting number.

We do not use induction in a generalized way. We deduce a "phase induction" to MU, where we have extended the series as long as this particular series is going to go for now — it is open to change, without absolute finality. In this way we can be specific about the series and generate our numbers.

In the conventional proof of the largest counting number, for the purposes of the argument, n is assumed to be absolutely the largest. It is thought therefore to be disproved as such by the addition of another unit. If the reasoning were consistently applied it would say STOP, you cannot go beyond n, because you have really said it is *absolutely* the largest. You are now prevented from disproving it to be so, or you will be breaking your own rule. You said it is the largest and now you are contradicting yourself! If you wanted to move on to n+1, you would have to have a rule that says "as a mathematician I reserve the right to add a number, even though n is being considered the largest. I am not bound by the 'absolute' rule for n." This ambivalent ghost assumption is built into the conventional proof. But when everything is asymmetrically connected, this position becomes self-contradictory. As we have seen, the contradiction happens every time you go from one absolutely exactly final unit to the next. But if one assumes this inconsistency into the numbers, as is currently the case in mathematics, then of course the proof is correctly deduced. The rule is broken in the assumption. Conversely the logic of change allows us to change the greatest number without inconsistency, as part of the way a series is distributed.

Before we continue I would like to quibble over just one small statement in the above quote. "A rigorous proof is simply a sound deductive argument, meaning that it starts with statements *which we know to be true* and then makes small steps, each step following from the previous steps, until we reach our conclusion." I am sure that Nelson is not trying to claim omniscience on behalf of the axioms of mathematics. So I threw in the italics with the idea that he would no doubt agree that it might be more accurate — though less clear for his purpose, since it opens doors to philosophy — to say, "which *we assume* to be true." This slight alteration gives the math a more open-ended character, grounding it a bit more in the same earth as the sciences it describes. Meanwhile the distinctions between a theorem and a theory still apply.

Once again, it is notable that all scientific evidence to date, provided by our most powerful technology, shows asymmetry to be all-pervasive. Prof. Frank Close, author of *Lucifer's Legacy*, where the story of asymmetry is told, was head of communications at CERN, home of the Large Hadron Collider. Awareness of nature's asymmetry seems to be growing. In Lee Smolin's *Time Reborn: From the Crisis in Physics to the Future of the Universe*, asymmetry is thematic. As a founding member of the Perimeter Institute for Theoretical Physics, Prof. Smolin's perspective provides a shared context in the interpretation of data using Platonic math.

## Decimal Intervals

Continuing in the pursuit of clarity, let's further inspect the way numbers asymmetrically unfold at a fundamental level. Considering the intervals . . . infinitely repeating decimals asymmetrically advance for as long as some smaller and smaller decimal is added. One might even think they would continue beyond the point or threshold where we might choose to start the next unit — blending the unit we are dividing with the next. On the asymmetric number line, it would almost seem that the numbers could overlap, each number increasing beyond the threshold of the next, though they lose definition. The numbers might seem to be approximate enough to allow an unspecified Extremely Small Fraction (ESF) or MU — where we leave off subdividing — to extend the number past the beginning of the next number. The next number would not be counted until it has become exact enough no longer to be confused with the one before it. But it's not quite like that — that would be a slippery slope into the confusion mathematicians rightly fear when it comes to loosening the borders of numbers.

The decimals that are being repeatedly added must always be smaller and smaller than the unit of the preceding decimal — even if the units cannot be absolutely exactly defined. Still we might scratch our heads and wonder why, given an infinite number of bits being added, the number doesn't get huge, eventually. There is a hidden illusion or double standard.

The point is that you can't insist forever that you are always adding a smaller and smaller fraction.

The incremental additions wouldn't increase the number beyond the next because of the built-in assumption that the additional decimal must always be smaller — forever. The assumption that the decimals must always be smaller is a vital organizing feature of arithmetic that keeps confusion at bay. But the "forever" is another story. Asymmetrically speaking, you can't say, "always smaller *forever*."

"Always smaller forever" is the assumption that keeps the decimals always falling short of the preceding decimal place but always continuing. Numbers with continuing decimals are assumed to go on "forever." If you don't just say something like "they can continue only as long as we continue counting," then you are assuming an absolute infinity. There's the double standard: an absolute infinity that keeps opening up. Here again is Plato's paradoxical ghost, or a better term might be "shadow," in keeping with the shadows against the wall of the cave. Plato compared us to people bound in a cave in such a way as only to be able to see our shadows, so that we take the shadow play as reality. (How he could figure on telling us this with no more than shadow language is a mystery of good fiction.) In a poetic sense, decimals that just seem to keep going do taper off into the shadows, or into the light, or into a story. But we do leave off counting. It is important to note that when we say "count," we do not need to be totally literal about it. The term "phase induction" is one way to describe counting beyond the need to nail down (or write down) each number that we wish to identify. There are many ways of counting or doing math, and creativity will discover many more, but taking infinity for an absolute would be miscounting — which might qualify as a shadowy illusion. I will leave off with the metaphors before Halloween and move on to the next paragraph.

If we can't say, "must always be smaller forever," but we are still going to continue, a threshold of change must take place. It's nature's polarity bringing us back from verging on the impossible pure symmetry of absolute infinity or constant repetition in one direction. The previous number is finalized when we go no further with its extremely small decimals, but continue on the line to the next number.

Numbers with repeating or seemingly endless decimals appear to taper off, but as long as anything at all is added, they grow as the series changes, as though riding a wave that tapers off but only ends when we leave off counting. On an asymmetric series, the decimals don't really go on forever, but they can continue — just not into pure symmetry. The repetition builds a threshold of tension until nature's polarity brings about a leap into the next unit, space or place. Like a wave, so you can't exactly indicate at which decimal the next unity merges in — at which point n followed by a series of decimals is succeeded by n+1.

By trying to make numbers absolute we build the confusion of the paradox of increments that are "always smaller forever." The numbers in the series sort of fall all over each other trying to be larger and smaller at the same time. While asymmetric numbers might appear to be fuzzy and overlapping, the truth is that they allow us to be more specific about how a series can be organized and develop.

Likewise in the example of Cantor's diagonalization argument in the previous chapter, another problem is raised for set theory when the set of decimals cannot be categorized symmetrically in one-to-one correspondence with the counting numbers, because we don't know exactly where the decimals (and their counting numbers) end. Asymmetry would keep them from all ending in that same questionable absolute required for the argument to work — while still providing us with the numbers to work with. Asymmetric numbers can slip through the diagonalization argument (Chapter 21, Figure 3).

## No Point of Symmetry Between Units

Another thing we cannot do in an asymmetric series is to have a point where the previous unit exactly meets or turns into the next unit such that it becomes a point of pure symmetry between them. The attempt to achieve point symmetry, as told in the story of the Lady of the Lake, builds tension — and the circumference of the circle around its center point fails. Each time it regains its tension and repeatedly fails, it can be made to reverberate with the polarity of asymmetric change, like a drum. This broadcasting effect of individual forms of near-symmetry is a characteristic of their open-endedness. The way the near-symmetry breaks has to do with the specific circumstances (or conditions) of its context or environment. In a math environment we could call this "mathematical tension."

While we were sitting out on the porch with our barbecued salmon, salad and wine, Rolo expounded somewhat on the ironic connection between these simple deductions about circles and the extremely complicated tangle of string theory. Rolo had the *Discover* interview with him and loosely quoted the following interesting statement by cosmologist Max Tegmark in response to the question, "Can you give a simple example of a mathematical structure?" Answer:

> The integers 1, 2, 3 are a mathematical structure if you include operations like addition, subtraction, and the like. Of course, the integers are pretty simple. The mathematical structure that must be our universe would be complex enough for creatures like us to exist. Some people think string theory is the ultimate theory of the universe, the so-called theory of everything. If that turns out to be true, then string theory will be a mathematical structure complex enough so that self-awareness can exist within it.[24]

After which Rolo went on to quote Peter Woit in *Not Even Wrong*: "The fates of supersymmetry and string theory are linked . . . these ideas are either both wrong or both right."[25] And here Rolo realized that he was losing us for sure.

But he threw out the following remarks just to show that he was done, and we should feel free to change the subject afterwards: "Whatever one thinks of Woit's book, he really hits the nail on the head when he says, and I quote from memory, 'The necessity for spontaneous breaking of supersymmetry is a disaster for the whole supersymmetric quantum field theory project.' In other words, they are stuck on absolute symmetry. They know it must break somehow to be descriptive of nature. But how? They can't get from that part of their math that describes the asymmetries to that part that is intrinsically assuming absolute symmetry, and back again. They need to find the asymmetric ground where the non-existence of absolutes means that the symmetry is always already broken to some degree. Until then they will be lost without a compass in a sea of infinities and parallel universes, doppelganger people, and all the rest."

We listened in silence to the crickets playing chorus to the brook and watched the fireflies for a while.

\* \* \*

Numbers like pi, where the decimals just seem to keep on going, opening up, going beyond, bring us the direct sense of the power and mystery of asymmetry in nature by standing as evidence that pure symmetry does not exist. Leaving aside for a moment that nothing exists in the absence of asymmetry, we can fantasize a world where absolute pi happens. In such a world we could access all the repeating decimals of a number at once. Everything would already be counted and known, without any process of opening up. All the decimals of pi would immediately be known, if anything absolute could be known at all. We would have a God's eye view of pi, leaving aside the other side of the ancient paradox, where that view would be cancelled by the escaping numbers. Sometimes the actual world seems as though we are always trying to pursue those decimals and so many other things to the bitter end, in search of the absolute. But the true intervals and their decimals are like partially open doors between numbers and poetry, where it's not all "just numbers," and poetry is not limited to words.

\* \* \*

The power of asymmetric infinity is that it cannot be stopped absolutely. No matter how small they get, the overriding reality is that the decimals can keep on going, adding to the number, as long as the rule of the absence of absolutes is not violated. Numbers with seemingly endless decimals exist because it's the nature of all numbers to continue asymmetrically into the next, because no series ever repeats exactly, because it cannot be stopped completely. Nor can it be correctly assumed to be already absolutely counted and included, out to some absolute infinity. Numbers that can keep on going like pi are a succinct statement on the nature of all numbers, even though some appear to stop.

\* \* \*

Numbers that have repeating decimals have extremely low asymmetry, like the 2s discussed earlier in this essay and in "Totalitarian Math." These "orderly" numbers require the existence of "crazy" numbers with decimals that have extremely low asymmetry *at the other extreme*, where there is near chaos in the way the decimals are *almost randomly* distributed (bearing in mind the impossible paradox that pure randomness requires the lockstep symmetry of exact repetition). In this way the fundamental asymmetric polarity shows up in numbers.

* * *

The finer the divisions of a unit get, that is, the more we divide each unit up in smaller and smaller subunits, the more we are tightening up the line and making it more exactly symmetrical. This is because we are approaching the paradoxical symmetry of that Platonic infinity. This calls into action the polarity of the River of Asymmetry and calls for change. Arithmetic is always a dynamic process. You don't need calculus for that.

Fortunately, the asymmetric arithmetic works out much the same as we conventionally know it. Each successive number can be seen as a threshold brought about in some way by nature's creativity. If we want to call it quits and assume an end to the decimals before the next number in a sequence, we can of course do so, as long as we remain consistent with the understanding that the next number or unit is not absolutely disconnected from the numbers that precede it.

The issue of free will in association with mathematics is becoming a recurring theme, as we keep saying things like "call it quits." But, we can describe the way the asymmetric reasoning affects our numbers without having to know how it is that we decide to "do some arithmetic." Whatever it is that brings about a decision to "do math" engages the effects of the reasoning and the reach of any series in the context of MU.

* * *

Another aspect of the asymmetric logic is that it is impossible to subdivide a unity forever without destroying its finiteness — its ability to be divided. The conventional meaning of "forever" or "infinity" is not precise enough and results in the Platonic paradox again. In trying for perfection, the logic loses its precision where we are unable to ascertain that a unit is being divided.

Put another way, you can only subdivide a thing within overall approximately finite boundaries or thresholds — up to a point. As such it is still a divided unity. To try to do more (using a Platonic infinity) is to use a double standard. It's the same self-contradiction of wanting a line to continue forever but also stop completely where you want it to stop and how you want it to stop. The unity is effectively destroyed as a meaningful object by the ambivalence. Curiously, this ambivalence is what happens in the absence of identifying a fundamental polarity in numbers.

\* \* \*

There's that old conundrum used by the philosopher Zeno of never arriving at a destination by approaching it a fraction of the remaining distance at a time. Asymmetrically speaking, this is just a bit of interesting nonsense, since it assumes its own problem of self-contradiction by insisting that the destination remain perfectly constant even though the remaining distance is continuously changed by being reduced. The distance and the destination defined by the remaining distance are themselves absolutely separated in a sleight of hand that denies the question of what kind of a series we are going to have: a Platonically infinite one, an absolutely finite one, or an asymmetric series? Again, the unity that is being whittled away is destroyed as a meaningful object, unless the asymmetric connection is made to the destination.

The Platonic number being approached gets to remain absolute while the changing incremental increase creeps forward in its direction. This is the double standard of conventional arithmetic. In the asymmetric series, the destination becomes indistinguishable from the eventual marginal extra extremely small fraction of the decreasing distance. We are able to deduce that this indistinguishability is present as a basic characteristic of numbers, something overlooked by the absolutist perspective. Asymmetrically speaking, for the purposes of this operation, we can leave off counting the approach at an extremely small fraction and go on to the number being approached, knowing that no absolute gap can separate anything from anything else.

Plato made use of Zeno's paradoxes to advance his own absolutism, and they are still a problem for mathematicians and philosophers to this day.

If the fractions try to advance to a Platonic infinity, the whole operation of trying to divide a unity infinitely ends up making no more sense than attempting to divide nothing, which math does not allow for the good reason that there is nothing to do. It's like attempting to divide nothing because, in the end, there is no absolute finality in the unit to divide. No unit is absolutely final but, within practical limits, division is of course a handy arithmetic tool.

Rusty gates vanish in time. No unit is exact enough to remain forever waiting while you approach it forever; it dissolves, so to speak, into the threshold of breaking near-symmetry, into the asymmetric continuum, the River of Asymmetry, instead of supporting a Platonic ideal of pure symmetry. But if the operation of incremental creep stops, then, because change is ubiquitous, we can continue on and connect with the number approached and left standing — because by stopping we participate in the definition of a context where another unit is possible.

Looked at again in another way: You can't really say that it can never be reached as a number. It would be absurd to say, "This specific number that is not anywhere can never be reached." What exactly are we referring to that can't be reached? There was never any Platonic number to fall short of. (Not to dwell on the front wheel of the monocycle.) In fact, in the sense that a number is in part merged into the fundamental asymmetry of the series, it has been reached. And the number — like all things already created — has already been a part of the continuity. The rest of creation — including any further numbers — has yet to happen, in time, space or otherwise.

This reasoning of course goes beyond arithmetic to involve the concept of infinitesimals and limits used in calculus. Without going into mathematical detail, the calculus still works asymmetrically, but for a somewhat better reason, and the "flattening" of infinity could prove helpful in other mathematical ways.

\* \* \*

Counting asymmetrically, by the way, time matters, because time, as described later on in this book, is one of the ways things change. Time is not something that can be completely separated out of the River of Asymmetry, although it can be emphasized with a special axis to represent time, as such. In the same way, different dimensions cannot be absolutely separated, but they can be unfolded and collapsed back into each other to get perspective. But an "infinite number" of dimensions is out of the question, which, again, could be helpful in many ways, as Rolo would be happy to point out.

The conventional treatment of limits in calculus — where they are never reached — is based on the Platonic absolute ideal. All limits *are* reached asymmetrically. In order to keep the numbers in place and to maintain their integrity, you need a largest number within the context of MU — or an extremely small fraction, as the case may be. It need not be specified to any great extent, as long as it is acknowledged.

\* \* \*

In future, math teachers may not have to try to make sense to their students in explaining how the curve on some graphs approaches the axis forever but never reaches it. It does — just the way it looks. Nor will statisticians have to try to fit nature with purely symmetrical bell curves.

Basically, the one axis shouldn't remain so finite and absolute as an axis (defined by the asymmetric number it intersects on the other axis), while the curve is extended to a nonexistent absolute infinity. The extension of the series must assume the open-endedness of all the numbers.

The more your results depend on the double standard of a Platonically infinite extension of a series, the less dependable they are. In calculus, for example, we can arrive at a correct answer in the usual way, without having to depend on the Platonic philosophy of limits, which was developed after the calculus itself was in use.

I remember a professor going to the blackboard and simply drawing a horizontal line that was supposed to go "off to infinity" at both ends and then claiming to bisect it into equal halves by cutting it in two with an arbitrary vertical slice, as though his piece of chalk were a sword. I doubt he thought he was acting randomly, but if asymmetry is the rule in all things, then it might explain a vague feeling of the absurd in the performance of proving a theorem. Asymmetrically speaking, you can't bisect a line in any meaningful way until you have established the context of approximate limits of MU at each end. Otherwise we are assuming that we already know where and how the line will continue at either end, when no one can know how the asymmetric continuum will proceed in the development of all Creation, let alone know what has already been created. It would be to assume a *final destination* with some ideal of absolute infinity, while pretending otherwise. The universe and all Creation would have to be perfectly symmetrical. Unwittingly or not, we would be assuming absolute knowledge, that we are omniscient, playing God, marking the center of the symmetrical universe.

The philosophy of asymmetry puts math into a larger context. It's the natural consequence of connecting numbers to concepts that are not really numbers and without which we have no numbers. The non-mathematical concepts cannot be unmade or separated out with a final disconnecting divide.

Treating infinity as a sort of constant number has allowed mathematicians to generalize a series into exactly repeating units, thereby randomizing it and consequently losing control of the language here and there. Perhaps this is partly a result of assuming or hoping that everything is numbers, or that everything can be pinned down by numbers. This can unnecessarily complicate, derail, or unbalance the math. Generalizing on a number in this absolutist way has the effect of disconnecting it from anything and calling into question its very presence, as we have seen towards the end of Chapter 6, with the onion in the maze.

* * *

Watching the waves on a river or by the ocean, it's easy to enjoy the evidence of asymmetry. It's got to be a creative process if it doesn't repeat exactly. The poetry in nature can be found in nature's numbers.

Pi brings out the fluid, organic quality in all numbers, and, as we can see by squaring a circle, in asymmetric geometry. Pi stops where we stop counting, leaving a specific pattern, a specific pi with an arrow, so to speak, because nothing repeats exactly. The number pi shows how the diameter fits and grows asymmetrically into the circumference of a circle. Pi is a generalization (as described by Samuel in Chapter 6) with a loose end — where the specific pi of the circle in question stops with a finite number of decimals. The number pi says that there are no perfectly closed circles. Each number pi is making such a statement from different but connecting contexts, in the same way as it appears in different places in this text.

Pi repeats asymmetrically in smaller and smaller increments, forming the circumference, growing, changing in size with the extremely small decimal or MU. Yet pi continues to define or describe a unity — the circle. Pi shows how units are like the onion — not absolute. Pi also shows that there can always be more units, more circles, because the units can never be absolutely defined — finished off.

As pi grows, the circle changes shape. Its asymmetrical shape is connected to MU, where we stop counting pi. Pi is about 3.14159265, but with the asymmetric number line, the decimals can continue to be added until we decide to continue with, say, 3.15 and beyond. It's like rounding off the numbers for practical purposes, but with a difference, because there is a connecting leap to the next chosen number.

\* \* \*

The usual means of abstracting a series off into the distance involves substituting variables like x, y, or n. This technique of induction locks in a randomness that assumes "the right line" to maintain the number line illusion that shadows our thinking. The would-be random, pure symmetry tries to happen when the presence of the variable assumes exactly repeating units.

We often use a letter like n or x to mean any number of some specified sort. But substituting the variable typically contains the assumption that numbers can be random. The absolute randomness of variables like x assumes a number line that is both sequential to absolute infinity and finite. This is similar to the assumption that the chosen line became sequential randomly, eliminating choice along with the mathematician.

A coin can never have close to a fifty-fifty chance of landing heads or tails without defining, limiting the circumstances. Will it be taken by the wind? Will it be lost in the grass? By what road did the one with the coin arrive before the energy of his or her arrival culminated or partook in the tossing of the coin? Such limitation requires a narrative, a choice, a connecting asymmetry. It can never have a purely symmetrical fifty-fifty chance without the Platonic double standard — at which point it would not exist.

No coin is tossed forever. There is no ultimate, final and infinite, absolute god to toss it forever. A computer tossing an imaginary coin over and over is a rare occurrence, and the longer it does it the rarer it becomes, defeating any objective of demonstrating randomness as a fundamental, everyday reality, until it finally has to break down or do something else.

If exact repetition happened just once, the asymmetry would cease to exist and the cosmos would be entirely random like a purposeless drum machine beating time for a finite span before stopping for no more reason than it began, except for the fact that it would never have begun if even the possibility of exact repetition existed — that is, the possibility of nothing ever happening.

Any natural drummer or musician knows about a nice tight beat, relaxing the beat, or about stretching the beat. None of this musical emotion and rhythmic sense would be possible without the asymmetric nature of true infinity to give us pressure and texture in rhythmic patterns, like sex. Rhythm has direction because of infinity's asymmetric polarity.

The illusion of pure randomness depends on uniformity (symmetry) and can appear either organized or chaotic and without rhythm or sequence. Such symmetry would be absolutely cold and flat, waveless, lifeless, or as Frank Close put it, "bland." Except that it does not exist. Such a state could have no way of happening without imposing absolute limits on asymmetric infinity — an impossible task to complete. So the door to absolute chaos can never be opened, not even just a crack. That's the nature of truly infinite power.

Each unit would have to be perfectly separate from its neighbor in order to be perfectly defined as equal without variation. Each unit would have to be identical, in fact, not equal, so all units would turn out to be the same unity viewed under an illusion, if such a totally undifferentiated unity were at all possible.

True infinity, mathematical or otherwise, does not just sit out there "somewhere" at the end of some magic line to the end of the rainbow. It moves and has power in many specific ways. It makes the rainbow possible.

The infinite is not random. This may be one of the most liberating and intuitively self-evident facts in the world.

\* \* \*

While reading Samuel's essay I decided to stop him there. I did get his agreement, and there was an informal vote on the matter. If we had let him continue any further, who would have wanted to read Rolo's story of the female genie — the jinniyah?

## 23. The Jinniyah and the Greatest Number, by Rolo

There was a man who went about the town proclaiming that there was no largest number. This would not have mattered if it had not got to the ears of the sultan who ruled this part of the land of the Arabian Nights.

The ruler was not pleased to hear of this, because he prided himself on being the largest of anything in just about every respect, as long as he approved of whatever it was, and he approved of numbers in a big way.

So the man was called from the streets and asked to account for his affront before the sultan himself.

"So you say there is no largest number!" said the Great One to the lowly one.

The lowly one bravely replied that it was so.

"But I see no number at all." the sultan replied. "And you are a man of little consequence. You have no numbers about you of anything worth my notice, so how do you say there is no largest number when I see about you no number of anything of account. No largest number! What impudence. Why do you talk such nonsense? Are you trying to offend me? Or have you taken leave of your senses, having lost any number of anything you might have once had? No largest number! You have no numbers at all! Perhaps I should take pity on you and have you put to death immediately and painlessly."

"It is true that I am of little consequence, Your Munificence, Your Majesty, however this makes it all the more true, all the more real, how your greatness and splendor shine forth by comparison, so much so that it has no end, none that any mortal can see. And since surely you shine with the righteousness of the Almighty, O Commander of the

Faithful, there is no number of anything that can count the rays of such infinite brilliance. It shines on without end and has no greatest number."

"Your flattery is well received," the sultan replied. "Not unexpected, but accepted nonetheless. I will only say that you are still in danger of losing your life if you proceed with this refrain of there being no largest number, for it may amount to blasphemy! God Almighty is but one; however, that one is the largest number, as you must well know! And if you persist in denying Him, you will forfeit a quick death for a slow one."

Seeing himself trapped in a confusion between the infinite and the greatest number, the man trembled in panic, only glad that he was already on his knees before the throne. "Perhaps, O Marvel of Marvels, we have found the riddle of the cosmos?"

The sultan grunted with pleasure. "And now that you have bound yourself up in this riddle, how do you propose to extricate yourself?"

"Ask the jinn! The jinni!" the man blurted out in desperation.

The sultan roared with laughter. "The one in the bottle? Or the one in the lamp!"

When the laughter of the court settled down, the man, encouraged by the merriment, suggested they ask the jinniyah. "She would tell us . . . or she might dance!" he added in hopes of diverting the topic.

Silence befell the court. "If she agrees to dance — we will hear her . . ." the sultan cautiously replied, though he had been assured all his life that the jinn, male and female, were safely locked in their bottles since ancient times. He preferred the tale about King Solomon sealing their fate with a ring of power.

Then the man with all his heart wished for the jinniyah to appear. It was accepted in those days that this might happen. There were tales of a female jinni who might still come to help a person in need. It was clear to all concerned that this man was in trouble, and so they all waited to see what entertainment might or might not come of it.

A woman appeared at the entrance of the throne room. She was dressed as though she had come straight from the harem. She was unannounced, and it was forbidden on pain of death for any woman to go about unaccompanied. Boldly she advanced to the throne as the courtiers held their breath.

Before the sultan could say anything, she asked him directly and without ceremony: "How many do I represent?" She gave him such a

## 23. The Jinniyah and the Greatest Number...

look of confidence that he hesitated on the possibility that this might indeed be the famous jinniyah herself, disguised as one of his wives.

He had so many wives that he could not be sure to recognize them all on sight. This one had the sensuality of wisdom and was not one of his recent acquisitions. "I can see by your expression that I am not the one!" she continued. "So how many do I represent?" She twirled around once, letting her garments flow outward slightly as the light reflected off the jewel in her belly button, and then she resumed a sensuous but practical pose. "How many?"

"How many what?" the sultan roared in frustration.

"Precisely!" she replied, and twirled once more, coming round to look him in the eye, her shoulders straight, her body relaxed.

He was sure she must be the jinniyah. But this one was out of control. "Since I am not the one," she continued, "how many am I? Am I two?"

She twirled once more and stepped to one side. This time her former image remained in place, so that now there were two of her. She twirled again, and there were three of her in a row. There was no longer any doubt who she was. It was the jinniyah, three times over.

"Ah!" said the sultan, "you are the jinniyah—"

"How many?" she persisted, speaking from all three positions at once.

"Three!" the sultan responded reflexively.

She twirled once more. "Now what is my greatest number?"

"Four!" he blurted out, unable to think of anything else to say but the obvious.

There was a bit of laughter heard throughout the court. He glared at her helplessly, feeling ludicrous. The courtiers realized which way the wind was blowing and went silent.

She twirled again. "And now?"

He tried to restrain himself. The sultan resolved to say nothing. But then the courtiers were finding it difficult to restrain themselves, so he decided to try the alternative strategy and he said: "Five."

"What is my greatest number?"

He did not appear to know. There was a silence. He was the schoolyard bully who has not done his homework. The jinniyah gave him a maternal look. "At this moment, in this place, in this throne room, in this palace, what is my greatest number now?"

"Five!" The sultan cried out in anguish and embarrassment.

"Correct," said the jinniyah. The courtiers were dying in fear of laughing.

In terror he watched her twirl once more. She kept turning in a graceful dance until the five images were folded back into one.

"Now, is there a greatest number?" she asked.

"When, O jinniyah? When?"

"Precisely."

Suddenly the man on his knees jumped up and threw his arms around her and then stepped back to exclaim, "That's it! When! when! You must ask when! You must ask where!"

"You are so right, you must be specific," she said, and stepped forward to take hold of him in a dance that would save his life.

"Like the king, I was generalizing—" He felt safe. They spun round. "You cannot generalize like that about a greatest number."

They turned again as the ruler watched in confusion.

"Continue," said the jinniyah.

"This is not just any genie! This is the jinniyah!" he said for all to hear. "You cannot use a symbol to represent any number and use that to say there is always one greater! Somewhere, there is always a greatest number, to be specific! Otherwise, no numbers at all! No place, no time, no context, no number!"

"And a time and a place without numbers," she added, rolling her eyes towards the exit with the suggestion of a nearby destination.

They spun round faster and faster as he continued. "Here we go once, here we go twice, ah ha, and here we go three times! Each one the largest, each one the greatest, each one so — *wonderful* — until we have found where we will stop. At our greatest number!" Wild with pleasure, this mathematician was dancing with the jinniyah, twirling and twirling until they whirled out of the throne room in a trail of light and back into the streets until the dance ended, and the jinniyah disappeared.

The grand wazir came to console the sultan. "You see, you were right, after all, O Great Majesty, there is a greatest number, after all. You were correct, time and again—"

But with each word the sultan looked more humiliated and the grand wazir more patronizing. He saw the look on the sultan's face, and the mistake grew, and the courtiers saw it and began to formulate their own versions of the event.

The tale spread far and wide, and changes came to the land when it was clear that the sultan was right, that he was so right that he was wrong. He felt his power slipping away with his moral authority. He would ask himself, "How many do I represent? How many numbers? How many of which numbers? Who am I, after all?"

The questions reverberated throughout the land until, after many a thousand nights and a night, there was an Arabian Dawn on a Middle Eastern dream. People began to count the vote, and the man from the streets won. The genie was out of the bottle.

However, to this very day most mathematicians believe it makes sense to prove that there is ultimately no largest number. But there is always a greatest number, now one number, then another — it just keeps changing with circumstances, so long as there are any numbers at all. Numbers aren't everything. You have to know when to quit.

## Rolo's Postscript Rant

I found the following postscript at the end of my manuscript for this story about the jinniyah. Since we cut off Samuel, we decided to keep this for the reader to get a bit of a further insight into why *Zen and the Art of Monocycle Maintenance* did not happen. Notice that I must include myself among the "math people."

\* \* \*

Hey math people! If you say there's no greatest number — which you do — you're saying there must always be another number; you're saying there are always more, but, still, you've counted them already — to infinity — contradicting yourselves. How can there always be more if you've counted them all already? Unless you have a largest number, you can't really define your series. Have you really counted it or not? Without a largest number to establish the asymmetry of going beyond, your numbers fall apart. This happens if you try to disconnect your number line and its infinity from the rest of existence by saying that nothing can follow the numbers but numbers, and they must follow each other off to infinity. This is like saying numbers are everything, because what goes beyond can only be a number.

This is not really going beyond and not really infinity. It allows you to put what you are calling "infinity" in a box, protecting your pure symmetry from the universal asymmetry. As a result, you can develop an argument that says that there are totally different kinds of infinities, such as the infinity of odd numbers going out forever and the infinity of even numbers going out forever, and thereby apparently keep the odd and even number sequences and their infinities entirely separate. What you are really doing is already defining infinity and your number line to suit your purpose; the ghostly cultural assumption protects the icon of absolute symmetry with an absolute disconnect!

I know, you just wanted to do math — but by disregarding the rest of the world, you are confusing infinity with the sort of absolute you imagine a constant number to be, mixing up your math, like the hero in our story. The Platonic infinity, being a largest absolute, is really a largest number. This is contrary to your symmetry-based theorem that says there can be no greatest number.

In the case of the odds and evens, they really go out to an extremely large odd number (or an extremely odd large number) and an extremely large even number (or even an extremely large number) and remain asymmetrically separate as long as we assume them or choose them to be so. In this way we don't forget that numbers, like everything else, connect with the whole of existence, and they are not everything.

P.S. What's that again? How come math assumes math is everything if we don't know when to quit? If we don't quit counting, then we do nothing else but math. In practice, the reality is that we do quit counting the intervals between numbers when we go on to the next number and we do quit counting larger and larger numbers, even though we theoretically assume we do not. That assumption is a denial built into the culture of our math. It's a gate that we try to keep closed. But we do in fact quit and continue with other things — that's observable. We just need to recognize it in our reasoning and check out the unfolding consequences, where a stream of fundamental connectivity becomes a magic carpet for many things, consciousness, even, in the form of a genie, no less! But you have to be willing to stop. A *finite* number cannot be finite *forever* — it's against its nature. Long before forever, we just leave off holding onto the numbers; we let them go and do something else.

Thus I almost spun out with my monocycle, enjoying the ride. And by the way, leaving me roiling away in this romantic passion with this issue of greatness, in case the reader is wondering, there *are* mathematicians who single-mindedly *do* believe everything can be stated mathematically. One who has gone to the extreme of this idea is that Max Tegmark fellow introduced in Chapter 22.

Throughout his career, Tegmark has made important contributions to problems such as measuring dark matter in the cosmos and understanding how light from the early universe informs models of the Big Bang . . . In a series of papers that have caught the attention of physicists and philosophers around the world, he explores not what the laws of nature say but why there are any laws at all.

According to Tegmark, "there is only mathematics; that is all that exists." In his theory, the mathematical universe hypothesis, he updates quantum physics and cosmology with the concept of many parallel universes inhabiting multiple levels of space and time.[26]

Now, while I cool my heels, Lola will take the math and its fiction to the next level — with "Aquilah and the Lamp," further demonstrating, by the by, that:

## WITHOUT THE HUMANITIES,
## THERE CAN BE NO THEORY OF EVERYTHING,

all of which adds up to something more than a theory.

# IV. Aquilah and the Lamp, by Lola

> The timeless view of physics ... has shown its impotence ... But if we embrace the reality of time, we make possible a time-asymmetric physics within which the universe can naturally evolve complexity and structure. And thus we avoid the paradox of an improbable universe.
>
> —Lee Smolin, *Time Reborn*

## 24. Awakening

She awoke from deep dreams. As she came to consciousness, she looked over and saw her cat, Millameowsimous, the cat of a thousand meows. It seemed to be as awake as a cat can be, but she sensed that it was dreaming its life, on autopilot, with the aid of instinct — and something more. Then she looked around the room and realized she was still trapped in the lamp.

Of one thing she was certain: she was conscious to some degree. She began to recall the conversation she had had about a thousand years ago with the philosopher who kept arguing that he was not conscious at all, that such a thing as awareness was an illusion that in fact did not exist. She smiled at the memory, and like one joke after another, it was soon followed by the recollection of that other fellow who had insisted there was no truth. He had had to stop himself from insisting that every word he was saying was — untrue.

Buoyed by the memories, she arose and stretched, ready to meet the challenge. It had been far too long since anyone had called on her consulting services. As long as she had agreed to be an absolute slave to anyone who rubbed the lamp, she had had plenty of business — far too much, for that matter. Now she had slept without being awakened for so long that even the dreams of a genie could no longer provide the illusion that she was not trapped, "Trapped by ignorance?" she asked the cat.

It purred.

With a magical wave of her hand, she tried to leave the lamp. "Even if it's all just a dream of consciousness, it's solid enough," she sighed.

Millameowsimous purred on and on, then stretched her sleek form, sloping down low on powerful hind springs being reloaded for action.

Then Aquilah remembered that there was a key to exit any bottle or lamp. It was a legendary key, said to have been known before the enslavement of genies in hierarchies, hierarchies wherein they had to wait for someone to conjure them before they could taste the external world. The key was said to have been forgotten because too many genies had got caught up in the master-servant cycle of dependency. She shuddered at the thought and left it at that.

The other reason the key had been lost was simply the lack of time available to reconfigure it. It had always been taught that an exit key could be fashioned by reason and applied with physical strength. One of the reasons she had decided to put out her shingle as a consultant, apart from the attempt to cast off the dependency of master and servant, was that it seemed increasingly that whenever she began to work on the ancient key, someone would call her up on a mission in the external world. Now that she demanded her freedom and no one seemed interested, she had fallen asleep, only to awaken in an age when few genies were called upon anyway. She soon realized that the time was now both an opportunity and a desperate necessity.

In a flash and a shower of lights, she ascertained once more that indeed no exit had opened up. She would have to craft or conjure a key. She remembered the hint given her by a wise and elder genie, that there was no universal skeleton key. But a key could be configured for each specific situation. One just had to know enough of the history of the key to continue it. She looked again at Millameowsimous.

The cat winked at her.

Then she remembered that the last thing she had done before becoming too drowsy to think was to consider the implications of anything — bottle, lamp, or otherwise — being absolutely final. Her dark eyelids and long genie lashes had got so heavy so fast that she had just made it to her silky bed in time. What had come over her? Now she wondered how her cat had fared over the centuries.

Did the fact that she could find no exits from her bottle really mean that it was absolutely final? She felt a bit dizzy. The magical cycle of power and illusion that had enslaved genies had been wheeling along for so long that this genie had woken up. Perhaps the vicious circle was not perfect. The wheel was not a self-contained perpetual-motion machine, forever yanking genies out of bottles for slave duty or drugging them if they wanted to be free. It needed sustenance from outside — or inside — its circumference. Where had it been getting its energy?

Without knowing more precisely the nature of this beast, she shook off its ancient effects with the aid of a new century in early progress in the world at large, where the beast had lost interest in genies and was feeding elsewhere. She stood up and stretched. She lay down and stretched again, developing herself into some of the yoga positions for genies. These are like the poses adapted for humans, but without the same physical restrictions, since genies can take many shapes — though not any shape at all, she was reminded again and again. "I have become stiff with sleep!" she said to the cat.

Genies use shape shifting to think; it is taught in genie school that quite often a thought must be preceded by an action, in the absence of which it cannot find a way to be thought of — as thoughts are physical. One thing leads to another.

As she concentrated on remembering how to think without physically trapping herself in her own illusions, she began to vaguely recall an ancient tale of genies in bottles. It was all a matter of keeping a sense of direction. But how? Again and again, she tried to recall the physical context and the times she had heard or read the story, clearing her head until she was able to reassemble it all. Here's how it has come down to me.

## 25. Genies in Bottles, by Rolo

It says in the Book of *The Thousand Nights and a Night* that Solomon's ring sealed the genies in the bottles. There were things that Shahrazad had to say to save her life. The subtlety of her stories is found when, in spite of this imprisonment of genies, genies are to be found in story after story.

It was said that there were ever more powerful genies in the cosmos.[27] When one of these genies needed extra help from an extra powerful genie, he or she had only to rub the lamp and the greater genie would appear to the little genie and his or her wish would be granted in a spirit of goodwill and good reason. Sometimes the greater genie would have to turn to an even greater one, and on occasion the request would go far and wide until a genie who was powerful beyond their comprehension would grant the request and provide a planet, a solar system or even a galaxy, if there were sufficient reason and good will. He or she would rarely do so on his or her own but joined with others of like powers, and they would make a Day of it together. Then it was up to the smaller genies to do their part and the people to do theirs on the new planets along with the rest of the animals.

One thing the genies would never do was to elect among themselves a dictator, a supreme genie to be God over all creation for all time, to have all their powers at his or her command. Not that the request didn't occasionally arrive, where some impulse led to a considerable amount of pressure for this God to be granted to all creation. But the genies generally understood that such a thing was impossible. Experience showed what power struggles would ensue and what devils would come of it, where some powers would demonize other powers more than usual, the stakes being so high. So education was important throughout the cosmos, where it never ended and never ends — because with education things keep opening up, as we discover that they are not already opened up all the way and not everything is known for all time. Genies learn that no one will ever know it all. Courses in infinity are taught on any planet where genies might show up. And one of the oldest truths about infinity is that there is no absolute symmetry. Because infinity opens up in so many different ways, it would have to have opened up already and come to an end before you could find any absolute symmetry. Because you can never be sure of your symmetry until infinity stops opening up! This is a key point to the politics of the cosmos. A single God of all creation would have to be absolutely symmetrical where it counts — right in the center of the God's power. To pin one's hopes on such a center leads to political chaos and despair.

This is a hard truth for those whose request has been repeatedly turned down. Many of these souls realized that unless the genies were in a bottle of some kind, people would have the perspective to figure out the political situation. With genies in little bottles or lamps, people would be emboldened to imagine that there are no further levels of power beyond — just the absolute power of a perfectly centered god. So the disaffected, in denial, began to circulate the story of not only the genies in the bottles but one story that Shahrazad rightly, in her position, left untouched. It's the story of the genies within the bottles belonging to the genies who were locked up like Russian dolls with the seal of Solomon to ensure that one God would win out.

She left that one alone because, like many of her stories of genies out of lamps and bottles, it had a variety of tempting sequels — this particular sequel was not circulated for a long time, because it tells of how they appeared to escape. She did not want to tempt herself with the unleashing of stories of escaping God (in keeping with tales to escape the madness of her husband). So she did set the stage for eventual degrees of liberation. The escape was possible, the seal not having been crafted as it might have seemed. Sealed with words, it was undone with words.

Solomon was a wise man, it is told, because he built not just the famous Temple of Solomon but also a temple to the goddess Astarte and helped bring prosperity to his people by making peace with his Pagan neighbors. Some things are not meant to be known, according to the "powers that be." This temple of Astarte is one more quest that Shahrazad left for future historians and archaeologists.

You may know from Sir Richard Burton's gusty translation that she had to tell a different story every night to keep an extremely self-centered, autocratic ruler from murdering her, according to his resolve to marry a woman every day and have her executed the following day, in order to restore his honor, for what it was worth. Shahrazad could not tell many things. In a way, this is how she became a jinniyah in a bottle. She was not free. However, by creative action and a series of fantastic stories, she saved herself and the other women who would have been murdered. It is this spirit of feminine freedom that beguiles us in the *Arabian Nights*. By involving her husband in the fabulous asymmetries of stories that call forth even more stories, Shahrazad was able to remove his deadly fixation.

\* \* \*

The secret of Solomon's temple to Astarte, no secret in its day, was bottled up using the fiction of his ring and its seal of absolute royal power. The seal was said to be so powerful that not only did it bottle up in lamps and other commonplace but mysterious containers, genies of many kinds, but genies within bottles and lamps in bottles and lamps with genies who could not beak the seal. So any genie in a lamp might come across another lamp inside the vast mysterious interior of the seemingly ordinary lamp that contained him or her, but never could he or she call upon the genie in that lamp to get any of them out of there. It was complicated beyond imagining, such was the absolute power of King Solomon and his god, so they said. The way out was part of the great Ineffable Unknowable, and the genies could never communicate this Unknowable, or communicate much at all, caught alone as they were in the hierarchy of bottles in that one bottle tossed into God's Cosmic Ocean, in our story.

The story of how they got free is quite simple and always has a number of possibilities, depending on where you live; the answer must have roots. The right and natural thing must be said to un-spin the lie. The answer must be sufficiently rooted to stop the spin. This can take time, patience, and a great deal of effort by many who may even be oblivious of what the community is doing and where they are in history or which planet they are on. It is true you need passwords — but they cannot just be secret ones. They must also be open. Even in stories such as "Ali Baba and the Forty Thieves," where he needs to know the secret, magic words, "open sesame," the words are only effective in the context of the story. And where would the story be without its people and places, including a place and time for the storyteller — and so forth?

The words that would break the spin on the seal of Solomon were words of Solomon's own wisdom, of inspiration and reason, of love and logic. Sometimes just one word would do by itself, but it must connect up in creative ways with other words and actions, like the stories of Shahrazad. Words that bring hope, riding in on waves that say: nothing is unknowable! Nothing is unknowable because the infinite keeps opening up, building bridges of opportunity for all to find out the why and the wherefore and the way to the next stop.

* * *

In our story of how the genies get out of the Russian bottles of genies in a cosmos of escalating power contained by one god, a young girl finds a lamp in an antique store along one of the scenic back roads of Maine. Having been lucky enough to have read some of the tales of Shahrazad in school, she buys it and brings it home, places it in the garden, and when no one is looking, gives into the temptation to pretend she is in the world of the *Arabian Nights* and rubs the lamp. Education wins the day, for the same reason that we have the *Arabian Nights*, and a jinniyah appears from the lamp.

After she had become accustomed to the genie in her life, she began to realize that the genie was a soul, just like her. Then she wondered how she, a simple girl, had escaped the power of the seal, to be able to free the genie. Then she asked herself if the genie was really free. Then she asked the genie, "Are you free?"

"So many ask the genie to be a servant," came the reply. "So many ask to be a ruler and ask in the same breath — though they may not know it — for a supreme god. You ask whether I am free. The answer to your question is yes, I am Liberty. I can call myself Liberty because there is no supreme ruler. You have freed the genie of freedom, and on behalf of the genies who are now flying free of their romantic prisons, I thank you!"

"You're all welcome—" The girl looked around for any sign of the escapees. Assuming they preferred to remain invisible she continued, "But you must have always been free — even in your lamp, Ms. Liberty."

"In a way — how else do you turn around a wrong story? You have to see inside the genie's lamp in order to have a lamp in the story. You have to put yourself inside other people's prisons to save freedom. We genies have put a part of ourselves there, like the nested Russian dolls to show how things would be — and how it is." Then she smiled. "Everything is know-*able*; that's what creates a mystery to discover, to find out; knowing creates more questions. You know me for the same reason you said the magic words, 'Are you free?' So we are friends. Together we can find out things we would never have discovered alone."

The girl's eyes widened, "Even you can discover things because of me? That's a mystery, for sure."

"This aspect of me was able to escape the lamp and discover this garden and have this conversation because of you. In a democracy, as a wise man said, all politics is local. The rich and powerful can only be liberated at the grass roots. If they don't find their freedom by helping their liberators there, they will fall. Their destiny becomes their prison. It is a foundational idea in many stories and faiths and for good reason."

"So, are you running for office?"

"Sure, why not!"

"I've got to tell my friends about this!" Then she paused reflectively. "It takes time. I'd better be sure they've read some of those old stories and break it to them slowly. They might get culture shock or something. I need time to find the right words and the right words to find the time, a little like Shahrazad. I see what you mean; I don't think every aspect of me is free, either. Maybe you should wait on that run for the Legislature."

"All right then, when the time comes, you run, and I will be your Muse."

The genie did not go back into the lamp but remained in the garden, appearing from time to time in a world that was that much more like the *Arabian Nights* is supposed to become, where you can read them by a lamp in comfort, without having to be caught in them, when the magical possibilities liberate us from the oppression, and the lamp is Liberty's torch.

One day this young adult was over at a friend's house, and they were in the garden to pick some fresh mint for their iced tea, when they saw a leprechaun leaning on the shoulder of a statue of a garden gnome by the wishing well. After catching her breath, her friend said, "Quickly, catch him, and we'll have the three wishes or the pot of gold!" But the other restrained her, saying, "No, let him be, and we'll always be free."

The leprechaun disappeared. Her friend looked at her and said, "What do you mean, free? Are you free?"

"Cool out, drink your iced tea; I'll tell you a story."

They twisted the mint and mixed it with their tea in silence until the other replied, "We just saw a leprechaun—"

## Back at the Waterfall and the Pond

While discussing which stories we should include in the book, we realized that we were increasingly observant of the effects of the afterglow of the day on the garden, as it mixed with the rising light of a full moon.

"The fireflies almost seem to be signaling us," I, Lola, commented.

"Yes," said Samuel, "it's true that people have always noticed the way nature sometimes looks at you personally, as though some great soul has put on a local disguise, some elaborate costume made of flowers and greenery, or like the Green Man looking out of a tree at you; sometimes I think the rapids in the river look like the paws of a sphinx in front of the bearded face looking at you from out of the waterfall."

"Of course the clouds—" said Alice.

"The weather," I sighed.

In Maine! Where the seasons go round in a theater of four acts and many extreme scenes.

## 26. Quill Pen

Millameowsimous was circulating round a large, spherical, red, clay bottle with a long neck and no handles. It was sitting on its broad base on the mosaic floor next to the Persian carpet. After rubbing up against it a few times, the cat stood back, sat down and waited with especially big eyes. Aquilah joined her, and they both fixed their attention on the stopper. All she had to do was lift it, but for some reason she couldn't recall what was in that particularly large jug. "That's odd," she said. "You'd think I'd remember that—"

"Mrrt," said the cat.

"I might as well check," and she reached to lift the stopper, but stopped herself. "What if there's a genie in there?"

"Mrrt."

"What if there are infinite numbers of genies in bottles in there. They'd be quite frustrated with me by now, I think! What if my falling asleep has kept them in there all this time? What if some of them don't sympathize with my philosophy of freedom and liberty for all? Better keep the stopper on—" and realizing the conflict, she added, "at least for a while, until I sort things out. It's not like my heart isn't in the right place, I hope.

"Of course it might just be an extra bottle of olive oil I forgot to store away when I was getting weary." Then she saw the ship in the bottle on the mantel over the fireplace. "Who might be in there? Oh my, I really must get out of here!"

The cat purred. The purring reminded her of infinitely recurring streams of things in her dreams.

"On second thought," she replied to the purring, "if Liberty really is in all the bottles and lamps, I don't think it's in her nature to go on ad infinitum without ever stopping somewhere. It would seem — immodest, kind of arrogant, really, if not downright — omnipotent! Omnipotent—" It didn't sound like Liberty to Aquilah, especially from inside the bottle, or inside some unknown number of bottles before the last stopper could be popped for some outside air. As she tried out the word "omnipotent" a few more times, it reminded her of the force that had got the genies in the bottles to begin with — the omnipotent god, which had turned out to be a case of mistaken identity. It was coming back to her now. The fragments were assembling themselves.

"Where is the Land of Maine?" she asked Millameowsimous. "I certainly never heard of such a place. It must be a message in my dream, coming from the outside! Dreams do that sometimes, don't they?"

Millameowsimous strolled over to a large, round, glass door that was of an opaque light blue, in contrast to the multicolored curved glass walls of the room. She stopped and looked back, then sharpened her claws on the wooden doorframe. Aquilah got up to let out the cat. Then she followed her through the verandah and into the biosphere, the lamp. This was another dimension of creation, to make life tolerable for genies. It was part of the deal with the hierarchy, the deal that had got them into bottles, lamps, and other containers. The genie sighed.

They went out to the waterfall and the pond. A playful millwheel turned lazily under the shower from the falls. It powered a music box that contained a vast collection of recordings. Aquilah skipped a flat stone across the pond. The ripples lapped up against the bows of a daysailer at anchor. She knew that no matter how many days she sailed the pond, she would never be able truly to sail out of the lamp. Not until she figured out the key.

She knew that a piece of the key that had to do with current, active change itself, so it had to be crafted to each requirement, bearing in mind the long-term rules of change. Change, she remembered, is the fundamental ABCs of genies. Usually they just "get it" and don't have to think about it much, like a gift of music from the Muses. "Abuse the Muse and knowledge is lost," she remembered from somewhere. So now, she realized, if she really wanted to change her life, she needed to understand — "What?"

Staring into the waterfall, she began to wonder where it fell from — ultimately. What fed the pond? Where did it go? Why down? — in a lamp? A lamp where?

"Understand what? Understand gravity?" she asked her cat with a sudden feeling of despair.

Millameowsimous loved to sit by the millwheel and watch the fish milling about nearby. Aquilah had named her accordingly, adding on syllables for the fun of it, in tune with Milly's playfulness. So it was Milly for short.

"I need a name!"

Milly looked at her.

"I need the name of the key."

She thought for a moment. "Why do I need a name? Names are fanciful and romantic, like genies. Keys are logical. Naming them is one thing, knowing them is another. Knowing them means I have to think! Genies are romantics, genies are powerful; they can just act! We use magic. Since when has a genie had to do the drudgery of thinking! The magic just comes; it's a gift." She paused. "A gift that can be a curse—" She skipped a few more stones while Milly watched closely.

Aquilah picked her up and cuddled her. "Oh Milly, you are sheer magic. But you are a work of nature — and that's science. I'm going to have to do some thinking. But it's been so long!" She placed the cat back down carefully, contemplatively by the pond.

"Millameowsimous, we've got to go back and find a version of the key in Father Time's old storeroom. It's been so long, I can't remember where I put it exactly. But I know where I keep old keys and things like that. I'm sure I've still got the one I used when Old Time built me that storeroom. I never really found out what he needed to store in this particular lamp, so I never locked the room. I suppose any place with a history has a storeroom of some kind. Perhaps I can even use the key to the room to derive the way out of here by thinking. I'll have to be logical and just do it — applying the key is the key." She sighed. "You know, Milly, we jinniyahs are no better than those hopelessly unthinking brute male genies who haven't had a thought of their own — or of anyone else for that matter — in a long, long, time." She sighed again with a few memories of romance, and nothing more came to mind.

"Mrrt."

\* \* \*

We now need to make several deductions in order to give Aquilah's story the structure it needs to prevent it from just being another tale of "going back in time." This is especially true where asymmetry is concerned, because the absence of absolutes means that no one can go back in time in the way that such a journey has been conventionally understood. To go literally back in time requires pure symmetry, otherwise how to retrace the footsteps of time exactly? So that is out of the question. But we can go back asymmetrically.[28]

Things do change. As we have inferred from the Transformation Proof, there is nothing that does not change. If change were to stop, obviously, nothing would continue — not even time. So time can be thought of as an aspect of the nature of change. It's what we sometimes identify when we experience the fundamental continuity. We experience certain kinds of changes and we say "time passes."

Time is rhythmic and can change in unexpected ways, not being able to repeat absolutely exactly, no matter how accurate the clock becomes. Its asymmetric character also means that time cannot be fundamentally broken. Changes could take place where time would become unrecognizable. But no absolute limits can be placed on the basic nature of change, the fundamental continuity.

So we can no more go back in time than the Lady of the Lake could return to the place where she began the ring of pi. But this does not prevent us from going into the past asymmetrically. As changes happen in the present, the relationship of present to past changes; the context inhabited by the past changes, thereby changing the past — like roots growing into the ground with the branches of a tree growing out. The relationship between past and present means the past is alive in some way in the present. The present reaches into the past. No one in the present can avoid being part of the context of the past and causing changes in the nature of the past accordingly.

These changes — though they may be as extremely small as the most repetitive differences in the divisions of time — are a part of the way physical consciousness changes. Likewise, nothing is completely lost when new layers of the past are created, like the onion in the ground. The reality of how the past used to be when it was in a different context remains in changing ways, like a continuously readapting object that can fade and be rediscovered. For anything to be truly lost, something would have had to end absolutely. And nothing is ever so completely known that it loses its mystery entirely.

Sometimes it is possible to be more of a part of that process of the present accessing the past, in a way that is more intimate than usual. Genies have a way of visiting the past by accessing this characteristic of the nature of change, they being creatures of transformation, even when they've lost the reasons for their abilities and the Muses have all but given up on them.

Aquilah danced and wiggled and played one song after another, tried to turn herself into one sort of key after another, tying herself into every kind of yoga knot she could imagine, but she was unable to find a way to work herself into the past, along the corridors of eternity to Time's Storeroom.

"But Liberty must be here somewhere, if only a cat's whisker, a look, something to guide me into that interaction of present and past. I just need to find that wiggle room and follow the way the present opens up those deep layers of Time's maze." Exhausted, she looked at Milly, who was watching the fish in the pond.

The weariness reminded her of that assignment she had avoided in school. The professor had warned her that she would one day need to do her homework. Or she would risk losing the key to balancing her powers. Instead of looking for a key, she now began to wonder where she had left her favorite quill pen. Then she remembered she had already started the essay. But something had worn her out. And it had taken her forever to find that pen. Now she picked up the thread of energy and went to find the writing desk.

Genies, like all sentient creatures, are vulnerable to being corrupted by power. This weakness being recognized among them, some were all-too-easily convinced that they needed to be enslaved, though other words than "enslaved" were used by those who overpowered them with false logic. She would need to rectify that.

She set up her desk by the pond. It was more fun going to get it than just using magic. She enjoyed the way it would ingeniously collapse to be carried. Likewise she loved the quill pen. It was old times again. Milly curled up for a nap to dream by the millwheel.

Aquilah looked up, visualizing the world beyond her sphere and the classical image of her professor as depicted in art by the Ancient Greeks, Urania holding a globe of planet Earth and wearing a cloak embroidered with stars, her eyes looking at the sky. "This is for you, Urania. Please accept my attempted essay from within this world, even though it is late."

# 27. Aquilah's Essay

In this environment where I live there are no absolute finalities, no exact repetition, and accordingly there is no perfect symmetry. This I remember as basic. From this I must craft a key.

Before me there is a pond. The surface of the pond can never become perfectly symmetrically flat. The falls can never become totally turbulent. Between these non-existent poles is another polarity. I will call it the "polarity of creation." There is that word "Tao," but I am not sure what has become of it. The poles of creation may take many forms, as things change, but everything happens between them.

These poles happen because the impossibility of the absolute condition means that things are diverted from achieving it. This redirection is a changing phenomenon. It amounts to a sense of direction in consciousness, and as all genies know from the ability to materialize and dematerialize objects on demand, consciousness is a physical thing, and all things are somehow also forms of consciousness. So with this sense of direction, let us proceed. O Urania help me, for I do not feel at home with this strange style of writing essays! My cat has fallen asleep, and I must stay awake.

Now, if we were able to proceed in a perfectly orderly manner, it would be the same thing as proceeding in perfect chaos, as the two are really the same random impossibility — the perfectly exact repetition of exact order and of course the chaos.

Instead, we can proceed (I am repeating that word again; I will come back and fix it later) in our characteristic and asymmetric balance or imbalance, depending on how we fare. We cannot be absolutely neutral, as all constants have a non-symmetrical, an asymmetric bias, just as every point points somewhere. (Urania, I sound so intellectual!) We cannot proceed with pure, constant motion, nor can we remain absolutely immobile. Absolute inertia does not happen, as general relativity concurs. "General relativity"? The Muse has sent me a direct message from outside the bottle! This is a new term to me, but it arrives accompanied with the insight to understand it — but in a different way. Different from whose understanding? Who is out there, Urania? But not to get sidetracked, I can see that even though it shares the pure symmetry of the "Newtonian paradigm" by assuming an ultimately timeless and absolutely symmetrical "block universe," Einstein's paradox seems to work quite well a lot of the time — what have I said! Oh well, another paradox. I must take a break now.

\* \* \*

Returning to my essay, Urania, I feel I may be making progress with the key. I feel a new confidence.

So worlds come into being in the balance between these two impossible positions, fictions of pure chaos and absolute immobility or unchanging repetition. All the changes we experience are in-between, so to speak, in a balance that has fundamental direction. It being conscious in various ways, we could call it a "universal instinct."

Now that we know we have a compass, let's get our bearings, let's try to read it.

There is an organizing, creative principle at work that keeps all of creation from exploding into pure chaos or collapsing into an amorphous absolutely chaotic blob or a single point of extinction into pure symmetry or anything of the sort.

There is a fundamental connectivity; before there is any complete break there is always a transformation. This is where genies get their power. I didn't think I would ever have to write all this down.

Any changes in the direction of absolute immobility or absolutely chaotic action would eventually be accompanied by tendencies or pressures for changes away from that impossible state. The impossibility of the "non-poles" is a kind of repellent. Things just can't go there, so they have to change accordingly. Or, because they change, they don't go there. Because the non-poles are nonexistent, they don't really have any effect, so there are lots of reasons why things don't "go there": it's the manifold nature of reality. That's its power, its creativity. If things are going to exist at all, they must change. So the way of change has all the power of existence itself. And because things can't just suddenly slam up against the nothingness of an absolute — there being nothing to encounter — there are degrees of change toward and away from the impossible pure symmetry of the absolute.

I am — we are — going to get out of here after all, Urania! But I must keep writing.

Degrees or tendencies toward absolute immobility and degrees or tendencies toward absolute action or chaos are attracted away from the impossible absolute state in a continuous changing balance in motion. The water goes down over the falls specifically the way it does, in part because the special stillness in the pond above it cannot be perfectly still; the degrees of immobility in the pond are possible because the water cannot rush in absolute chaos over the waterfall. In the absence of absolutes they balance each other, the waterfall and the pond. And so each has its own quality or personality in the environmental community, if I might put it so. There is a polarity here to be further explored along that ancient River of Asymmetry.

Looking outward, if there is no absolute immobility, and the universe is always in motion, then this polarity is fundamental. It is as basic to the electromagnetic spectrum as it is to water, gravity, or anything else. Electromagnetic spectrum? Where did I get that from, Urania, O Muse? What are these flashes of insight from the outside world? Am I becoming some sort of a genius? Apologies, Urania. Or did you inspire that one?

So, why doesn't the water fall up, at least in this lamp? After all, I don't know where my lamp is.

In the process of creative changes between the poles of creation, the spherical condition came about in the form of orbiting bodies, among other things. According to our rules for asymmetry, in the sphere there is a balance between the twin impossibilities of an absolute center and a perfectly symmetrical circumference.

Let's take the example of a planet. It cannot collapse to zero, into the perfect symmetry of an absolute center. And the planet has matter. This is the same as saying that if it is not going to be nothing and be a planet, then obviously it must have matter of some kind. What is the matter? (O dear!)

In a sense, the land is pushing up and outward into spherical existence, redirected from any absolute center of the sphere. But why the geography and geology? (More terms!)

The planet cannot become perfectly spherical. In the avoidance of such an absolute shape, there is a balancing pressure downwards, distorting, as it were, away from the absolute perfection of a perfect sphere. This crumpling downward force would be gravity. (That genie Einstein called it a "warping of the space-time continuum." Got that! But there's more — what happens when we change the meaning of the term "absolute"?)

The outward manifestation away from absolute centralization or chaos would appear as matter (light or dark), and the inward force would be gravity. But without the one you would not have the other, so they are different aspects of each other. With the land rising up in time, *en mass*, you get waterfalls. Not that the land ever had to rise from the central focus of the planet's core. It is kept "afloat" and in motion by gravity and the absence of an absolute center, in the balance. It's a question of the characteristic balance of the gravity and matter as the orb achieved density and shape. It's a curious fact that no perfectly circular orbits and no perfectly spherical celestial bodies have been found. (At least, come to think of it, I never found any in my travels.)

Why does the gravity crumple downward, or "warp" inwards? Why doesn't the manifestation of the outward accumulation of matter just keep on going out? Because if it did, it would achieve absolute symmetry, achieving a perfectly infinite Platonic circumference. (I remember that man, Plato!) There would be nothing to stop it at any point, and such nothingness would be absolute in the ancient paradox. This would break the rules of asymmetry. So the sphere is flattened, shaped, and warped in characteristic ways and according to its relationships.

Or as wonderful ol' Omar K. might say, were he to write an essay: if, on the potter's wheel, the circular bowl never becomes absolutely round, the edges are possible with something beyond. This is what gives us our shapes in creation, including our space and time. It is the power to go beyond asymmetrically that allows our boundaries and thresholds to take shape and come into physical being. Here's my quote, Urania.

> I watched the potter thumping his wet clay;
> And with its all oblitherated tongue
> It murmured: "Gently, brother, gently, pray!"
>
> . . . .
>
> "What! did the hand, then, of the Potter shake?"[29]

## 27. Aquilah's Essay

If we are going to have a planet at all, there will be a force to push back from perfect symmetry, back down toward the central focus of the planet's core, allowing for a varied landscape on the surface boundary of the planet and requiring rhythm in layers going down to the core. The sun likewise is layered, including layers of heat distributed, with some hotter outside the cooler ones. It's the maze. Gravity would not affect the planet in pure symmetrical lines inwards, but would change in patterns throughout its structure.

The sphere of influence of the gravity would be wider than the planet, going beyond and fading out, failing to reach a pure and infinite circumference. It would be wider than the planet because the nonexistent, perfect sphere from which the force of gravity is the diversion is not confined to the eventual surface of the matter. If it were so confined, then the matter and gravity would be in a relationship of perfect symmetry, as would be the center and circumference of the sphere.

Correspondingly and more obviously, the effect of gravity could not fall short of the outer boundary of the planet's matter without losing the landscape to space.

So objects beyond the surface of the planet are affected by this gravity. Also, gravity would have the wave patterns generated by the breaking symmetry of circles and spheres and so forth. Such objects emit waves as they achieve thresholds in the redirection of energy from the impossible.

From the smallest particles to the largest orbs, the tension within objects in fundamental polarity in our universe brings with it gravity, even when objects group together and no longer look like spheres. (Where is that term "quantum gravity" coming from!) Asymmetry connects, macro to micro, from the particles of matter to the planets and stars. So, according to this idea, Urania, the material of an object is not just built around the absence of an absolute center of gravity in the object as a whole, but matter also happens in conjunction with the absence of any center of symmetry in its asymmetric particles.

Likewise, since the gravity is there to avoid absolutes in nature, and if it is true that all absolutes, like the non-poles of creation, are the same nothingness that does not exist, the absence of an absolute center of the sphere is as much a reason for the phenomenon of gravity as is the absence of an infinitely symmetrical circumference. Even though the various kinds of pure symmetry are really the same nothingness, the location where the symmetry breaks or fails or is turned away from the absolute makes a difference in the way things turn out and create space and time as different aspects of the changes. So we can think of gravity not only as pulling but pushing the universe apart asymmetrically. So the universe must be expanding more than it is contracting — as I seem to remember out there. But one day it might contract, whichever, as long as it is not in the fictitious balance of pure symmetry. In the absence of anything absolute, gravity pushing, as compared with the familiar pulling, is like the "dark" side of some energy, but still visible when you consider that nothing can fall instantaneously.

In the absence of absolute poles, we live in a moving balance between poles of extremely low asymmetry, with the speed of light as one pole and the solid mass of matter as another asymmetric pole. The more you (Urania?) approach the speed of light, the more you conjure the balancing necessity of increasing mass. What is not included in relativity theory, is that the speed of light is not absolute, after all. For the balancing effects to function, you need asymmetry in the absence of absolutes. As one approaches the extremely low asymmetry of light or extreme mass, changes take place attracting away from the impossible pole of either condition. Relativity theory works so well because the error is extremely slight in the difference between the absolute condition and the changes wrought at such low asymmetry, where pure symmetry is but fiction. But such errors in the fundamental nature of reality can be extremely consequential.

Extending this idea a bit further, O Muse, if the fundamental continuum is physical, and therefore no single line can exist without having a physical presence, then circles are really more like wheels. If so, then the wheel would have material and gravitational effects like the spherical objects. Taking this further again, any wavelike rhythmic phenomenon that repeats and has a cyclical effect — yes, energy — would be a form of matter and gravity with mass, as the Einstein genie might agree. This energy's associated mass might accumulate in some way like a succession of wheels. Objects might be materialized, or in the reverse process they might vanish (or explode, if we are not careful). And it's just possible that waves, including light, are slung along by gravitational effects over distances, even beyond the speed of light. Change has no absolute limit, so the light might change beyond Einstein's absolute limit. Perhaps it would no longer be called light or whatever it had been. The material involved could be as subtle as consciousness and difficult — but not impossible — to measure. In the absence of absolutes, there will be wiggle room —[30]

* * *

Aquilah looked at Milly. "I think I have enough of an essay. I can already feel the balancing effects of the discipline of the attempt to write it. I feel the thresholds along the cyclical waves, like tingling particles along my body. The power that has kept us here is based on the illusion of a single pole of absolute perfection and symmetry. I see through it. I can visualize a way. That's all this genie needs to get us out of here without blowing ourselves up."

The cat woke up. They both surveyed the daysailer. The genie visualized it as an impressionistic painting, a rhythmic pattern of particles on the move. "Milly, we'll sail to the 'key'! I should have known it was just a play on words—words to get us here." She took the mooring line that was looped through the buoy and hauled the little sharpie to the dock. "Curious shoal-waters design," she mused. "I don't recall her looking like that. I wonder where New England is."

Aquilah called forth a wind from just the right direction, and they sailed with close-hauled asymmetry at just the right angle until the present moment began to feel somehow timeless, enlarged, and the past gave way.

They arrived at a sand bar on the edge of a cove, just as the bottle was about to be thrown into God's Cosmic Ocean. The genie and her cat disembarked, and before anyone had the time to stop them, she lifted the stopper. They sailed away to the present, in time to be free.

In future, if anyone briefly asked, it was often replied that the genies got free when word got out that God had failed to properly cork the bottles, drunk on power, of course. But many scientists explained that in fact the genies just found the exits via nature's asymmetries—and at least one cat. There were arguments about a dog.

# V. The Tea-Room Scenarios

> Whether we ever get to know about them or not, there
> are very probably alien civilizations that are superhuman,
> to the point of being god-like in ways that exceed
> anything a theologian could possibly imagine.
>
> —Richard Dawkins, *The God Delusion*

## 28. By the River

On the night of the salmon barbecue, there was considerable discussion about how Aquilah and her cat should attempt to escape the bottle — specifically. It was decided that there should be a break in Lola's story — about here.

All four authors strolled out under the full moon to watch the waterfall at the end of the garden. The old milldam was about eight feet high, heavily eroded, and about fifty feet long. There was no trace of the millwheel; only the few rusted bits of iron remained. The ones Samuel had taken a hammer to and pounded over and into the crumbling cement one dry summer, for safety. Now a sheet of water curved over the length of the edge, spreading a thin, glossy reflection of the night, a thunderstorm having replenished the pond.

Rolo commented that the moonlight seemed to reverberate along the falls, as though the sound of the water were coming from the moon. The other three allowed the poetry of the comment by adding to it in their own ways.

After referencing the way parallelograms of slate along the stream channeled whitewater down toward the Kennebec River, Alice said she wished the story of Aquilah could have continued, although she understood that this was not meant to be a fairy tale. They were supposed to be writing philosophy.

"Maybe we can do something about that," said Samuel, stroking his beard as he watched Alice's Mayflower features in the silvery light and shadows. With her blond hair, she is so ethnic, he thought to himself — in the context of the Arabian Nights. There she is, dreaming intellectual fantasies of flying carpets.

The waterfall seemed especially quiet to them for a long moment, although its muted texture reflected the impossibility of any of them knowing for sure that the others also heard the increasing silence in the scene.

The reader might now wonder briefly who is narrating the story. Has Aquilah escaped? Is she now one of the Muses? Does it matter?

Samuel stared at the waterfall. "It's iridescent in this light, especially culminating at the base. It almost looks electrical, like lightning."

"There could even be a storm god in the waterfall," said Lola, enjoying a chance to prolong the mythmaking.

"Zeus with a water nymph — but that sounds a bit dated," added Rolo. "Perhaps Thor and—"

"Right where the pond bends into the falls, that's the sex," said Lola.

"And the mystery," continued Rolo, gazing at his wife.

"The seeming perfection," said Lola playfully. "No wonder people believe in God! And having just one god, it kind of breaks the tension, gives resolution to all that magic, when it just seems to be too much. So easy to understand, especially when some god answers their prayers."

"Or some other thing answers—" Rolo commented.

"And they're so sure who's on the other end o' the line!"

"Who is?"

Who is what?

"So sure."

"Not sure—"

"Who's not?"

"Who's on first?" said Lola.

"After you—"

"Somebody stop them," said Alice to no one in particular.

Samuel intervened flatly, "Of course this genie story could just as well be about a Jack-in-the-box."

"What?" said Alice.

"Sure, you know, a children's tale about Toyland and the fellow who gets stuck in the box because the mechanism fails."

"That's right," said Lola. "But whatever the tale may be, it must of course have rules. For example, our genie cannot just do anything. The interesting thing that makes this tale of genies a bit truer than it might otherwise be is that we have a solid reason why she cannot do just any random thing she likes."

"Sci-fi and fantasy writers know there have to be rules," Samuel agreed with relief, "the difference here being the Transformation Proof.

"Typically in a story of magic kingdoms, powers are bestowed from superiors to inferiors, from kings down to knights, and so forth, all the way down from the gods. But there is another kind of limitation on power, getting back to the question of writing philosophy — with Alice longing for fantasy." He smiled, and his eyes twinkled.

Alice allowed herself to watch the moonlight sparkling there. "So?—" she encouraged him.

Gazing away to the river he continued, "So — Aquilah will use her natural limitation to create a way out. And we will share in her limitation."

"What limitation?"

"That neither she nor anyone can achieve the absolute. That there is no God to seal her fate forever."

"So she found the illusion," said Lola.

"And that augmented her power," added Rolo.

"She got the balance," Lola confirmed.

"And broke the seal," said Rolo.

"The seal of Solomon's ring was a fake. It was flawed, a usurpation, not really his." Lola replied. "And we could tell a story of how the limitation reversed itself upon the ones who had misused the power." They were working up another scenario.

"So how does she use it, specifically, this limitation we all share?" asked Alice, who was now focused on the potential of another world intersecting with theirs. She inspected the way the water broke over the dam. "Or maybe we should change the question to something more like: who is she? *Getting out*, at this level of specificity, has become more of a technical genie question. Or, like you said, Samuel, a mechanical question for the Jack-in-the-box. Aquilah does her homework. We need to be asking, just *who is* this genie, anyway? And what about her Muse, Urania? Perhaps a Muse can embody herself in the characters of a story?"

A cat passed among them and went to the riverbank to drink. They all watched it move the way animals can so easily steal the show.

"Is that your cat?" asked Alice.

Samuel shook his head, "Not that cat."

## 29. Infinity and The Book of Changes, by Rolo

"**M**illy! Milly! Here kitty—

"Now where's that cat o' mine?" Aquilah looked out into the gathering of listeners. No trace visible of the cat of a thousand meows. As she scanned the gaps between the individuals, looking for any movement that might give a cat away, the flick of a tail or the reflection of cat eyes, she allowed a silence to fill the tea room. She was surprised to find that no one else was talking. All the tables of patrons had joined her discussion, bringing up chairs or sitting on big cushions on the floor. Now the silence was profound. Then she heard the purring. She looked to her left. There, relaxed against the well-used shine of the wooden counter, next to the pastry cart, was a tall, powerful, bearded man in blue jeans and a checked shirt with Milly in his arms, caressing her as the motor revved.

Millameowsimous had the ability to change her stripes, so she had to be recognized the way you recognize someone regardless of what they are wearing. To do so in the case of a cat required some of the talents of a genie. "Milly! Where have you been this time?"

"Oh, she was just on the threshold as I came in to see what was happening here," the man, who looked like a god, replied instead of the cat.

Milly leaped down and in a couple of bounds was in the genie's lap, where they relaxed on one of the bar stools.

One of the reasons for the attentiveness in the room was the storyteller's ability, like her cat, to change costume while acting out the parts. In response to questions from the group, Aquilah had filled out the story of "Infinity and the *Book of Changes*" into interrelated accounts, giving the themes more and more background until she had covered far more than the version sketched out below. The Transformation Proof and its consequences were thrown in as explanations in the course of the advancing drama, to better understand the storyline and the characters and even to discover some of the secrets of the world in which they all found themselves. They had arrived from many walks of life, some having died. The more recent arrivals of the latter group were in a heightened state of curiosity. The genie had woven a world for them all, with childlike motifs to reassure them. But always there were threads that they felt went further, more questions beyond temporary borders. Now there was an intermission — and a silence that seemed to touch a pool of eternal, preexisting wonder.

* * *

One recurring question had been whether Aquilah, being a genie, was actually creating their world, sort of making it up as she went along. Her answers, although often emphatic, had left some doubt — to the point where she seemed to be encouraging the doubt, without wanting to scare them. Some of the apparent illusions that she had generated had seemed to carry the entire show to other lands under different skies and even under different stars. "Doubt can be a powerful force for positive change!" she had exclaimed, when one newcomer to the tea room wouldn't let go of his question, no matter where they seemed to be at the time. For many of these patrons and travelers, philosophy had become more than a game.

Especially at issue was the way the sexual polarity of the changes in the story of the *Book of Changes* was diversified by being represented in numbers, leading to a succession of symbols that can develop a narrative that may have little to do with sex. For example, there are key numbers in question: three is the number of lines in a trigram; two trigrams make a hexagram of six lines. One builds up a hexagram by throwing yarrow sticks or flipping coins.

Using coins, one side of the coin can represent the female sex or yin and is traditionally symbolized with two in-line horizontal lines (or a single line with a space in the middle). The other side of the coin can represent yang, the male polarity, drawn as a single line with no interval. Therefore, after flipping a coin six times, one possible result might be drawn like this:

```
——————    ——————
————  ————    ——————
——————    ——————
——————    ——————
——————    ——————
————  ————    ——————
```

These six lines form the image of *ting*, a Chinese word for "cauldron." The lower trigram signifies wood, wind, and things that are gentle. The upper trigram stands for fire and things that cling. One can visualize the lines from the bottom up as representing the legs, the belly, the handles, and the carrying rings of the cauldron, in addition to all the cultural and historical associations of this object.

These six lines could be interpreted as a symbol of good economics, where giving nourishment to the people is a major theme, and where the refinement of civilization is in the provision of health and nourishment to all. This is a responsibility of leadership and parenthood, as understood in the tradition of the providers who serve nourishment from the ting. It is likewise a symbol of the common good and the state, where public service is supposed to consist in caring for the people. By extension, in more recent times than when the *Book of Changes* developed, the ting represents a government of the people, by the people, and for the people.

Much more can be said about the meaning of ting, arising as it does from simple, binary combinations, here of yin and yang, the relationship of sexual creation, brought about in a nonrandom fashion, like the water of the pond breaking in near-symmetry over the falls. There is a mysterious doorway, a balance in these transformations, where extremely low asymmetry — rather than closing down absolutely — projects a horizon, a true chance for all, not just a random one.

While the genie's questioner was an economist, he had kept insisting, protesting even, that Aquilah was seducing him and that her seduction was including him in the creation of the world of the tea room and beyond, stretching to all the curious places they were visiting. He recognized that he was not alone in this relationship. So there was that nagging question about having a choice and taking responsibility. If nature is not random, then just what sense of direction does she have? What is her motive? And were they all just being carried along willy-nilly in some grand seduction? What if he stepped outside the tea-room door? Did he or any of them have that choice? Were they all building a world of flaws that would one day come round and bite them in the ass, he wanted to know.

Without breaking his stride, he continued, "It's all very well being masters of our universe and creating our own destiny, but we're so damn ignorant! Am I expected to just go along and believe, like a free-marketeer, that as long as I buckle my swash and stand forth, a magical invisible hand, all-knowing with infinite justice, will ensure that the haggling around supply and demand and all the backroom deals are somehow guided to culminate in the ideal society? I don't think so! What about the other invisible hand that keeps pounding, oppressing, and senselessly destroying? The same malicious hand that took Adam Smith's image and turned it against itself—"

The genie had raised her hands in a calming gesture, then placed them on her hips and rolled her eyes. "You are so right! And I understand your urgency, Mr. Smith. But really, for one who is asking all the right questions, you can calm down while I buckle my own swash—" Thereupon she turned into a genie in a typical pirate costume, complete with sword, black boots, bandanna, and a braid of long black hair that she finished off quite seductively with a small silver clasp in the shape of a star.

The questioner sighed and sat back in his chair to become one with the audience again.

\* \* \*

"Kings and sages have tried to control the *Book of Changes*. Lao Tzu told me that it cannot be done. The gods have said it cannot be done. But kings and sages have tried many times, and the Book has not got any smaller with their commentaries," said the genie.

In recalling the story, Aquilah confided to the patrons of the tea room about the time she and one of her lovers had sat opposite each other, flipping the three coins to form each of the two trigrams of each hexagram. Tails were designated as yin and heads as yang. They had started with the traditional yarrow sticks and, instead of a seduction, had moved on to coins, as the game of prediction became increasingly competitive. They had ended up trying to outdo each other in materializing the most evenly balanced coins, to see who could make them fall the most randomly. Finally, sidetracked in this way beyond frustration and in the attempt to play the gentleman, the exasperated Ahmed had exclaimed, "All right! Aquilah, you win! You are the most balanced and therefore you are clearly able to materialize the most perfect coin! There is just one problem with that—"

"We can no longer foretell anything," she interrupted.

They sat in silence for a while before laughing.

"What we need is for one of the elder genies to influence the coins for us."

"But how do you know which elder genie to call upon. There are many Ancients who still don't get it—"

There was a pause as they listened to the breeze flow with soft summer eloquence through the weeping willow and along the stream over the colorful stones of pink granite and turquoise.

"Get what?" asked Aquilah cautiously.

"It!"

"What it?"

"In any case," he continued, "we might as well just ask directly, instead of playing this silly game."

"Oh but Ahmed, what would the Muses who inspired the *Book of Changes* say to that? There are many who like to communicate this way, with all the symbols that go beyond words."

"True, my lovely, true enough!"

"And then there is the slight issue of travel. In order to speak directly with one of the elder — and wiser — genies, we would have to travel, and who knows if there are any worthy of asking, here in this beautiful world. Or if there are, they may not want to be disturbed. We might have to go through formalities and ancient traditional social rituals to get so far as a hello! Some genies like the indirect, more asymmetrical approach, ya know."

"Yeah, tell me about it," he replied.

"I'm sure I don't have to, knowing the civilization that produced you and your kin—"

"An entire civilization — bottled up! And now you're our great liberator. So what's the secret? How did you do it? Or was it that cat of yours, the one with the long name and repeating, wavy stripes? What if she hadn't gone back to the bottle in the room where you woke up? What if your little Milly hadn't felt like rubbing up against the bottle where we were all waiting for you to finish your essay? Waiting for you to pull out the stopper!"

"Oh stop! But in a way, it's true — the Muse was like a small animal, a cat overlooked by the Absolute. She lived in the shadow of the vast illusion that is always worn by the Absolute, the one that moves like a hooded nothingness. The secret is called Urania."

"Urania overlooked!"

"The illusion of the Absolute is vast." she repeated. "The Absolute ensnares itself. You'd expect that with such immense ignorance overshadowing the world, there would be plenty of unseen, secret rescuers who could have come for us, even in broad daylight, and uncorked the bottle."

Ahmed sighed, "It's the old question of *whose illusion*, isn't it? and just who this Absolute happens to include. If we ever learned anything in school, it's not just 'the One,' and that's just one reason why it's not absolute. I suppose we shouldn't really call it 'the Absolute' like that, because it reaches out for us with that same sarcasm.

"So I'm not surprised it was a Muse; they are extremely difficult to count. I mean their numbers keep changing — and their leaders, Apollo was one of their leaders. If you start counting their leaders, then where are we?"

\* \* \*

Free at last, Aquilah was enjoying a tea room in a village where she had come to rest at the base of an old, eroded, grassy pyramid, where it was rumored the gods occasionally strolled along the sides on the encircling terraced pathways, discussing the state of the world. With a few old coins she had been entertaining the patrons by interpreting the hexagrams with the ancient Chinese *Book of Changes,* playing the Gypsy fortuneteller. She liked this town and wouldn't mind being accepted as a resident.

Now an entire pirate's chest of gold coins and jewels was open with the wealth spilling out, coins rolling across the floor to be lost beneath the tables and chairs or scooped up quickly by those newcomers who happened to be seated on the floor.

Others watched with amusement until the genie thrust her sword into the treasure chest, lifted her hands into the air, and spun round several times. She slowly brought her hands down in a wavelike fashion over her attire, and her costume changed yet again. There she stood in rags, like a homeless person, and the treasure, the sword, and all the coins in the room had vanished. "There is a story about the one who called himself the King of Heaven," she began. "He collected all six lines of the masculine polarity into a hexagram and called it 'the creative force of heaven beyond which there was no further power.'

"Such was his power that the King threw the yarrow sticks many times, and they repeatedly gave the hexagram for heaven, which is traditionally represented like this."

With a flourish, she materialized a black, diaphanous screen with the six golden lines.

―――――――
―――――――
―――――――
―――――――
―――――――
―――――――

"Assuming he could do this any time he liked, he arrogated to himself absolute power.

"However, a goddess let it be known that all six lines of yin, the feminine polarity, were still beyond heaven's realm," and spaces formed down the middle in the lines.

――― ―――
――― ―――
――― ―――
――― ―――
――― ―――
――― ―――

"The King decided to include a trigram of each polarity and declared that now his realm was all-inclusive. Then to make his point clear, he placed the male trigram over the female trigram and said it represented Heaven's rule over the Earth, declaring it to mean that his rule and his word were absolute. He also meant it as a warning: there would be no further changes. The lines arranged themselves accordingly into the hexagram that we know today as P'i or Stagnation."

Meanwhile the entire tea room began to feel like it was being transported in space and time, but only slightly.

"The goddess let it be known that now a trigram of yang was left outside his realm and that she had placed it in a hexagram with the remaining trigram of yin in a variety of patterns according to the wishes of the people.

"The King inquired which people were to be found beyond his realm. The goddess let it be known that only their wishes, some of their dreams remained beyond him. What should that matter to him?

"The more he wondered about it, the more it mattered. Still his realm was not secure and absolutely complete. The more he thought about it, the less complete his world appeared. Then he realized that the goddess was outside his domain! It made him feel foolish to have overlooked the obvious and fanned his anger.

"He accused her of performing some magic against his Realm of Heaven. She let it be known that far from it being magic, it was simply nature's infinitely changing balance.

"The King demanded that all the trigrams be gathered into his realm and that rules be made to set limits so that nothing beyond a hexagram of six lines should exist. In keeping with his image of a ruler of nature, he kept to the two polarities, male and female of the Tao."

The following list replaced the hexagram on the tea-room screen.

Number of different lines: 2
Number of positions: 3
2 to the power of 3 = 8 trigrams possible:
mmm fff
mmf fmm
mff ffm
fmf mfm
Number of different trigrams: 8
Number of different positions: 2

8 to the power of 2 = 64 hexagrams possible,
as per ancient tradition.

" 'Where is your infinity now!' demanded the King of Heaven.

"The goddess let it be known that the meaning of each trigram had yet to be established.

"The King instructed his sages to set forth the exact meaning of the trigrams and hexagrams, and of course they obeyed. They commented at length on the many precise symbols, such as the lake and the wind and the trees and the little fox that gets his tail wet. The King thought to imprison the goddess with symbols and words and especially by enslaving the citizenry; she seemed to care about them, though he suspected she just wanted to steal them from him.

"The goddess let it be known that the people who used the *Book of Changes* wondered how they should interpret the symbols to apply them to their lives and to answer the questions they have about their future in the Realm of Heaven. The people were wondering, because the soothsayers on the streets were reluctant to add anything to what the King's sages had decreed. The dreams of the people continued to escape the Realm of Heaven on the wings of the hexagrams.

"The King passed a law forbidding the *Book of Changes* to be circulated or held by anyone except himself and whoever he should designate. He had his warriors terrorize the people into handing over all the copies of the *Book of Changes*, and the books and scrolls were burned, except for the King's collection, locked away in a special vault. He had a number inscribed on the vault and attributed sacred significance to it.

"The King of Heaven became terrified of this thing called 'infinity.' No matter what he did to impose a limit, always there was something more, something creative. It was the Tao, it was liberty. It came to be known as the name of the goddess who spoke on behalf of the people. They knew her as a goddess of love, and they let it be known that she was elected. Now she had the power to overthrow the King of Heaven. For this reason the goddess of love must all too often be a goddess of war.

"The more fearful he became, the more disorganized was his realm. Encouraged, the people organized, and the ascending hexagrams toppled the hierarchy, rebalancing the world."

* * *

By this time the patrons were looking about the room and wondering what world the genie had in mind. They had traveled together as the hexagrams changed on the screen, until Aquilah began to wonder where her cat had got to. As she called out for the cat of a thousand meows, the burly godlike character had entered the tea room with Milly in his arms, and they were back on familiar ground.

## 30. Alice at Tea

The profound silence of the intermission was broken when another newcomer in the town asked the question that turned out to be on more than one mind: "How does one 'let it be known'?"

"Something always gets through," the genie replied. "No matter what, there is always a signal that goes beyond any obstacles and oppression, the same way this genie got out of the bottle. Or was it a lamp? I sometimes forget — from the inside things look different.

"Anyway, the democratic impulse is one of the most fundamental signals of all. That impulse is a vote. You may not know where it goes or what it might bring, but there is no communication more basic than the vote, and it gets a response from those who are tuned into the conditions of the signal's source and to the very essence of nature's sense of direction. The signal doesn't go just anywhere or to just anyone; it has a specific pathway to find and follow, and it takes time. That is why more is needed than just a signal; the vote needs to be augmented, amplified by the right sort of action, a reaching out that will be sure to find a response in the long run, if not before. It has the power of inevitability."

Aquilah waited. There she stood in her genie pants, her genie top, with the bare cocoa-colored midriff with understated muscles, the shapely arms, the curved highlights of her cheekbones, all reflecting the same light in the room, where she would shift her shape. She seemed a combination of costume and actor between acts.

She looked for Mr. Smith, the one who had been asking about the invisible hand. He had been roaming the room, checking details of furniture and wall hangings, ever so often upturning empty coffee mugs and teacups to read the crafter's inscription, trying to track the changes. He felt her gaze, looked up and smiled. "Here I am! You still haven't answered my question. What sort of characters can we hope for, what heroes who have the power, elected or otherwise? Are there any real heroes and heroines to hope for?"

"Okay, Mr. Smith, we have so far established that we are talking about a truly cosmic, physical, living consciousness, ever changing, always in motion, with some sort of balance and a nonrandom sense of direction." Aquilah held her pose, arms to her side, shoulders back slightly.

Smith folded his arms.

"In the absence of absolute finality," she continued, "there is immortal consciousness happening all around and within us. That means soul. What else is soul but a self-aware life that continues? Furthermore, its physical nature means it is open to discovery by scientific means. What we mean by a 'soul' is more like an immortal body. Like any object, it has layers. It's complicated."

"Like the onion," added Smith with a touch of irony.

"Precisely." Aquilah slowly began to lift her arms in a curve up each side of her body, hands cupped upward, and feathers appeared in their wake, feathers of turquoise and gold extending from her body through concentric patterns like the wings of an eagle. She continued the curve until she pressed her hands together above her head with the sound of a gong, and the wings turned into a shawl, which she gathered round her shoulders. "Right away there is the issue of a center of individuality that continues."

Smith and some others tried not to be impressed.

"What could be the self-conscious focus of a soul?" asked the genie. "It cannot have that impossible absolute symmetry. No consciousness can have a continuous, perfectly centered focus of individuality. We have established that pressures would build to redirect such focus and break its impending symmetry."

She lowered the shawl to her hips and held out the ends so that it fell round her curves, and she smiled as she slowly moved the shawl out one way and her hips the other, and her breasts, with typical genie cleavage, moved with the shawl. Then she stopped and briefly moved her head side-to-side, Egyptian style, with a deadpan expression. Then, without moving her head, she looked from side to side, her eyes heavy with mascara. She rolled her eyes. "Am I being too self-conscious? Or just mechanical?"

No one said a word.

"Asymmetric changes," and she slowly, casually reversed the

sensuous relationship between hips, breasts, and shawl a few times as she spoke, allowing her neck and facial expression to relax with the flow, "ensure that universal life can continue forever, without ever achieving pure symmetry in eternal continuity. It's the nature of asymmetric infinity. Eternally changing continuity will not achieve pure symmetry. It's the nature of change, to which absolute symmetry would put an end. Remember?"

She threw the shawl up into the air, and it kept opening up in waves of scenery that quickly replaced the tea room with the garden by the waterfall and the pond. Samuel was standing thoughtfully by the tomatoes. The audience was still seated, but on wooden garden furniture on the comfortably overgrown lawn. The sound of the waterfall turned into the hushed voice of the genie. "And even if it were possible, such centrality of awareness would not be able to see outside itself. There would be no other truly individual selves. It would be absolutely finite — the only one."

The scene vanished and everyone was back at the tea room. Aquilah stopped, then lifted herself onto the counter and sat there dangling her legs, leaning forward slightly, hands on the counter. "To speculate on what it would be like if the Absolute existed gives us an idea of what we are approaching when we try for such pure symmetry of being. We would be closing ourselves off to others, even as we closed down the universe, ultimately destroying all Creation."

Next, continuing the formal lecture in combination with the slight seduction, she suggested that it might be more in keeping with the answers if she were to change clothes — again. In the blink of an eye, she was wearing blue jeans matching closely the faded sky blue of the jeans on the bearded man near the other end of the counter. She continued while buttoning up a blue-collar shirt, as though finishing to dress. "Because it has cosmic balance, nature cannot have a single cosmic center." She finished a button, leaving the rest. "The more it does so, the more it is drawn apart and redistributed. So nature, the universe, or the cosmos as a whole never amounts to a person, soul, or deity, with any long-term individual, immortal sense of self. Thus God was disproved in Alice's essay.

"Which reminds me — should I be wearing something more formal for a philosophy lecture, do you think? With all these words like 'asymmetry' and 'absolute'? Am I out of sync with my delivery? And, being female, maybe a dress or a skirt and blouse?"

## 30. Alice at Tea

The audience looked as though it might get bored with the wardrobe act, so she let it go, saying, "Magic does get tedious."

Then the genie placed in their minds the image of Alice. They all remembered her in Aquilah's full version of "Infinity and the *Book of Changes*." Alice was the one who had said the authors should be asking the question of *who* — who was this genie, anyway? Smith was brimming with the same question.

\* \* \*

Alice, a descendant of puritans, was giving that tale a good twist, as those ancestors "turned in their graves," as the saying goes. But Aquilah had left hanging the question of whether the four authors had been able to finalize their book and who would do the finalizing. It was generally considered to be something the genie would get back to eventually. It had become a major issue, bound up as it was with some other fundamentals.

Ah Alice! She is here somewhere. She can remain invisible and only just acknowledge herself by referring to herself in the third person as the narrator of this part of the book — be a little coy and peek out of the bushes like a spirit or fairy — a pixy? She had been to the West Country of Britain and had been quite taken with the possibility of some pixie lore being true. Sometimes Alice had seen lights, colored lights that would make good pixies, like Tinker Belle in *Peter Pan*, though she was said to be a fairy. Or perhaps Alice should be a little more direct, even, dare we say it, symmetrical in her approach? Sweet Alice, emerging from the environment like spring, possibly, or deciding against it — receding like the sap in the maple tree into winter. She fancies herself a tree spirit, now, a nymph!

Some of the patrons of the tea room, on the other hand, had got it into their heads that Alice was at least as powerful as the genie herself and might even be an alias for the Muse, Urania. As the genie continued with her lecture, wearing the sort of blue jeans and shirt that Alice might, these patrons became increasingly worshipful, imagining that this was indeed Alice, disguised as the genie, who was letting them in on some of the act by making the genie look artificial and more than a bit weird with all that gobbledygook. They felt so privileged and ogled the genie so closely that they missed most of what she was saying.

"In the same way," Aquilah continued, "the more a circle develops a center or focus," she glanced at the oglers, "the more it disintegrates at that center after a while — and from ever being a perfect circle. The lack of focus can become comfortably numb."

"What genie talks that way!" one whispered to another.

If Alice, however, were a Muse and could inspire a great variety of subjects, and if this were the Muse Urania, then it all made perfect sense, Urania being the Muse of astronomy. In modern times this would include cosmology and all the math, science, and philosophy that apply to the universe. Astrologers could still claim her, of course, in keeping with tradition. But she would sound intellectual. This must be Alice in disguise and not some genie, they concluded in whispers.

"As long as it persists," said Aquilah, prolonging the lingo of asymmetry, as it came back to her increasingly, "the tendency for symmetrical centrality is reset continuously with a succession of thresholds in the avoidance of the absolute condition. Eventually the circle becomes something else. The ways that these coordinating events accompany each other are as various and manifold as nature's imagination. The circle drawn by the draftsman or the seemingly ideal circle in the mind of the mathematician, and the pot on the potter's wheel will all have balancing, thresholding events right on their borders or somewhere in nature connected to the developing symmetry, to keep nature's balance in motion." She was speaking evenly, weighing her words.

"That balance of asymmetric infinity might manifest like the explosion of a collapsing star that has reached so much symmetry in falling in on itself with its own gravity, so reinforcing its internal symmetry that it blows almost chaotically apart."

The scientists in the room picked up their ears.

"If you want to know how I uncorked the bottle sealed with the ring of Solomon, the bottle that was cast into God's Cosmic Ocean, there's a hint. I added my own power to that of the Absolute, reinforcing the symmetry of the bottle top until it blew. The thing was to have the balance to ensure that we all didn't disintegrate along the way. For this, I used a corkscrew."

The worshippers of Alice nodded knowingly.

"Meanwhile, there were those on the outside who just needed me to wake up to a few things and act accordingly, write my essay. They knew I would have to wake up eventually. How they knew and who they may be — that will become more evident as we go, Mr. Smith.

"A planet dies or falls into the sun; the stars burn out while new ones are born. Nature tends away from being a single, perfectly focused center of awareness, knowledge, and individuality. Eventually, the more nature reasserts any circle of individuality, the more it builds pressures to undo it. Attempting to maintain intense and unbalanced individuality could lead to catastrophic disintegration. Asymmetric pressures must build to right the balance of change.

"The same is true of foolhardy romanticism that celebrates chaos or the crazy ideas of the communists who call for the sacrifice of the individual in favor of the state. The same is true of the Medieval Church that taught that the individual was originally sinful and one should sacrifice one's earthly life for the greater glory of the one Creator and His promise of Heaven.

"The sea of cosmic consciousness never achieves individuality itself — nor chaos. We have to conclude that many ancient ideas of a single, exclusive god will have to be updated where a monotheistic mythology has overwhelmed the asymmetric facts of many overlapping traditions. The fiction has got out of balance with the nonfiction, confusing the two and ultimately devaluing the power of the mythology, as well as the facts experienced by the people over time.

"So, my friends, do we just disintegrate into a cosmic conscious soup when we die? Are you having your last cup of tea? Will only the genie have the power to keep changing, while you will not? Is this what you have come to hear, at least some of you?

"Are you curious about what polarity there could be to allow a soul identity to collect and become a focus of self-awareness that would have that open-ended quality that assures participation in the immortality of the universal consciousness — while avoiding that disintegration of symmetry, which maintains the balance in nature? Does immortality extend to you, the individual? This is the fascination of some genies more than others. This is the question of *who* — Mr. Smith. Who we are, and can we become anything further? Who is behind the appearances of nature — and does Alice have a Muse?" She winked at the worshippers of Alice, making them more attentive.

Some of the patrons held their coffee mugs tightly in sweaty palms, their teacups rather too gingerly, or turned them thoughtfully on their saucers. One stared into the liquid and thought of tea leaves, another of the universe, a saucer of solar systems with only his reflection floating in it and nothing more.

"This is where the truth habitually gets missed. This is where the tension can get so extreme that we just opt for non-existent extremes and lapse into the false promises of chaos and absolutes."

The patrons were remarkably calm, as her words held them with a palpable, rhythmic assurance, even though this mixture of words and transformations might be preparing them, as individuals, for extinction. Was this a goodbye, a civilized finale, as their lives were about to fade out — a way to see them through without the shock of immediacy, the absolute being out of the question. Such notions were taking hold of the patrons as the novelty of recent events began to wear off.

"But if nature is making sense with a balanced sense of direction, then we are being guided with basic wisdom of some kind. But how do we know the wisdom is even aware of itself," Aquilah pursued. "Does the direction, perhaps, just happen to be a wise way to go? A good path? Is its good character empty of soul? Maybe we go that way? What do you think, Mr. Smith? Am I still seducing you at all?"

Smith felt unfairly singled out by the word "we."

"You can call me Adam," he offered, while wishing to engage the genie as much as possible. To be swept away to a tomato garden and back at the swish of her shawl and all this talk about *who*, to which, he acknowledged to himself, he had been party, had long been culminating in him in questions of sheer survival. He realized, having surveyed the room, that he was not the only one who had become focused on existence itself. They were not just philosophizing. He decided that the longer they all continued having tea and chatting together the better. Accordingly he took up a hypothesis with a will.

"What if, after all, *sex* is the fundamental polarity of life forms?" he asked rhetorically. "And is even more so the more conscious the form of life?" He picked up on the genie's style of delivery. The worshippers of Alice looked up at him. A few smiled playfully, wondering if he was special.

At this point, I, Alice — even though it will hardly discourage my worshippers — will come out of the greenery and metaphor, not to say "closet," to say upfront that, as narrator and no more, this is how I imagine Mr. Smith might have taken up the line of reasoning, even though I very much doubt that he did anything of the sort. But had he done so, here it is.

* * *

## 30. Alice at Tea

I will assume that Adam Smith continued like this. "We are looking for a focus of awareness, of being, that cannot become an absolute center. What about being male or female? What if we cannot become the absolute male or the absolute female? Could masculinity or femininity be the focus of what can become a soul? Like the yin and yang of the hexagrams in your story, the polarity could take many more forms than just sex — in the way that sexuality, through the transformations of reproduction, takes many forms, not just our sex organs."

Aquilah welcomed the break while the quiet man along the counter poured her some tea. She slid back down onto the barstool.

The patrons took heart, giving the speaker every conceivable benefit of the diminishing doubts about their viability.

"Let us hypothesize sexual polarity," Smith continued shakily.

"The soul could never be absolutely male or absolutely female. This means that to be male a soul must feel incomplete without the female, open to the female, seeking the female. So a man who feels totally independent of and indeed superior to the female is losing his masculinity.

"I am speaking from the male point of view, but reason says the same goes for the female.

"Likewise the soul would lose its integrity and tend to fall apart if the two poles became internalized inside the soul as it tended in some extreme way toward the impossible symmetry of having the two in one. There would be a deceptive false balance of directly opposing opposites. The outward openness that we are looking for would be lost. It would become more and more like the cosmic sea where all the patterns, including sexual polarity, arise. It would tend towards becoming the impossible single god and be redistributed without a center before it ever got there." *How am I doing?* he wondered to himself ruefully.

"It's interesting to note that if there is too much symmetry or androgyny in similarity between the sexes, then we can rely on the lack of pure symmetry in nature to throw off any extreme tendency for that kind of false equality to build a pure center of equilibrium between the sexes. A creative balance would be called for that would involve something more."

I, Alice, might as well add a bit of magic for Mr. Smith: Aquilah swung her legs out and the jeans flared with red silk up to her knees, and white stars fell out of the flares and sparkled into invisibility. She looked over at the man who had brought in Milly. He raised a hand, palm facing her and said he was fine, thank you. She left him alone in plain jeans.

After allowing the event to pass, Smith continued his exposition. He was now really hitting his stride. "As long as the individual polarity remained incomplete, as male or female, then the open-endedness would be satisfied. It seems that what we might call 'soul' could develop around a single pole of sexuality. We can imagine the rhythmic patterns of the cosmic sea being guided to take shape and identity like a soul fingerprint around a single sexual pole in a creative sexual polarity. This polarity would be more of a sense of direction than a center.

"If this were the polarity of the more experienced souls in nature, in fact, the fundamental polarity of the most experienced and conscious individuals in the universe of consciousness," he looked almost prayerfully at Aquilah, "then we could or would have to conclude that sex is the fundamental polarity in nature. Nature's sense of direction would be closely involved with the sense of direction of such beings, being nonrandom, as we have already concluded. The particles of physics would follow the physical currents of consciousness. We would have to establish that nature is guided by what have been mythologically referred to as gods and goddesses, although we can only guess at what lies behind the mythology, what truth is projected on the wings of fiction, as the poets might say.

"A universal civilization — or a universe of civilizations — would be more likely than the cultural trappings that have paraded through our meager history so far, masquerading as gods and religion."

He didn't want to appear to be kissing ass.

* * *

Here in the narrative Alice gives the cat something to do: Milly, who had long ago curled up and was sleeping on the countertop, started up and meowed, eyes wide and questioning. Some patrons, encouraged by Smith's monologue, laughed and applauded her timing. Millameowsimous kept meowing until she was offered a sardine.

Smith was glad to pause, acknowledged the critique and continued, having fussed over the cat as long as he dared. "It would be fundamental polarity, because it would be the polarity of the basic guiding lights of

## 30. Alice at Tea

the universe. Sex would be the polarity of the consciousness of a soul who is able to consciously access the cutting edge or the foundations of the fundamental, asymmetric continuity, your River of Life!

"So the clothes do not a goddess make! Perhaps that's why they are portrayed sometimes in the nude or partially so."

He couldn't help eyeing the genie casually and winced as her unclothed image took a brief but tranquil form in his mind.

"Inspiration beyond mere lust, possibly," he responded aloud and continued, encouraged, "the bigger picture being that the open and incomplete nature of either side of the sexual equation ensures that no absolute center can form in the soul and no pure symmetry can happen between the sexes. In fact the inverse is true. There is a fountain of creativity in the soul that shows up in its many kinds of relationships. The moving balance between them will avoid becoming some kind of a fixed fulcrum or universal center between or within male and female.

"So there is no ultimate male or female soul; rather the sexuality expresses itself in a vast multitude of souls in many ways, without any one or ones ever being the original creators or parents of the universe."

\* \* \*

Aquilah slid off her pedestal and joined the man in the matching color of sky blue. She rolled her eyes; they linked arms and smiled disconcertingly. Smith stopped.

"Don't mind us, Adam Smith," she said.

"I think you have me confused with the economist. Please call me Adam. Look, I'm clutching at straws here."

"Please finish, or I'll have to dissolve you into the cosmic soup!" She smiled even more disconcertingly, wondering if it was wrong to tease him.

"The absence of absolutes," Smith pursued heatedly, "is like a driver of creation, and change is where nature's balance is found generated in the field of the possible, the Field of Action!—" He looked shiftily from one to the other, "Without there ever having been the pure symmetry of an absolute beginning or end."

"As has been mentioned already," said someone somewhere.

Adam looked over his shoulder at the ingrate. "I see you're still there. Maybe if *you* keep talking—"

"I speak therefore I am!" exclaimed another, raising his mug in a salute. "Go for it! We're all with you." Glancing at the two powers standing before them, he added, "I hope."

"The open-endedness," Adam Smith resumed his lecture after swallowing hard, "is the beauty and mystery of creation that gives us our logical way of discovering how it works. And there is a natural, instinctive way for people to relate and for communities to develop in all their relationships, including strangers, friends, families and acquaintances — right? Likewise, this philosophy emphasizes the productive potential of teamwork over the idea of just making it on your own."

He paused. "Anyone else care to jump in here?—

"There is plenty of room here, by the way, for sexual preferences and situations. Being immortal, once the soul gets going in nature, it can change and incarnate in various ways. It does not always remain the same. This does not prevent the male or female soul from enjoying the polarity of the sexual relationship by expressing the sexuality of the opposite sex. A gay man is still a gay man. He can't be gay unless he is a man. Likewise the lesbian must be female. It would not be impossible for a male soul to be born into a female body and so forth. Asymmetry produces variety. Again there is no absolute male or female."

\* \* \*

Aquilah moved away from her friend and raised her hand. "That was very well done; have a seat! You certainly did your homework, Adam. Don't worry, you will not be disqualified from existence. Perhaps, if you had been with the wrong genie, you might have ended up in the wrong place at the wrong time, but not this time. So have a seat, or continue roaming, as you wish. I will take it from here."

"It's just love, isn't it?" said Smith, unwilling to go, and as though he were owning up to something. "The polarity is about *the other*, just the other, isn't it— It doesn't have to be sexually different — just *other* than the other individual. Because they are different — there's your polarity. Understanding?— That's love." He sat down among the worshippers of Alice and wondered if he had answered his own question about character.

"So," said the genie, "should I just let you fade away like one of my dreams?" Aquilah's sky-blue attire began to fade until they could

## 30. Alice at Tea

see the wooden paneling of the counter right through her. Some were relieved to see her go; others weren't so sure. On balance they felt safer with her than without, and she regained her full physical form.

"The votes are in, she continued. But we need to establish ourselves on a more regular basis, don't you think?"

Even the regulars at the tea room, who had showed up to witness the latest scenarios, had become uneasy about all the transformations and about who was calling the shots these days. They had begun to feel the need for some roots, lest the whole affair now turn into a flying carpet that one day gets snapped into oblivion in the breeze — end of story.

Everyone here took it for granted that they were all on a journey of some kind, no matter how long some had stayed in town. There was a curious absence of history in the region, as though they needed reminding. One of the habitués of the tea room and its adjoining tavern asked the genie to seriously address this question, to go deeper. The idea was well received, especially by those who figured that whatever the genie focused on would happen. "Yes, get her to go deep!" a voice called out, and there were some backup calls, "Yes, go deep!" Deeper, please!" "Don't stop now!"

"I think we need another intermission," she replied. "How about some more tea, coffee? Whatever you like; the bar is open; it's on me. Just place your orders, just let the waiters know what you would like. Take a break! We will reconvene, I promise you."

With the utmost caution they called for refreshments, as though their lives depended on it.

"I recommend the scrumpy!"

\* \* \*

"What does this mean if we go deeper? How deep?" asked the genie in all seriousness. "We need to find some foundations. Absolute unconsciousness is no consciousness at all. No consciousness, no continuum, remember? Absolute unconsciousness does not exist.

"If there is any awareness at all, then it is awake — to some extent. Consciousness is self-awareness — that's its nature. If it is awake at all, it is aware of itself, at least some of the time. It can be awakened.

"This must be one reason why we dream — because it is impossible to be totally asleep continuously. Though we may be unconscious now and then, it must be temporary. We go deep into the unconsciousness of our soul history and rise to the surface and subside again and again, and not only by sleeping! Sometimes we are more lucid; at other times we get carried away. Change is rhythmic, like reincarnation, a natural consequence of the impossibility of a one-of-a-kind lifetime. But that's another story. For now, to understand that there is polarity in consciousness, waking and sleeping, by degrees dreaming, lucid, and deluded, is enough.

"If consciousness has that sense of self in some way, then it has the polarity of soul — and it wakes up now and then. It has its moments! The polarity of soul is fundamental to consciousness. It has always had to be sufficiently self-aware in the long run to be a consciousness. There has always had to be enough soul polarity to support consciousness in the cosmos. If that polarity of soul were absent, then there would be no self-awareness at all. Absolute unconsciousness means no continuum and no universe. This does not mean that every part of the physical reach of the consciousness has to be a soul center — no. Homogeneity would reign. Instead the soul wears the physical awareness like a body, until it wears out and changes.

"Meanwhile, we have identified the balancing continuum as developing its manifold characteristics with a sexual polarity. Of all polarities this one must be quite fundamental, as it needs the additional polarity of being both subtle and obvious, like consciousness itself. And it feels intimate to one's very soul. The openness of nature's consciously guiding sense of direction would include procreation. If this were some obscure and secret polarity — as sex is often treated in moral systems — then it would contradict love and the free and open desire to provide equal opportunity to all, including a balanced understanding of sexual relations."

She paused. "Oh but what have I said now? I've touched on a desire to provide freedom. And how can we wish to provide freedom without understanding relationships to some degree? How can we understand relationships without experiencing love? Love provides opportunities. The polarity of sex can lead us to put ourselves in each other's shoes. But it would have to be obvious, big and open — but subtle! Like love.

"The animals, not to mention other forms of life without any brain at all, they would be confused as hell by an esoteric guidance system fundamental to the consciousness of which everything is made, but accessible only to a superior intellect or extraordinary insight. What sort of pinheaded polarity would sit at the top of that hierarchy of awareness, micromanaging procreation, while hiding its own sexual involvement, its sexuality? A god who is above sex is disconnected and cannot lead. Such a one would be like the most labyrinthine bureaucracy. Of course, let's not be confused about leadership pressuring us to have sex; that's not freedom. We are talking about attitudes of moral superiority.

"Sexual polarity has got to be obvious, and it must be natural to the most developed soul consciousness, giving off a big — cosmic — signal capable of arriving in some of the most subtle ways—"

She stopped and thought for a moment. "We could say that love is the polarity. Is that too generalized? Love needs to be grounded to be true. A father's love, a mother's love, are different and compliment each other in providing parenthood. Sexuality plays out in many ways other than just having sex between individuals. As fine as that may be, it is specialized — highly specialized, sometimes." Someone giggled. "Sexuality allows specificity of many different kinds through personality and genetic development, giving us all the family and community relationships."

Millameowsimous yawned and curled up again in comfort.

Aquilah reached for her cup of tea and a mille-feuille, one of the tea room's specialties, each flaky leaf of pastry separated by the lightest cream, with thin icing on top — the genie was enchanted by the taste, inspired by a far greater power than hers.

She turned to the godlike man on her left. "What do you think? What do you have to say about all this? What is *your* math? Can you ground us a bit more?"

The following story was in later years recorded and published in books of tales of regional history that sold well beyond the borders of the town. Here is one version of the narration. The original was given in different voices over time on behalf of the visitor who appears to have first told it, newly arrived as he was at the tea room.

## 31. The Gingerbread Variable, by Rolo

The baker made X's and N's and Y's for the mathematicians' barbecue. One of these variables came to life and ran off saying, "Can't catch me!"

The running variable was stopped and asked why by one of the guests. "Because I can go as far as I want when I want; I can jump from here to eternity just like that! Can't catch me! I can contain infinity in a single bound!"

The mathematicians agreed that since they used the variable to prove that infinity could be contained, the variable must be right.

Then one of them wondered aloud, "How can this variable not be caught, if the variable always does what it's told?"

But another assured him that it came to the same thing, whether it was the mathematician telling the variable what to do or the variable doing it by itself.

"Choice is not an issue?" the one responded.

"You have no choice but to do math, my friend," came the jaded reply. "You are like the artist who must paint!"

"Can't catch me!" the variable called out the challenge, repeating like an automatic program.

A nearby fox, waiting for a handout, challenged the variable. "Jump infinity!" barked the fox. The variable jumped and jumped, but always there was more to jump.

Exhausted, it stopped and claimed that it had done it by jumping from one number to another, leaving infinite subdivisions in between. But the fox wasn't satisfied. "There's more!" he barked, "Jump infinity!" The variable had to keep jumping because there was more, no matter which way you look at it. So it answered the challenge, and jumped this way and that way, becoming increasingly erratic and random-looking until it broke apart, leaving only crumbs.

The fox was dismayed because one of the mathematicians had

promised him a variable if he would wait and behave himself; now it was in crumbs.

After looking over the crumbs, a guest commented, "Well that just goes to show that you can't tell where any number ends."

Another argued that you could count the crumbs.

The fox yawned.

A physicist confirmed that you can't say where the particles are exactly in all respects. And if you can't say where it ends, you can't have an exact replica or any exact symmetry. "Even if one crumb looks like another, the fact that it's in a different space or happened at a different time means it's similar but there's no exact replica. You can't entirely separate the thing from its time and space.

"The power of the creativity," he continued, "is precisely that one thing can be so similar to another while still adhering to the rule of having to be different, considering the forces preventing any exact repetition."

He paused.

"But it's a creative, connecting force, so you would expect similarity to be created to communicate the direction of the changes. It's got rhythm and direction, like music. So it's not restricted to having to be very different, even though there is no exact repetition. It's amazing! And the lack of exact repetition is everywhere along with the creativity. Because, if there's no exact repetition, then everything is always being created, including the similarities! That's why it connects."

"It's a question of focus," said a languid philosopher. "The more you focus on the details of a thing, the more you realize that it can't be repeated exactly, because you can't find the absolute details in absolute detail, whereas, of course, when you are less focused it's clear that you have not established exactly any definition sufficiently to repeat it exactly. You don't exactly know what to repeat! It's no good assuming something vague is exactly repeated. So you don't get absolute symmetry either way. Nature has focus — more or less — without which nothing would be identified at all. Focus is what happens when everything is alive," he concluded, as another variable ran by, boasting, "Can't catch me!"

"These variables are all the same!" someone was heard to exclaim. "But on second thought, not exactly—" A variable stopped nearby and turned into the number three. Someone swept it up and took a bite. The fox watched patiently.

"The only three of its kind," commented another guest.

"Which doesn't guarantee any especially good flavor," answered the other as he ponderously chewed the arrested variable.

Another mathematician said that if you can't repeat exactly, then there's no absolute randomness, "That's how the cookie crumbles." She made haste to continue. "By assuming a number line of exactly equal units, the numbers are randomized even though they might appear not to be when they look sequential. Random is choiceless. So infinity is everywhere keeping the units ever so slightly approximate and totally connected. But there's something wrong with the way quantum calculations are made using probability and statistics—" She turned to the physicist, "But you seem to know that."

"Our fox can take responsibility," the physicists replied.

"But why is it creative?" asked another guest.

"The fox?"

"I mean, how do we know it will always continue to be creative?" Then she raised her hand, "Wait! I think I've got it—"

The fox watched her hand.

They waited. Some variables ran past.

"Because, because . . . one thing we do know is . . . that it's the very nature of this infinity to surpass any attempt to put an end to it. You can always go beyond as long as there's a boundary. This is continuously proven every day of our lives.

"And it's creative because . . . like you said, you can't repeat anything or any part of anything exactly, can't repeat anything exactly at all . . . but something similar can happen, can be created. That could only happen if there's no ideal template, no Platonic ideal. So things develop creatively; I don't know what other word to use to describe it, the unfolding process. There's your choice!

"Also, also—" A variable ran past, and she continued, "It doesn't have to repeat but it can. You don't have to pretend or assume infinity is counted already; in fact you shouldn't! Infinity just goes beyond . . . that's it's power. It just keeps showing up as you discover specific boundaries and definitions. In fact it allows you to discover them. It's counterproductive to assume it's already counted. Just leave off the divisions and go on to the next number, as long as you need to, in order to be specific.

"If you over-generalize with the variable, like saying it can be any number, it loses its meaning, and the math becomes unbalanced, counterproductive. Possibly destructive! If you try to be too absolutely exact with the variable, saying it repeats exactly, accommodating absolutely equal intervals, it again loses its meaning, like carrying out a decimal beyond the point where it's relevant to the thing being measured, to absurdity. Both kinds of imbalance creep into the math if you assume symmetry in exact repetition. So . . . when you're done counting, just quit for a while and decide to do something else."

They waited. The fox waited. Then they burst into various conversations.

After considerable discussion, they eventually came to the conclusion that they must be living in a real, mythological world, as the baker's gingerbread variables continued to run past, challenging, "Can't catch me!"

"I think we're a bit slow," one of the guests commented.

"Slow?" asked another. "In what way?"

"Isn't it obvious that this world is a living, created mythology?"

Another variable ran past.

"Like a dream?"

"Dreamlike, but physical—"

"So we can change things!"

"To some extent, in time."

The fox decided to rebel and snapped up the next variable as it ran past. Then the next and the next. As the very mild hint of ginger eventually caught up with him, he began to spit them out.

Witnessing the fox, one group grandly chose to pay the baker a visit to ask him to put a little more ginger in the bread to give the variables more "direction, more character—"

"They're nice . . . but a little so-so," said the philosopher. "A bit random and crumbly, dry," commented another, "but sustaining nonetheless — up to a point."

"Bland, just bland," said the philosopher.

The baker was indignant and told them that the bread was the ultimate and used by the priests to represent the God of all Creation — without, of course, the ginger and yeast. They should be grateful to get gingerbread at all.

They retired in a huddle and came to the conclusion that if things have direction because they can't be random, because they can't repeat exactly, then there is clearly a polarity in infinity, a unifying polarity, a rhythmic balance. Without polarity there is no direction. Where there is direction, there is some sort of polarity. They further concluded that this polarity was so unifying that it connects all things and is the way individual things happen to be themselves. And the polarity is always there in many ways itself, many kinds of polarity. The polarity of infinity, they concluded, was so basic, that neither pole of creation could be both poles. There never was and never could be a single pole of all creation. If this were to happen, infinity would cease to exist and absolute symmetry would rule a disconnected, non-creative universe that would in fact have no way of even beginning — an absolutely symmetrical beginning, being no beginning at all. No choice. And, of course, no menu.

"Not even bland," agreed the physicist.

Encouraged, it didn't take them long to figure out that the polarity of life must be conscious, since consciousness could never be excluded from such a widespread connectivity as this definition of infinity offered. It would always have avenues to discover, to explore. So even our thoughts are physical realities.

They added to this the realization that the polarity itself could not repeat without developing rhythmic individual "fingerprints" that would each be conscious, in fact, a soul, like a maze of physical consciousness gathered around a central polarity — an advanced self-awareness — in relation to another pole of creation, eventually.

"The soul is really a body within the mortal body," said one, "and there is a body for every kind of lifetime experience." The soul would develop as long as it remained creative and its creativity was assured by the fact that it could not become both poles of creation and thereby extinguish itself with absolute symmetry. It could come close but could not succeed in the impossibility of absolute symmetry. It cannot become God, so it is basically secure.

The relationships between these souls would develop over vast areas of time and space and from the slightest newly formed soul of a special animal to the most balanced and aware souls who would be able to understand the plight of others, because the polarity had led them to the knowledge of true infinity, building bridges of insight into the viewpoints of others. These great souls would not shut out others; they had realized increasingly the reality of the connective, creative force. These cosmic souls, who are sometimes called gods by smaller creatures, develop immense powers and technologies with balance and a natural sense of direction, by understanding the power of love.

Those who didn't "get it" when real opportunities were offered might continue to shut out the connectedness of life and even work against it, hopelessly but repetitively, even obsessively, while their own selfishness would shut them out and restrict their power from what the power of infinite love has to offer.

"So love leads the way!" a philosopher of math concluded. "And no one-off, absolute lifetimes, but instead rhythmic repetitions of lifetimes that hopefully create a better world as we realize things about life on this mythological planet!"

Then they speculated on the nature of the basic creative polarity of life that would allow such development of character and came to the conclusion that it may well be sexual. They just couldn't come up with any more basic polarity in life to satisfy the requirement that no individual can become or encompass both poles to become a perfectly symmetrical, monotheistic being. It was a seductive hypothesis.

Then one of them just suggested that love of one another is the polarity. "Love is the most fundamental consciousness, and sometimes it's sexual."

"Or when you're horny," someone said, almost as a question.

"Love of one another," they repeated thoughtfully, each in their own way.

The maze of the soul must be gathered round a single pole for relationships to develop and for the soul to grow. It grows with love, that musical rhythm of infinity.

So, the more "godlike" and symmetrical the soul tries to be, the more likely it is to get crumbly with "feet of clay." No one becomes God, not even God. There is no love in it to make it possible.

They excitedly considered the existence of gods and goddesses, and thought of ways to ask them things. But, to be specific, they concluded that they ought to ask the baker's wife about the gingerbread.

"You folks sure know how to take the long way around to figuring out the obvious!" she said. "That man of mine has been the only baker in town for far too long. Just who does he think he is, anyway! Why, if I were independent and had the confidence of some of the likes of you, I could give him a run for his money." And she described some of the most mouthwatering pastries they had ever imagined, while giving them some samples she had baked on the side.

They decided to back her, "put their money where their mouths were," as one said, and soon there was a new bakery in town, along with an uproar about her involvement with these hometown intellectuals — about the trouble with education giving people "ideas."

People responded by building a new school. There were fierce debates about paying for it. About teaching sex education. And eventually, to the delight of the old guard and their old God, the local tabloid, with the morality of an appointed judge of character, never stopped giving out excuses to anyone who wanted them about the baker's wife. Excuses not to invest in the school, not to taste the delights of the new bakery, not to explore the world and meet new people, not to be tolerant of our differences and inclusive in our communities. People with individuality were attacked for not conforming to accepted modes of behavior. It seemed that nothing was untouched by the new bakery. And there can be no doubt that the baker's wife, whose name was Molly, was, in a variety of ways, beloved of many. Folks even told stories of how a god was seen at the bakery. Some said it was just Puck. Others claimed they had sat down with one of the great goddesses for tea in the new tea room opened at the bakery. Others said she was obviously just a pixie.

The tea room was a hit with all sorts of people, and more and more would drop in there to taste the amazing variables, which were a specialty of the house. The Reverend Henry Singleton was a gregarious, fun-loving man, who was so specific about his god as to follow Thomas Jefferson's example. Privately on his laptop computer, Singleton enjoyed updating the Bible, and — not to fall into the fundamentalist trap — would cut and paste the best parts, leaving out all that embarrassing stuff, like Lot's incest in the cave after the flood (having first offered a daughter to those strangers at the door, before God's genocide, oddly sparing Lot and a few others, but not the pillar of salt). And parts advocating slavery and genocide, while adding in a few lines of his own with the word "democracy" here and there, since the reverend had discovered its complete absence in either Testament — a shocking omission, when one considers that democratic ideas had been a civilizing force for at least five hundred years before Jesus is said to have spoken of important things. But how to explain away the command by the last of the Great Prophets, Samuel by name, to David — to return to the field of his victory and properly finish the job by finishing off the surviving women and children. Singleton abhorred fundamentalism in all its forms. The tea room was for him a refuge.

So the reverend would drop in at the sign of The Baker's Tea Room

Tavern and chat round a table of friends, in the way seventeenth-century coffee shops had generated the ideas of the American Revolution, back in his old world.

In conversation Singleton was adamant about what sort of god his was, especially surrounded by all those Pagans and their gods. It got to the point where he had become so dissatisfied with having to generalize about his god with nothing more than the most general word, that is, the word "God," that he just burst out one day in the midst of conversation about gods, "By Jove, I'll call him Jehovah, by God, I will! Or why not just Jove? That must be his name, in fact. Whether it is or not, that's his name as far as I'm concerned, from now on: Jove! There's a name for the sort of god I look up to. A god's got to have a name or two, or he's no god at all! I for one won't be reduced to calling him Hey You!" He raised a mug of cider, and they all drank to that.

From then on, he would refer to Jove rather than just God, and his friends knew who he meant. This also had the advantage of allowing him to distinguish Jove from the gods he began to refer to as Yahweh and even ol' Al, whose followers could be just as definite about Al's reputed *lack* of certain characteristics. "Just call me Al," they said he said.

Anyway, that way the reverend didn't appear to imply that followers of Al and Yahweh were misguided about God. Being specific enough made all the difference. They just followed another god or maybe they had another name in another language with other cultural metaphors for Jove, who was liberal and generous and inclusive in his love of variety. So as far as Singleton was concerned, followers of Al and Yahweh were exotic and welcome visitors to the tea room.

Things got so interesting there that one day through the door entered a visitor "from away," who called himself Jove. He was tall and burly, had a long, white beard — happened to be wearing blue jeans that day with sneakers and an open shirt. He was youthful but ancient and jovial. The reverend recognized him at once, though others said it was just old Atlas, who was in the best humor since he was free of the burden of holding up the heavens. He was there to let them know about it, now that there was a tea room in town.

That's how Atlas introduced himself — with this story. Holding up Heaven and all the rest had given him much time to reflect on the nature of spheres and all that that entails, including Urania. The exact details of his relationship with Singleton are still in dispute.

## 32. Molly

Those who had been at the mathematicians' barbecue that year were surprised to hear this character tell their story. Many voices at once began to discuss the history of the tea room and the nature of the narrator, until one of them asked about Rolo and for that matter the other three authors in Maine. Did they finish the book, or more importantly, who narrated the ending? The room fell silent.

"Who?" asked Aquilah. "Milly! Milly! Where's that cat?" The genie began to search among the tables until she just sat down amidst a friendly group who had casually been looking for the cat along with her, suspecting a game. After all, how can a genie lose a cat? Then again, it was a genie's cat — at that.

"Cats are creatures of borders," said Molly, the baker's wife.

"They certainly are!" her husband shouted from the kitchen, as Milly tore past the tables and out the door.

"Cats civilize us by reminding us of nature's own ways," she continued without missing a beat. "That's what reminded me. Did those folks over in Archon ever finish their book or not?" She looked at the genie.

The genie looked at her. They were remarkably alike.

Molly folded her arms. "Well," she challenged, "you managed to let us know plenty about those stories they were writing and all that philosophy — which, if you don't mind my saying, could have been wrapped up in a few good examples on the pastry tray over there — and all the rest, while you were goin' on about hexagrams and how hexagrams change into hexagrams like stories change into stories, being told by different storytellers, on and on, but you never said — now where was I?" She put her hands on her hips. "Well what happened to Alice's story? That's what I'd like to know. Is she still tellin' her tale or isn't she? And if she is, how does she know? That's what I was sayin' to these folks over here." She paused and the room was still quiet, so she continued. "Well we all have a lot in common with their world. And they with us, though they don't know it so well as we do, not being able to participate in our goings on as we do in theirs and all."

"So how do you think it should end?" Aquilah asked.

"Well it's about who we all are in the end, I think." She was a curvy figure in black slacks and a black blouse with embroidered pockets on both. When she put her hands in her pockets and leaned against a carved column and addressed her patrons, the colors of the embroidery were like lights in a night sky. The ceiling took on the appearance of a dome.

"Take Alice," she continued. "If she were to tell the story of what is happening here and now, what could she honestly say? I mean, how would she know what I am doing right now exactly — what any of us is doing?

"She might say a genie or some such told her. That would require a miracle in Archon, where some genie would pretty much have to appear to her or show up and make the case that this was a genie. That would be a story and a half! We'd be a long way from the end with that scenario — one person's revelation being another's madness. How should our genie dress for such an occasion? you might wonder. How much proof is proof? Might drive the poor girl off her rocker and no end in sight there either, just a whole lot of transformations and lights an' explanations! That would make a fine mess o' your romantics with your empiricists." She paused for effect, adding, "If you don't mind my sayin'." She could see that some of the intellectuals in the group had begun to take sides, while others were wondering what sort of baker this was, and whether she was putting on airs.

"No, the story of the genie showing up in Maine had to be fiction. There is only one way our girl can honestly tell this story, and that is to say it is inspiration based on what knowledge she is able to deduce from her Transformation Proof as applied to these circumstances.

"Alice cannot deduce that we are in fact in this tea room in this story as such and in detail. No, not yet at least. That is something in the future for the specialist, the technician, perhaps, given the balance required for the craft. But she can honestly say that she knows there are others out here somewhere and that there is communication of some kind among us all. She can also deduce that the communication does not have to be generalized and vague, but that it can be intimate. In fact, intimacy is in some ways its essence, where love is concerned.

But still it is indirect, for that is the how and the wherefore of it all. If it were not at least a bit indirect, it would not have anywhere to go to communicate.

"Some kinds of communication, 'inspiration' we'll call it, allow a story to be told that is like the way the genie might appear, like what she might wear for the occasion, like the story she might tell, even to a high degree of accuracy — a story that if told might be heard without the trouble of her traveling to tell it. Inspiration can be specific, and it has layers like my pastries, I dare say, which, by the way, are made with the healthiest oils and ingredients." She inhaled the aroma from the kitchen.

"These layers allow a focus more on the story with the genie, than on just the genie herself. And as we have seen, genies do sometimes get tangled up inside their own tales!" She gave Aquilah a mysterious smile. "But inspiration, as the Muses say, is teamwork. If Aquilah were to show up and speak to Alice in Archon in Maine, it would require teamwork. Both Alice and Aquilah would have to be in the right relationship for the event, whether they knew it or not. In fact the whole state of Maine would in various degrees have to be in on it somehow, not to mention the rest of us!

"But with a story, Alice can accomplish more in many ways than just to describe what we are up to here this afternoon at the tea room in this particular community. Everyone likes a good story. And Alice's story even knows it's alive, if I might put it that way, in that it embodies us. We reach out with it as though it were an extension of our hands, our soul, our attire, even. Inspiration is available to all, not to be confused with 'knowing it all.' It's just a matter of having some relationship with the Muses, as the Ancient Greeks might say. And who doesn't, for better or worse! I mean, Rolo's monocycle is an inspired machine, but it's a good thing there is the balanced inspiration to keep it off the road — or should I say, on the road? Sometimes it requires a whole tea room full of people — but animals, as essential as they are to the environment, should be kept out of the kitchen!"

Molly looked around the room. "And who are the Muses in today's terms? That I will leave to you."

There was a surge of discussion and calls for more tea and some of those hot breads on the pastry cart. Suddenly everyone seemed rather inspired and the pastry cart returned to the kitchen empty, which left some of the patrons a bit suspicious of this Molly.

## 32. Molly

Milly looked from outside into the tea room, as the baker's husband turned back into the kitchen, and she followed him, tail in air like a question mark.

* * *

"So," said I, "this is the story of the Transformation Proof."

"Well, it sounds like a nice mythological community," said Samuel, "but how do we know they know what they are doing interfering with our lives like elves and the shoemaker, leprechauns, or worse!"

"Careful," said Lola, looking around the garden, past the tomatoes and over to the waterfall.

"Well," I replied, "I thought I'd let the guy who has had to hold up the Heavens have his say on the subject of social pressure. After all, he and Singleton have some explaining to do. But to save us the angst of hearing the whole conversation, I have a brief essay to lay bare the essentials, getting down to the questions of 'good and evil' and what to do about it, given the evidence.

"But first, let's not forget one of the very most inspired statements in all the works of the philosophers."

"Russell, on the sources of Plato's opinions!" intoned Rolo.

"Precisely and in full."

## 33. "The Sources of Plato's Opinions," from *A History of Western Philosophy,* by Bertrand Russell

PLATO AND ARISTOTLE WERE THE MOST INFLUENTIAL OF ALL philosophers, ancient, medieval, or modern; and of the two, it was Plato who had the greater effect upon subsequent ages. I say this for two reasons: first, that Aristotle himself is an outcome of Plato; second, that Christian theology and philosophy, at any rate until the thirteenth century, was much more Platonic than Aristotelian. It is necessary, therefore, in a history of philosophic thought, to treat Plato, and to a lesser degree Aristotle, more fully than any of their predecessors or successors.

The most important matters in Plato's philosophy are: first, his Utopia, which was the earliest of a long series; second, his theory of ideas, which was a pioneer attempt to deal with the still unsolved problem of universals; third, his arguments in favor of immortality; fourth, his cosmogony; fifth, his conception of knowledge as reminiscence rather than perception. But before dealing with any of these topics, I shall say a few words about the circumstances of his life and the influences which determined his political and philosophical opinions.

Plato was born in 428–7 B.C., in the early years of the Peloponnesian War. He was a well-to-do aristocrat, related to various people who were concerned in the rule of the Thirty Tyrants. He was a young man when Athens was defeated, and he could attribute the defeat to democracy, which his social position and his family connections were likely to make him despise. He was a pupil of Socrates, for whom he had a profound affection and respect; and Socrates was put to death by the democracy. It is not, therefore, surprising that he should turn to Sparta for an adumbration of his ideal commonwealth. Plato possessed the art to dress up illiberal suggestions in such a way that they deceived future ages, which admired the *Republic* without ever becoming aware of what was involved in its proposals. It has always been correct to praise Plato, but not to understand him. This is the common fate of great men. My object is the opposite. I wish to understand him, but to treat him with as little reverence as if he were a contemporary English or American advocate of totalitarianism.

The purely philosophical influences on Plato were also such as to predispose him in favor of Sparta. These influences, speaking broadly, were: Pythagoras, Parmenides, Heraclitus, and Socrates.

From Pythagoras (whether by way of Socrates or not) Plato derived the Orphic elements in his philosophy: the religious trend, the belief in immortality, the otherworldliness, the priestly tone, and all that is involved in the simile of the cave; also his respect for mathematics, and his intimate intermingling of intellect and mysticism.

From Parmenides he derived the belief that reality is eternal and timeless, and that, on logical grounds, all change must be illusory.

From Heraclitus he derived the negative doctrine that there is nothing permanent in the sensible world. This, combined with the doctrine of Parmenides, led to the conclusion that knowledge is not to be derived from the senses, but is only to be achieved by the intellect. This, in turn fitted in well with Pythagoreanism.

From Socrates he probably learnt his preoccupation with ethical problems, and his tendency to seek teleological rather than mechanical explanations of the world. "The Good" dominated his thought more than that of the pre-Socratics, and it is difficult not to attribute this fact to the influence of Socrates.

How is all this connected with authoritarianism in politics?

In the first place: Goodness and Reality being timeless, the best state will be the one which most nearly copies the heavenly model, by having a minimum of change and a maximum of static perfection, and its rulers should be those who best understand the eternal Good.

In the second place: Plato, like all mystics, has, in his beliefs, a core of certainty which is essentially incommunicable except by a way of life. The Pythagoreans had endeavored to set up a rule of the initiate, and this is, at bottom, what Plato desires. If a man is to be a good statesman, he must know the Good; this he can only do by a combination of intellectual and moral discipline. If those who have not gone through this discipline are allowed a share in the government, they will inevitably corrupt it.

In the third place: much education is needed to make a good ruler on Plato's principles. It seems to us unwise to have insisted on teaching geometry to the younger Dionysius, tyrant of Syracuse, in order to make him a good king, but from Plato's point of view it was essential. He was sufficiently Pythagorean to think that without mathematics no true wisdom is possible. This view implies an oligarchy.

In the fourth place: Plato, in common with most Greek philosophers, took the view that leisure is essential to wisdom, which will therefore not be found among those who have to work for their living, but only among those who have independent means, or who are relieved by the state from anxieties as to their subsistence. This point of view is essentially aristocratic.

Two general questions arise in confronting Plato with modem ideas. The first is: Is there such a thing as "wisdom"? The second is: Granted that there is such a thing, can any constitution be devised that will give it political power?

"Wisdom," in the sense supposed, would not be any kind of specialized skill, such as is possessed by the shoemaker or the physician or the military tactician. It must be something more generalized than this, since its possession is supposed to make a man capable of governing wisely. I think Plato would have said that it consists in knowledge of the good, and would have supplemented this definition with the Socratic doctrine that no man sins wittingly, from which it follows that whoever knows what is good does what is right. To us, such a view seems remote from reality. We should more naturally say that there are divergent interests, and that the statesman should arrive at the best available compromise. The members of a class or a nation may have a common interest, but it will usually conflict with the interests of other classes or other nations. There are, no doubt, some interests of mankind as a whole, but they do not suffice to determine political action. Perhaps they will do so at some future date, but certainly not so long as there are many sovereign States. And even then the most difficult part of the pursuit of the general interest would consist in arriving at compromises among mutually hostile special interests.

But even if we suppose that there is such a thing as "wisdom," is there any form of constitution which will give the government to the wise? It is clear that majorities, like general councils, may err, and in fact have erred. Aristocracies are not always wise; kings are often foolish; Popes, in spite of infallibility, have committed grievous errors. Would anybody advocate entrusting the government to university graduates, or even to doctors of divinity? Or to men who, having been born poor, have made great fortunes? It is clear that no legally definable selection of citizens is likely to be wiser, in practice, than the whole body.

It might be suggested that men could be given political wisdom by a suitable training. But the question would arise: what is a suitable training? And this would turn out to be a party question.

The problem of finding a collection of "wise" men and leaving the government to them is thus an insoluble one. That is the ultimate reason for democracy.

## 34. Streams of Paradise

In *Lucifer's Legacy*, Frank Close puts it like this: "If there is a credo of the Creation in modern cosmology it is that the universe was initially symmetric."[31] And again: "Physicists seeking the symmetry of the universe will not be happy until everything is accounted for and the sums balanced."[32] Why? one might ask. If the scientific environment where one is presumably trained to set out to discover what *is* — rather than accumulating evidence to empower one's claims — is exhibiting such bias in favor of symmetry, what about the rest of us? Must we be hoping and praying for the same final "answer" in our own, less scientific terms?

So, finishing up here, we might as well have a quick look at the depth of this social pressure and consider it along with the question of "good and evil." If we take the reasoning that flows in the absence of absolute symmetry, we can discover the nonrandom balancing act that is life. We have found that it exists between or in the absence of the "non-poles" of pure symmetry and sheer chaos. We have identified a pressure, an inspiration, an instinct, a seduction, including some reasoning and evidence, that build around basic polarities and return things from the extremes of either non-pole, and do a lot else besides. This persuasive effect is nature's balance in motion — not the symmetrical "balance" of sums referred to by Frank Close, though this polarity may be what the physicists and other seekers are really looking for.

In addition, we have deduced that the nonexistent non-poles themselves, of course, do nothing to encourage or discourage nature's balance in any way. (This goes with the warning label that the approach of extreme conditions can be dangerous — like the unicycle — at the risk of being extremely obvious.) Can we say anything more about this?

For the sake of this essay, let's define ego as the tendency to try to close the circle completely. "Closing the circle" can be regarded as an expression of the quest for pure symmetry in its many guises. This would be adverse social pressure. This is similar to the Buddhist metaphor of the "wheel of fire," of clutching one's wheel of fire. We are referring here more to the inability to "let something go," rather than just stumbling into symmetrical circumstances in search of true balance and such.

Symmetry-focused ego could become the deepest addiction because it is in denial of the fundamental connectivity. In denial, the addiction of ego automatically tries to repeat certain things exactly. The continuity or rhythm of life is lost as the obsession grows. The automatic or programmed characteristic would be the main ingredient of addiction. Each apparent success would be increasingly craved, having an addictive energy in the illusion that tensions are resolved. This kind of ego, in its raw form and on its own, would have difficulty thinking connectively, like a gambler who is increasingly attracted to the random symmetry of an "even chance." Feeling victorious would be mistaken for feeling the rush of nature's balance in motion and would encourage a false or usurping pattern of behavior.

For example, the "even chance" would be mistaken for justice and vindication. The illusion of success, based on short-term achievements, and the associated behavior would develop a falseness of character that would at times aggressively portray itself as the real thing. At other times the usurpation would call for great subtlety. Being so personal, the addiction of ego would be like the subtlest and most powerful of addictive drugs. It could behave like a computer virus, hard wired into the body and soul. As long as it had the upper hand, it would repeatedly attempt to gain more power at the expense of others whom it would supplant. It would also have a randomness about it, a kind of selfish indifference of the sociopath, as described by Hannah Arendt in *Eichmann in Jerusalem: A Report on the Banality of Evil*. This is a rather more complicated pattern of behavior than just being somewhat obsessed with getting something right. Since the false symmetry behind it all is both chaotic and organized, a great range of behaviors are accessible to the ego. But they have in common the lack of empathy.

Fortunately, the behavior would have false timing. The attempt to control natural behavior in others, or to exert excessive control over anything, would tend to fail in a variety of ways, large and small, often unsuspected.

Repeated insistence and failure would result in increasing irritation, anger and rage, as the circle that never closes springs open over and over, until the cycle becomes more and more obvious and control is lost in self-righteous violence, resentment, hopelessness, desperation.

This recalls Albert Einstein's famous statement about the definition of insanity being the excessively repeated attempt of same thing with the same result while hoping for a different outcome.

Hierarchical or egocentric institutions, without a democratic orientation, are susceptible to paranoia or just irrational fear where scapegoats are hunted, the hunters are hunted, and fear can become quite justified. The pressure of ritual repetition can be built and manipulated until it demands release in sacrifice or war.

All this should sound at least somewhat familiar and is a question of degree in society, where it can escalate dangerously or be balanced out if we act in a timely manner.

Asymmetry in nature would seem to give us the confidence that we do not need the ego, as defined, when we have the positive prospect of a deep, natural reason why dictatorships, empires, monarchies, and the like, along with their behavioral patterns, are hopelessly prone to conflict and failure. We can likewise accept that any religious system that is not tempered with democratic opportunities and aspirations will continuously break into schisms and their consequent battles, as recorded in history. Any hierarchical power system, be it a corporation, the military, or a religious organization, depends on democracy and needs to exist in a democratic context or it loses that balance and falls into the cycles of ego.

Excessively egocentric institutions and individuals who usurp the natural balance of the River of Life are caught in a complex psychology of projection and will accuse others of what they themselves are doing. It is typical of oppressors throughout history that they claim moral superiority and attack in the name of a moral code, a god, or claim to act on behalf of a formulated notion of freedom and democracy against "evildoers," and so forth. Things can quickly become disorienting with so much disguise. The target of the attack is often stunned because it's so untrue. Certainly this can be wielded cunningly in fiction as well as fact.

Bertrand Russell's statement on Plato, that "I wish to understand him, but to treat him with as little reverence as if he were a contemporary English or American advocate of totalitarianism," is an excellent example of the kind of balance needed to deal with the complicated issue of good and evil.

\* \* \*

I would now like to present another bit of prose, composed in a somewhat different voice, when I was in the mood.

Wherever paradise is found, in this world or in other places of the universe, the people understand that there are rivers and streams throughout its entirety. They know this in as many ways as the streams flow.

The reason for the rivers and streams is quite simple. They happen because of the way infinity opens up. They happen because infinity cannot be enclosed without exits. Infinity is the capacity to open up. Infinity is the cosmic connector. It can even close itself off, but never without allowing for a way out. This infinitely complex reality is often a subject for discussion in many areas of paradise, in many ways. It brings people together. This is natural when you consider what it means for a stream to develop, like a current in a river or within an ocean, as the infinite reality moves forward, enlivening words spoken in many languages and locations, where the actual word "infinity" may seldom need mentioning.

To always open up means that nothing is ever completely shut off, boxed up, and sealed absolutely in isolation. This further means that nothing can be absolutely repeated, for to repeat anything perfectly, you have to know its exact limits and its absolute borders. If you can't repeat anything exactly then everything is always being created. This makes for plenty of imaginative conversation in paradise; especially in paradise, because paradise is where we are close to the heart of a stream, close to the very nature of infinity opening up. Here, things are especially free and unboxed, unoppressed.

The way this freedom works in everyday relationships is that by the stream you can't help but empathize with others who are therefore not isolated. There are natural pathways to the feelings and inner experiences of another soul. These are sensitive ways of knowing how it is for someone else, not in-your-face, intrusive ways, but ways of honesty nonetheless. This balance is achieved in a natural flow of the stream because, quite simply, if nothing can be exactly duplicated or replicated, then there is no absolute symmetry, no randomness, no fifty-fifty chance, no series of absolutely equal possibilities to gamble on at the spin of a roulette wheel, no one to approach you randomly and insensitively.

Without randomness, the streams open up with direction and meaning. Your life has significance in paradise. It is a place where the power of love is recognized.

Naturally, where people really care what others think, and not just for self-image, they go for a vote on political matters. Paradise is run democratically, and everyone votes, unless they have a reason to abstain. People care enough to stay informed enough to vote with reason. They ensure that information is available. Their media systems are neither relativistic (where it's all basically considered a matter of opinion) nor are they absolutist; they have a realistic sense of direction that is grounded in evidence and expressed with logic amplified with imaginative examples. This does not mean that the people have perfect knowledge, far from it; it just means that they care enough and have the curiosity to research questions and change their minds when reason shows the way and the stream opens up. They vote to help out. They work with inspiration.

The further away from paradise a person falls, the more life is caught up in compartments, where voting might seem just a random thing with a very low probability of success on your own, a long shot, unless you cede your identity to a power block; life is lacking in significance, and you can't make the connection with society as a whole, and democratic government is perceived as distant or in your face. You find it hard to care and hard to believe that paradise can happen anywhere, at least not democratically — maybe in a kingdom somewhere or a dictatorship. You try to build your own little kingdom. You want to dictate how others should live. You develop a fairy tale of how life should be. You become simultaneously naive and cynical.

You find it hard to believe that anyone else cares; maybe you think you are the only one who does, but in another compartment you think it's cool to be cynical. You don't realize how naive cynicism is. If paradise is this real, then the cynic is naive. Your naiveté makes people wonder how deeply you really care and what you really care about. It gets more and more complicated until you opt for simple, unbalanced and false solutions, like the communist or fascist fairy tale with their heroes.

You miss the reality that is so close to you — so close that the more you deny it every day the more you box yourself in. The more your relationships suffer from you being boxed in, the less you can make the right decisions, the more you think it's all about finding your way up some hierarchy of credit and social approval. That becomes your American Dream. You sustain the super-rich to sustain your fairy-tale American Dream or its equivalent. You despise "the masses," the middle class.

You might become basically neutral on real issues, but excessively aggressive about the emotional subject of the moment. Then you just move to another subject without making much connection between them. You seek approval and become afraid to stand up for things you are able to see are true and against things you should know are unjust. You feel guilty and become entrenched, finding it hard to admit it when you are obviously wrong. You build an ego of mind games and lose track of yourself.

People you hang out with increasingly laugh to themselves about you and you laugh at them. Your humor degenerates into making fun of other people's perceived weaknesses. It can keep getting worse like a contagious disease, until the society goes to war on a wave of hate, like the Nazi crusade, with a holocaust, a genocide, as in Kosovo, in Rwanda, in the attacks on Native peoples in the Americas and elsewhere. The fractured and alienated society, worshiping authority and addicted to control, is brought together by a dictator.

If it does not get so bad as that, the messed up society can't see a dictator coming from foreign lands or arising in its midst. People lose the ability to know a real person who actually cares from one who is pretending to care; one who sees a hope of some aspect of paradise for his or her country from one who just wants to be in power. People lose the ability to imagine a real improvement towards a practical paradise; we become unable to distinguish fantasy from fact and lose the ability to enjoy and share dreams, flights of fancy, lucid and imaginative wit, a real sense of direction and excitement. The sensuality of life is randomly allocated to a place alternating with violence. The direction is lost, the love is lost, and we lose the ability to defend ourselves. Adults become like fake children — children being the real thing. Our children suffer from our lack of responsibility. The insecurity of immature adults and bullies fuels and further poisons their excessively competitive relationships to the point where they are uneasy even to see others enjoying simple pleasures, being with nature, taking everyday responsibility. (H. L. Mencken's definition of Puritanism: "The haunting fear that someone, somewhere, may be happy.")

In paradise everyone votes or abstains with reason, which is a vote in itself. They do this because the significance of that one act is so great, has so many things connected to it on the River, that to fail to be involved is to fall from paradise. Not to vote when you don't happen to be in paradise, is to fall even further, when you can least afford it.

So arises the question of the loss of soul. Can we lose our soul through such self-centeredness that we sort of blow apart like an exploding star that has achieved too much symmetry? Such evil is done by humans that one has to ask. Certainly it seems possible, except maybe for the saving grace of continuity.

Presumably history is remembered, recorded, in a consciousness-based reality. If anyone cared enough, a blown-apart soul might come together again in the relationships somehow. But the debt to be repaid would still be there, not because anyone would necessarily come asking for reparations, perhaps for fear of reawakening evil, but simply because the love that reassembled the soul could only do so by awakening some such unifying response. That organizing principle would have to care and could not continue to integrate itself without attempting somehow to undo the crimes committed. This is highly speculative and should not be confused with the heroic struggles that people endure in the attempt to improve things or just survive.

One is reminded of the age-old cycle of abuse, whether in cast systems where reincarnation was used as an excuse to "keep people in their place, because they are working out their karma through poverty and suffering" or in the ever-present immorality that says "riches and good health are a sign of God's grace — so if you don't have it, He's obviously not with you." With the circular corollary: "Let God work through you and give me your money, and thus awash in His Grace I will have the power to make you rich."

One of the ways to feel infinity is to listen to music and hear some real drums. Because the stream does not repeat exactly, it does not remain constant and flat or in a totally straight line, continuing repetitively, monotonously, without variation. So it does something in-between, something in balance, always moving, but rhythmically, in patterns that open up into other patterns, with art, with music. It climaxes where the near-symmetry breaks.

Everyday conversation in paradise has a rhythm of communication where the poetry of the soul finds expression with empathy and wit. Every region has it humor.

And when we vote, it is a simple affirmation of life, a rebirth after which things move into the next phase, without which the threshold is missed and a recovery is required. We can fall until we hardly know what we are missing. If paradise did not exist in many forms, times, and places — islands and pathways here and there in the landscape — then we would have nothing to miss and nowhere to go.

## 35. Atlas Speaks

"Ethics meets evidence where Atlas holds up the universe," I concluded rather grandly and with a bit too much wine. I waited for someone to comment that there's nothing worse than a drunk philosopher. In the absence of any objection I continued, "If we can deduce ourselves out of the box and into the world at large and back again with open-ended asymmetry, then we can say what we ought to do in specific situations, based on reason and evidence. When 'is' meets 'ought,' Atlas is relieved of his burden — at least somewhat, depending on how much responsibility the world is willing to take."

I leaned my arm on Samuel's shoulder, "Let's have a look at what he has to say. I think he's philosophizing again."

"No surprise there," quipped Samuel. "It's a heavy world." He passed me a draft of the following text that I was supposed to have written. I had had to enlist his help.

I retreated from his shoulder and looked at him with big eyes. "Heavy world? Hey, Mr. Atlas, it's just me here. Let's not get carried away, not just yet, anyway!"

"I think you were holding *me* up, sky lady!"

"That would make me an Earth mother as well."

"So that's how Atlas got the reputation for holding up the Earth!"

"One good story deserves another."

I saw Rolo look casually at Lola.

\* \* \*

Singleton, who had arrived at the edge of Heaven just after the incident of the scientist and the Pearly Gates, had had to be diverted somewhat from the usual sequence of events. Thus he had got out of step with his mythology. Having experienced the traditional build-up to the meeting with his Lord, he only found Atlas in blue jeans, sitting on the Throne — a giant in blue jeans.

Atlas had redirected him to the village at the foot of the grassy pyramid, and Singleton became a habitué of the tea room, like a refugee. Then one day Atlas joined the group with the above story about gingerbread. Now the one whom Singleton had eventually convinced himself to be God in Disguise was philosophizing, raising doubt after doubt, as a healthy matter of course. The reverend felt that he had all his life carried monotheism strenuously and patiently as far as was appropriate down the path of liberalization. This was the last straw. Atlas continued as the reverend hung on to his hat.

"The eighteenth-century philosopher David Hume, who was, by the way, a Hume-an—" This pun cracked Atlas up unexpectedly, and the audience had to wait until he collected himself.

"Human Hume made the point that writers were being sloppy in basing statements of 'what ought to be' on statements concerning what in fact is observable. We all know that statements can be divided into two categories, among others. There are 'descriptive' statements of 'what is' and 'prescriptive' statements of what we think 'ought to be.' Hume pointed out the common tendency to uphold a double standard. This 'change of mind' happens in the absence of an explanation of just how the moral ought-statements were got from the descriptive is-statements. This Hume-an," he paused and chuckled some more, "wanted to know how to infer a moral or ethical statement from a descriptive one. This inference would allow us to observe the world and know how we should act in order to be good instead of bad, or of course to locate ourselves somewhere in between. This, not surprisingly, has become one of the biggest questions, and not only in philosophy! Humans have a word for mixing normative or 'ought' statements with positive or 'is' statements; they sometimes call that the naturalistic fallacy. Sounds a bit rude to me," and he chuckled for an embarrassingly long time, until the audience wondered if he had had one too many at the tea-room bar.

When he had recovered, he looked out at the patient faces and apologized, "It's the pressure, the stress, and now the freedom!" The chuckle turned to a laugh with a hint of danger. "A bit of post trauma, no doubt! Or, to be fair, certainly with some doubt."

Singleton could take no more of this and got to his feet. "Since when does God philosophize!"

Atlas looked satisfied. "Took ya long enough!"

"What?"

"Good question! Well, we're going to have an election here—"

"What!"

"So I want to discuss some of the issues—"

"What issues?"

"So we can decide on what to inspire the hu-mans with for their book."

"Book?"

At this point, the scientist who had preceded Singleton at the Pearly Gates called out, "Are you trying to tell us that it was all an act? All the stuff about fixing the flaw? Fusing the gates? The Devil and all, the storm clouds? All an act?" He paused. "Just for me? In a book?"

Atlas said nothing.

"Well?" the scientist persisted. "Aren't ya going to say it took me long enough to react to your act?"

"Yes and no," said Atlas, standing there, human size, bearded and smiling, still in his jeans. "Yes an act and no, not just for you, as we are discovering."

"Well your jeans have shrunk!" someone called out.

Others began to repeat the question, as their existential worries returned. "All an act?"

"All an act?"

"An act?"

"An act, nothing more?"

"Who do you think we are?"

"What about the barbecue? Was I really at a barbecue, or what?"

"Yeah, what was that, anyway?"

"Hey, just what's goin' on around here?"

"Is everybody dead here? — or just me?"

Atlas raised his powerful arms in front on him and spread out his fingers and thumbs to quell the crowd. "All right, all right, *what is reality*, big deal, all right, settle down now. One question at a time."

They settled back into their chairs and into the big embroidered floor cushions. As the imposing figure was about to continue, Milly leapt from the counter onto his shoulder and stole the show.

"Well, that's more like it!" Atlas exclaimed. "You may not be the universe, but you're the world to me, Milly!"

Her motor started up, until it was magnified round the room, being a genie's cat, with a calming effect on the patrons.

"As Millameowsimous is trying to tell you, I am not God, not even a god, only a Titan!" he shouted, and the purring stopped.

"When I was so bold as to challenge Zeus on Olympus, he placed the weight of the heavens on my shoulders. What a loser was I! And Zeus remained supreme ruler. At least until the Athenians began to integrate him into their democratic ways. But they never succeeded in displacing his supremacy. No more than the Americans have displaced God, in practice. Well, perhaps I exaggerate, but then, a Titan has a right!"

Milly draped herself around his neck and over his shoulder, resting her head on her paws, looking down.

"Now, there are other stories that have me as a supreme ruler of Atlantis. And there's the tale of how I was fooled by Hercules. I don't know how he comes off as the hero in that one, after having tricked me into getting him those apples and taking back the weight of Heaven off his shoulders. But as you can see, times have changed somewhat." He stroked Milly's neck and shoulders, revving the purr.

"I'll admit that my reputation was not the greatest. But after the Christians had been in power for a while, I began to look a lot like their messiah. Almost like old times, when the Titans were in power! At least as far as I was concerned, with that heavy load on my back, I was as good as crucified by Pagans! With the weight of the world's expectations of a better life in Heaven on my back, I signified to the angels the suffering of Hume-ans." He chuckled again, still irritating some in the audience.

"Sometimes I have to wonder if those stories about that fellow Jesus bearing the cross up the hill didn't come down from *you know who*. But I'll be the first to admit, I'm not the only one to bear a cross of some sort. Remember this: wherever you find suffering, oppression, poverty, illness, and all the rest, know that the burden is connected. There is a universal burden. The cross goes asymmetric with the weight, and specific — highly specific — but always in some way the suffering of others is the burden being borne for you, unless you help. So help each other! The burden gets shifted, like when Hercules came along; it gets disproportionate. It's a longer story than you want to know. So help each other.

"Now Titans are a race of giants. In the books of monotheism you have giants, genies, and angels, prophets, and many others and many stories. Among the old timers, and I won't name names, the knowledge that there can be no absolutes, no pure symmetries, is old scientific hat. It was understood that because of the many connected addictions, in a world of people playing God in ways large and small, not to overly mention the gods, someone would have to *consciously* play the part of God, or we would all fall into the illusion.

"In fact, there was more than one part going, one for each of the versions of monotheism. I applied and was accepted, based on my long experience of bearing up under the pressures that favor the pure symmetry of a perfectly spherical global universe. This may have been represented in art in a literal sense, but it goes deeper than that, I assure you, with the King and hosts of Heaven, piled high, not to overly mention the weight of that throne." His voice boomed and reverberated, especially with the word "throne."

The ordinarily upbeat Singleton, who had slumped back into his seat, jumped up, shook his fist and cried out, "This is outrageous, bullshitting us like this! Who the hell you think you are, playing round with our most intimate faith and deepest beliefs! You should be ashamed! Shame on you!" And he sat back down with tears in his eyes, as though shaken by his own fist. "A lifetime of preachin' the gospel and bending over backwards to be acceptin' of others and then to die and be faced with such effrontery—"

"Well now, Reverend," Atlas replied, "I could say the same to you." And the Titan looked down at him compassionately with bushy brows. Milly was sitting upright on his shoulder.

"How can you say that?" Singleton's voice was like a prayer, full of a lifetime of arguing with the Almighty.

"I can't really blame you, Singleton. Who hasn't wanted a seemingly perfect moment to last forever? Who hasn't looked at a flower in bloom or heard music crescendo and felt that this is divine, like the water that curves before breaking into the falls, like the droplets that scatter in a rainbow in the seeming perfection of sunlight. I cannot blame you for your poetic soul, nor even for wanting a superman to worship. But I have had to bear the pressure of your insistence." There was a long pause, and Milly jumped carefully down to the floor with a supple cat thud.

"I'm not saying that playing God doesn't have its moments. But it's dirty work in the long run."

Singleton was staring at Atlas in shock. In a sudden reversal, this

## 35. Atlas Speaks

Titan had the moral high ground, which he seemed to have snatched from Singleton, who had cultivated it in homage to the Absolute. The truth was with the Titan and seemed to be insisting in its own right.

A sense of guilt began to overshadow Singleton's features; Atlas held up his hand. "No, no, I've heard enough confessions to bring the sky crashing down. It's opportunities I crave, opportunities for all! So, are there any questions?"

\* \* \*

The scientist, fresh from the Pearly Gates, said, "Excuse me, this looks like it's all above board, but I've seen some convincing showmanship in my time, none better than in the church where I grew up. I can see why you got the job, all right, not to pour cold water on the event, because it looks genuine enough to me. But let's just hypothesize that you are selling some highly refined snake oil. How 'bout proof. What can you prove to me about the fundamental motivation of the most powerful genies, souls, guiding lights, civilizations — whichever story you wish to tell — in the universe, in all existence? Because that's what it comes down to, doesn't it? Fundamentally, if consciousness guides the way, what is the ethics of the most civilized powers? What are the moral foundations of an open-ended, incomplete paradise?"

"An inspired question, thank you! How many would like to hear my answer?" A majority of hands went up, so Atlas relaxed and took a sip of tea that Molly had thoughtfully provided.

"The River of Life," he began in the manner of a sermon, "is always there, according to the Transformation Proof. If there really are guiding lights of the universe, the balance in such civilizations would tend to guide away from the futile attempt of completely closing the circle — or in my case, the sphere of the sky-globe!

"They would do this simply by being as they are, by nature. A free spirit, expressing nature's truth in its every action, would be a true guide in many ways, an inspiration, in fact. With nothing to repress such a spirit from the discoveries offered by the river that always flows beyond, one can only guess and wonder at the knowledge that would develop. Even so, we know things aren't always so easy. For example, it is all too easy to mistake interference into someone else's borders with the adventure of going beyond.

"So I must be careful not to jump to conclusions. We are looking at the possibility that there are civilizing souls who have always been here, who have somehow never been born, who have the eternal consciousness. Age does not always mean wisdom. There are plenty of fools about, young and old.

"The love of a free spirit would help guide the way, from within us and from without, but not infallibly. It's more like there's this vast experience available to us. To claim infallibility would be to reach for absolute knowledge in denial of the equal opportunity of nature's asymmetry. It's like assuming you have no ego. How to know when or where the threshold of that assumption begins? And as it gets going, so does the ego. *I have no ego!* What a thing to say!

"Gods who may have made mistakes, learned from their mistakes, and don't claim to be infallible are a little hard to worship, unless you're just trying to get them on your side. Such characters — call them gods if you will — tend instead to generate, to inspire, mythology, fiction, and ask the Muses what else. With good fiction we learn something as we go. We develop our abilities to know what it is like in the shoes of another, or in the bare feet of one without shoes. There may be more wisdom in the shenanigans of Mount Olympus than I know — or than the bards and playwrights had in mind. Not that I will let Zeus off the hook anytime soon!

"Theoretically, it would be possible for the souls who have never been born to be rather dim for a long time, and even today.

"This raises the question: what do we mean by age? Curiously, we must answer this before we get back to our fundamental ethics of good and evil." The sermon now had more the tone of a lecture or seminar.

"In the maze of relationships in the cosmos, polarity would develop into a new soul. So we would have a universe of souls who were created or who developed some kind of momentum and passed a threshold into selfhood among those who have 'never been born.' The more we discover about creativity and the River of Life, the more we find that the difference between souls who seem never to have been 'born' and those who developed a sense of selfhood 'later' in *time* adds to the plurality of nature's asymmetry.

"Remember that time is physical change; change is bigger than time. Creativity allows for changes in other kinds of lives than those in the time zones. The difference between souls in time and those in other zones would be like being born in different regions. Things change between regions. The regional differences would be ethnic as well. This gives us perspective on the notion that some souls were never born in time. The natural asymmetries carry a unifying democratic current with them in their open-endedness. This is a key point in understanding the motivation within the River of Life. Its asymmetric streams are oriented in such a way as to assure fundamental equal opportunity. This puts age in perspective and brings me to my next point.

"The essential connectivity of the River of Life is love in essence, in its deep democracy. Whatever the degree of soul consciousness, the River of Love is there. What do I mean by 'deep democracy'?

"The asymmetry of the Transformation Proof means that equality is more like opportunity than an exact repetition from one identical thing or person to the next. This is where we can resolve the conflict between individuality and what is sometimes perceived as 'equality' or the 'good of society.'

"Equality in a universe in motion is not static; it means movement with a sense of direction inspired by that fundamental connectivity that I like to call the River of Life. The River flows because of the adventure in the open-endedness of going beyond. We heroes and Titans just love it — once we get it! It is fundamentally not exclusive, as we have seen.

"This connectivity is a basic opportunity that shows up in many ways. It inspires personal growth and true individuality that shows up in personal relationships. The River of Asymmetry is equal opportunity in action. Working with this River of Opportunity has got to be good economics and good for the community. A good leader will always look for ways to increase equal opportunity; people will see the River in him or in her and in themselves.

"What we might refer to in our mythology as a 'democratic god' or 'goddess' would do no less. So no matter how powerful a leader becomes, the wise ones know that they are not above the River of Life. That River is where everyone's chances are moving.

"The balance of the cosmos requires that any aspect of it has this equal opportunity of going beyond, where the fundamental connectivity happens. Unfortunately, in places it is not so obvious.

"Opportunity is a way to go that is intimately connected with the fabric of specific lifeways. Therefore, fundamental opportunity is not repeated exactly, but has a creative horizon that is the shared universal horizon of existence to which we should all have unfettered access. So the more each one of us gets free, the more we all get free. This freedom is not a random or selfish thing and may not always look much like freedom to specific individuals. But it's true freedom that does exist and can be experienced as such, believe me!

"The fact that people and things can get complicated into situations where they are blocked into seemingly paradoxical knots, built into walls, or carry the world on their backs does not mean that the fundamental connectivity is not there somewhere.

"This connectivity is not accessed directly in every way all the time. In fact, if it were, it would be so self-centered as to be an absolute; so it fundamentally shuns such a state. What we really find is that it's the other way round where, in the absence of absolutes, equal opportunity develops freedom creatively, with pathways to travel and discover the meaning of freedom and individuality along the way. The patterns of life are meant to develop equal opportunity in a vast array of ways. Equal opportunity is being created to some degree in the way we live, and it is being blocked in some degree. Unfortunately, creativity has been used to block opportunity.

"We need to free up the world to help nature by increasing equal opportunity. Many people believe this instinctively and for many good reasons. Now we have more reason than ever and more need than ever on Earth, if that's possible.

"As for the question of evil at the foundations, I think you get the feeling I'm working up to it. But I need to acknowledge the vast extended unconsciousness of other individual things, like the rocks and the trees, and nature's manifold presence, the ecology of the River — unpolarized into selfhood, as such. What about these?

"These would have to be extensions of the creativity of soul consciousness, like a body. They are the way the soul is aware. Consciousness extends through them and manifests in them and takes shape in those ways and is aware of the objects by recognizing itself there; but the body and its creations are dependent on the soul, not the other way round. Otherwise my blue jeans might be falling down and the genie's genie breasts might be bursting out of her light-blue blouse, instead of these materials of apparel falling in with our guiding notions of dress. Not that we always dress the way we would like. This follows from the deduction that the universe would not exist without the presence of souls." He blushed.

"Just *what* are you suggesting?" the genie called out from the back of the tea room.

"Such an impressively civilized reality," Atlas continued unabated, "could be expected to connect with us through all kinds of tales from all over the world. Many folk tales and myths contain wisdom generated by the democratic impulse in the deeper connections we have found in nature.

"This now brings us to the question of what keeps us from the flow of the River of Opportunity. The only pressures that detract from the freedom of the River are those that push for absolute symmetry in some way. If it can be deduced that those pressures are subsequent to the continuum, then there would be souls who would be free and fair guides, even just instinctively — except insofar as they have buckled under the subsequent adverse pressures and not fully recovered.

"If the continuum is fundamental and asymmetrically infinite in its orientation, then the contrary pressures for absolutes must be subsequent in every way — timewise and otherwise. They are pressures only, based on a reaction to reality; there is no absolutely symmetrical foundation for such pressures to be grounded, pure symmetry and asymmetry being mutually exclusive, and asymmetry being abundantly present in nature."

Atlas looked at the scientist, "Does this answer your question to some extent?"

The man nodded and scratched his beard. "It is reasonable," he said, "to expect that if this bit of logic is possible on Earth, then older, vastly more experienced civilizations, who have in many ways embraced the River of Life, have figured out the basics and a lot more. Their science would appear as sheer magic."

Another hand went up. "Could the ego of pure symmetry and chaos — in its extreme form we might call it 'evil' — somehow take hold of the democratic continuum and establish a universal oppression?"

"It's too dysfunctional at the base," the Titan replied. "The clear insight, perception, and consciousness of a vast and varied community of souls aware of the River of Asymmetry would see the falsehood take shape in contrast and be able to predict the attacks in detail. Such a community, rooted in Creation itself, would have the fundamental power of Creation. Any reactive and therefore necessarily limited theft, usurpation, or imitation of such a reality would be found wanting, it's basic motivation being limited and counter to nature's democracy. Whatever the degree of harm inflicted by egocentric attacks, it would be clear from the foundations of the universe what was happening. It is important to note that since the very nature of reality would undo the attack, its undoing could come from surprising places where great knowledge might not be expected or even be present.

"Evil intent is futile and doesn't know what it really wants, but the terrible thing is that such reasoning doesn't always get in its way. But in the attempt to 'close the circle' so absolutely, the attacks themselves are self-limiting, even self-destructive. And there is always the universe beyond the attempted closing of the circle, where the creative River of Life opens up and is free. The core wisdom of love always finds life and expression somewhere by its very nature. But there is no reason for complacency. Freedom needs maintenance and protection. Otherwise we default to excessive symmetry for lack of caring. Under many circumstances this requires great effort. That's life, folks. Gotta find the balance, and 'so it goes,' like the man said.

"Symmetrical thinking and the resulting action cannot and should not always be instantly preempted. Doing so with such symmetrical opposition can increase the symmetry of the circumstances in even more unfortunate ways.

"But know this: Every reversal of fortune leads to a creative advance in the long haul of the soul. This is the natural result of the counter-pressures failing to close the circle, enclose the globe, or put the stopper in the genie's bottle once and for all. Whichever story you find yourself involved in, you are in a creative process, and if that process is blocked, you can be sure that there is something on the other side of the impediment that will one day allow those obstacles to fall into place and make sense in the development of your soul and its circumstances. The burden will become a constructive part of the path.

"Though I can sometimes put myself in your shoes and even take some steps with you, I cannot walk for you or carry your cross forever or remove your sins or pay the debt of your soul, no matter how much I might pray for it. If such a prayer were answered, in the long run, so to speak, I would become your usurper and use up your life. You would wither on the vine, and I would be an evil Titan indeed. So if you really want to help — help. Don't spread dependency!

"One more thing: Evil leaves a mark, but always fails to leave its *desired* mark in the creative process, as time changes history, and we do progress. Even so, balance, though fundamental, is elusive."

Milly leaped up onto his shoulders again, "Yes, Milly, you know

Aquilah and I go way back." With the hint of a smile, he looked at the genie and sighed.

"But there is another kind of prayer: it's the vote. You may not know it, but your hearts and minds — your very lives — cast votes all the time, and so here I am, for one. Now I'll leave you to vote on the other questions before the community." With that, Milly and the Titan sat down at one of the tables.

\* \* \*

The discussion that followed led some patrons to gather round the idea of writing some concluding essays for the book, so involved had they become in the reality of the project. They also joined in the discussion of what sort of book it should be — not that Alice and company were able to overhear them, as such.

Many patrons offered their support, motivated by the idea that it would further secure life as they knew it, adding stability — balance — to the tea room in its changing environment. They asked the genie if she thought Urania would somehow inspire Alice and the other authors to include these essays in the publication, as though a little bit of paradise were getting through, not that the writing would be all that great, one of them hastened to add, followed by general agreement.

Someone speculated that Alice might do well to put it entirely in her own words. Another concurred that to have Alice and the other three take the essays on board and anchor them in the book in their world could be the answer to grounding the tea room, not that they didn't appreciate the genie, they hastened to add, again. While they let it be known that she was welcome to stay as long as she wished, some felt that such an open-ended invitation carried an unwarranted level of risk.

The genie thought Urania might not mind playing "mail-Muse," delivering the gist of the writing, anyway, and it might even get picked up word for word in places, or even whole passages might find their way into the book — given the understanding of Alice that had been acquired and the consequent ability to write along with her, at least asymmetrically, indirectly.

There was a mild reaction forming meanwhile. A small band of patrons who had been passing through and were staying at the adjoining tavern finally decided that if this were paradise, they would have to keep searching. This was far too commonplace and lacking in the mysterious but vital ingredient that they could not quite identify but that they all agreed was the pure essence of any true paradise. They were having a bit of a struggle explaining this to some of the old-timers of the village and regulars of the tea room, who quite liked their region, thank you very much!

The travelers tried to explain that it was nothing personal and no doubt just a confusion over the word "paradise." That it was indeed very nice here, but no one seemed quite sure where they were, and it seemed things had to settle down a bit before any application of the P-word could be made.

One old-timer, who looked about in his twenties, advised them to take the turn at the edge of the village rather than the straight road beyond. "There's another gang headin' for town, and I hear they're armed to the teeth. It's true that they always get stumped by the ritual of numbers at the border and have to turn back. Best not to run into them beforehand, though. Some of 'em just never seem to learn."

*  *  *

There was some discussion as to whether a dog should be brought into the book somewhere. That would be here.

Once that was settled, Alice was leaning back in her chair on the porch, caressing the dog's ears, contemplating the task of taking over the narration from Samuel, when she had the idea of rounding off the book with some essays by some of the patrons of the tea room.

# VI. Stirring the Pot

This [data from the Kepler space telescope] means there are a lot of Earth analogs out there — two billion in the Milky Way galaxy. With that large a number, there's a good chance life and maybe even intelligent life might exist on some of those planets. And that's just our galaxy alone — there are 50 billion other galaxies.

—Joseph Catanzarite, astronomer
NASA's Jet Propulsion Laboratory

## 36. The Asymmetric Economy, by Anonymous Economist

Thinking asymmetrically about the economy, I will only attempt to say a few things to open up further discussion, the opportunities being vast. I will not explore the asymmetry between demand and supply, except to say that the price arrived at is good value depending on the quality of the forces involved. The economy deals with transactions or relationships where goods and services are exchanged between A and B and so on, involving some kind of money to pay the asymmetric price. Each transaction has its own history and characteristic price that is usually expressed in numbers. Economists have relied heavily on a narrow utilitarianism, using the concept of "marginal utility" to explain many things. This philosophy is amoral, driven by whatever is useful to whoever. If there is true quality, then we need to change our understanding of marginal utility in evaluating our prices. Something demanded by someone as extremely useful may in fact be quite useless to anyone. No surprise intuitively. But if we readjust our appraisal of markets and change our accounting practices accordingly, things will improve. (*The Price of Inequality* by Joseph Stiglitz provides a compass.)

So what is money? What does it mean to be motivated to "make money"? A basic issue in economics is the question of value, which is a question of quality, which is a question of the character of a thing — or person — and the question of behavior, an ethical question. Like I said, for the most part, this is to open up questions. A major problem for economists has been the absence of a logic of quality. Quantity is familiar to numbers. But we are more than numbers. Quantitative reasoning characterizes science and informs the social sciences. But things like "quality of life," "quality of place," have proven elusive to your math, to say the least.

The Transformation Proof can help. It indicates that there is what has been referred to as an asymmetric Field of Action, which has a balancing polarity with a sense of direction. In the absence of absolutes and their relativisms (as described previously in this book), *true* value, genuine quality, does indeed exist and can be quantified — if we know which is the *right* direction to measure. The problem has been to identify quality from other measurements. With everything in the economy in motion, how do we find this quality? How should we invest our time, energy, and money?

The enhancement of equal opportunity is the way. Investing in this human potential brings the greatest return in the long run, and of course that includes the health of the environment.

It almost goes without saying that the opportunity of a *good* education is essential to good investment in general and to the health of the economy as a whole. Demand and supply in the market can take many forms and many directions for better or worse, depending on our behavior. It may be surprising that it is possible to deduce an ethics of the marketplace from nature's empirical fact of asymmetry. This is an ethics that says it makes no logical sense — in fact it is an absolute absurdity — to just focus exclusively on "making money."

Our Field of Action, which includes the economy, is fundamentally good, not just because it is all-powerful in the long run. Its power is in its basic tendency to encourage understanding by offering opportunity to others, while avoiding and defending against absolutist pressures and demands, including what we call "adverse demand." Adverse demand encourages illusory supply, which encourages the sense that we are richer or poorer than we really are.

Adverse demand is part of the attempt to "close the circle." This is inevitably associated with a society that gives too much priority to exclusivity, losing track of its values, becoming a throwaway society that pollutes, displaying the behavioral patterns described by Alice in her essay in "Streams of Paradise."

With distortions of value, our prices are not reliable indicators of quality. To the extent that distorted value permeates the marketplace, we encounter the same difficulties that communism had in the allocation of resources, leading to collapse. The market needs reliable prices to guide investment in inventory and production, among other vital activities.

Distortions such as excessive inflation, undue recession, stagflation, depression, and so on are warning signs that we need to act as a community to recover harmony in the Field of Action. They provide the opportunity for a reality check. Representative government is the only way the whole community can specifically address and correct many economic imbalances. Allowed to function properly, democratic government improves the quality of the marketplace.

The connection between circle-closing behavior and market disruptions exists because there is a fundamentally good and natural direction in the foundations of the market, as a part of nature's asymmetry. Degrees of true value, real quality, and right action do exist, cynics notwithstanding.

* * *

To the extent that adverse demand is a component of the meeting of demand and supply where a price is found, that price will contain what I will call "Samuel's ghost." That ghost can come back to haunt us if the illusions build to a dangerous degree.

Demand and supply are manifestations of nature's ubiquitous, asymmetric polarity. In the absence of absolutes, market demand and supply find prices that are open-ended signals. In order to interpret these signals properly, we need to know about value. To the extent that the price is arrived at as a nexus where suppliers who are only interested in "making money" are trying to satisfy self-centered demand, the price, taken together with other similarly afflicted prices, will tend to lead the market down the wrong road and into the reactions of a circle that keeps popping open (like a bubble) and will just never close on "that price." A lot of grasping hands, visible or not so visible, lead to ruin.

Good government tends to protect the market and the people from adverse demand and illusory supply in a balanced way. The polarity of nature's balance requires that government find its direction in relationships that offer a corresponding opportunity to others. By avoiding a self-centered symmetry, nature's polarities flow in what poets might call a "River of Life" within the soul. A soulless market cheapens and keeps ruining itself.

Bertrand Russell said, "The problem of finding a collection of 'wise' men and leaving the government to them is thus an insoluble one. That is the ultimate reason for democracy." Or to put it differently: We should leave the government to an increasingly well-educated populace. Wisdom would grow with the understanding of what constitutes a quality education. This is because true wisdom is essentially available to all in many ways, subtle or otherwise.

Without wishing to tell you how to live, I can't help but add, on behalf of us all, that there is no equal opportunity (and no opportunity at all in the long run) without ongoing investment in each one's personal and environmental health, as a civilized society.

Basic to these features of the good economy is the good investor. Regardless of one's means, whoever takes real responsibility becomes a good investor, investing time, money, and investing personal energy, investing in those who care about the balance in everyday life.

The guiding lights of a fortunate civilization know that no one and no organization stands outside the economy. The attempt to do so would be like trying to exist outside of your own consciousness, a form of madness. The market moves when we move. The forces of demand and supply are larger than we might suppose. Along with goods and services, people demand and supply whole organizations, whole governments. To *demand* that we allow the "free market" to take care of itself and *demand* that no one intervene lest we upset the "free" operation of the forces of demand and supply is to *demand* a form of that same ol' paradox, which can only be supplied in a less-than-ideal manner, the true paradox being impossible. Instead, this adverse demand gets us dysfunctional markets, the accumulation of illusory supply, social upheaval and injustice with growing disparity of income, as the elite waste money on themselves. This is all very familiar, so we can learn from it.

The economist J. Bradford DeLong describes the paradoxical condition of the influential but confused Nobel laureate, Milton Friedman, in the following manner.

> He believed that almost all interventions in the economy were doomed to be destructive: only those interventions in the banking sector needed to keep the economy's stock of liquidity and flow of aggregate demand on an even keel were on average welfare-improving. But asserting those beliefs was rhetorically difficult: can you say that laissez-faire is the general rule but that there is one industry in which the government must be constantly intervening and one product — the economy's supply of liquidity, the output of the retail banking sector — where the government must be acting so as to make sure that

the right quantity is supplied whether the free market wants to or not? To try to make that argument is to expose that it is rhetorically weak, even if it is true. Better, Friedman thought, to take a different rhetorical tack: to say that laissez-faire is the rule, and that as far as the banking industry is concerned the laissez-faire policy is the one that makes the money stock of currency plus checking account deposits grow at a constant nominal rate of k% per year. But, of course, this really isn't a laissez-faire policy if there are shocks to the risk tolerance and liquidity preferences of the private financial market, and I think that the past eighteen months show us that there are.[33]

DeLong is referring to the collapse of the housing market, the banking meltdown, and the recession of 2007-09, a clear case of losing track of the value of things on planet Earth.

\* \* \*

When we organize in a civilized manner in communities, we make joint decisions democratically. Government is an expression of community. To be ideologically antagonistic towards representative government is to be against community and therefore elitist.

For the good of the economy, the government should invest in the grass roots and in such a way as to help those who have not yet benefited from as much opportunity as their fellow citizens. This should be the guiding principle when government invests to encourage aspects of industry, finance, agriculture, or any of the larger economic entities, as well as the small.

Sufficiently progressive taxation is an important way for the government to build community, the middle class, and enhance the health of the economy for the good of all, including those who have already benefited.

To move in the opposite direction is to build a class system that contributes to the eventual decadence and decay of the economy, a cultural effect from which no one, no matter how wealthy, can ultimately survive. The rich are particularly vulnerable to the effects of illusory supply, as they have so much. Progressive taxation is a good tonic for the rich.

No one makes it on their own. Fundamental continuity ensures that when we are successful, it is significantly because we are lifted up by a confluence of forces in the market environment and society, whether regional or global. Sometimes we call this "luck." Everyone who has done well in the market should know that there was a combination of luck or "good timing" that joined forces with their own skills and efforts. Anyone lucky enough to have been born to wealth has been given a special opportunity and responsibility to help the community. So we needn't always feel that taxation is taking something that is necessarily "mine." It is not. There is an inspired balance to a healthy market. To the extent that disparities of wealth deviate from this asymmetric sense of direction, the community must work democratically to heal the market with incentives, educational opportunities, and direct, measured redistribution of wealth.

Corporate hierarchies are especially prone to abuse of the market, because it takes truly inspired leadership to counter the symmetrical tendencies inherent in the undemocratic aspects of the typical corporate structure. Without going into detail, it is worth pointing out that the symmetries that develop as corporations get very large and powerful (without the mitigating benefits of democratic government) build a bureaucratic culture that repeatedly confuses money in the way that mathematicians can become overly platonic. But the illusions of a mathematician don't usually trigger the mayhem that has been unleashed by the misuse of math in some universities and in the banking system recently. The formulations bought and sold by financial institutions are a good example of the way money per se is regarded as a number, with the cold corollary of denial of its social connections throughout the community. The symmetrical attitude to the numbers of the "bottom line" is a selfishness that inevitably deprives others of their due, resulting in debts to society.

Even as the market moves with the River of Asymmetry, at any one time the distribution of wealth can come very close to being a zero-sum condition, where vast amounts of wealth in the hands of the few can only have been taken from the rest in various degrees. The Gross National Product of the United States, for example, has grown for the last three decades without any significant improvement in the fortunes of the middle class and those less well off. Where did the money go? It went somewhere: into the portfolios of the few who now owe a great debt. Much of the U.S. national debt can be identified as the debt of these relatively few individuals and corporations. The fact that it does not show up on their balance sheets and tax returns is a serious accounting problem, as well as a political challenge to every citizen to wake up and take responsibility. If the imbalances of denial and monies withheld are not relieved, the misplaced and overstressed levees and dams will break again and again, as the River of Asymmetry reasserts reality.

We often get the idea that we can outmaneuver and even take advantage of economic chaos. Sometimes we can, but ultimately no one can stand outside a market that cannot be disconnected from the asymmetric continuity of life as a whole.

Greed is not a good market driver. Individuals who try to accumulate wealth without the objective of participating in the economic balance of creating democratic opportunity and community attract to themselves imbalances in the form of debts to society. That much-misused term "karma" comes to mind. But when it's time to pay the piper, it can be an opportunity rather than yet another kind of misfortune.

Likewise if we act as though those who are less fortunate have "fallen from grace" in some way or are necessarily repaying a "karmic debt" to society, we can easily accumulate some of that debt ourselves. As Alice and the Titan have already shown, among the many inferences from the Transformation Proof, we can deduce that there is a primal innocence that gets attacked, and there is no "original sin." The piper's bill being only one means of many to right an imbalance, it follows that help offered needn't be the repayment of some debt, but rather a simple act of kindness.

\* \* \*

As an addendum to the brief comments above on progressive taxation, I would like to address the misguided opinion that money should be able to speak and influence elections as though money had the same rights as the individual soul. This is akin to the confusion in law between an individual and a corporation. The soul is not the body armor, the clothes, or the financial or corporate environment it inhabits. These are extensions of consciousness. What is the use of the right to vote in private, without interference, if we are subjected to unfettered political persuasion and attack from those with the loudest voices or the most money? Do we just pray to be rescued by even more powerful armies of financial muscle! Given such chaotic imbalance in the process of our democracy, a private moment for an informed opinion in the voting booth just becomes a technicality. A democracy that does not observe fair play in elections has no more chance of civilization than a market without laws and fair trade, or sports without umpires. Public financing of elections, where the community shares according to the progressive balance of their taxation, is the way forward to a healthy democracy, based on informed reasoning.

* * *

It is a vital feature of the Transformation Proof that no balancing effects can happen solely from outside the individual; we cannot disconnect ourselves from nature. In economic terms, if we want the market to recover some kind of equilibrium in a crisis, we have to do something about it — like President Roosevelt did during the Great Depression — because it doesn't happen automatically. Free markets are not maintenance free. To think that they are self-righting systems is to confuse freedom with an absolute.

Since asymmetry is fundamental, libertarian and neoliberal philosophy these days is mistaken in cutting back on the government that naturally should be the appropriate and sufficiently powerful means to help maintain the balance of the economy as a whole. Good government is vital to community. It is an expression of community. It is more helpful to think in terms of fair markets. The more we work for fair markets and fair trade, the more our freedom is optimized and the more we are engaged in the community as reflected in government.

The Transformation Proof sets in motion the logic of why markets alone are not self-righting systems. The influential economist Joseph Schumpeter had no logical foundation for the assertion that an economic recovery comes "of itself," and should be held to be sound only if it does come of itself. Happening purely "of one's self" is absolute symmetry. Nor is the old idea of "creative destruction" anything but destructive. The foundations of recovery are creative in spite of the destruction, not because of it. As already discussed by my friends in this book, "evil," to use the extreme term, is not creative as such. I would add that the idea of economic suffering as somehow healthy is a poor excuse for those who have the means to take advantage of business cycles, crises, and the misfortunes of others. I will leave it at that for now, as this is not meant to be a comprehensive ethics of the asymmetric economy.

There has, however, been an honest quest for some logic to support the idea of self-righting markets. It is an understandable illusion to confuse compelling experiences of nature's balance with the narrow concept of a "self-righting market" or the costly ethics of Friedrich Hayek's "spontaneous order" in prices, for example.

Nature's balance is in the fundamental asymmetry that encourages and inspires investment in equal opportunity. We are acting against nature unless we work to ensure that income is distributed fairly in ways that encourage equal opportunity for all. If we don't act accordingly and in a timely manner, therefore, things can slide very badly for centuries into dark ages — well beyond what we might call a "great depression."

\* \* \*

This chance of equal opportunity is of course stultified by requiring everyone to live at roughly the same socioeconomic level; such a leveling of society is just as pernicious as the encouragement of great disparities of wealth. The Transformation Proof predicts that one extreme accompanies the other in the close association of random chaos and perfect order, neither of which is functional or even exists in its pure form. The leveling of society will automatically bring about dictatorial, totalitarian hierarchies such as seen in the Soviet Union and China. The examples of aristocratic and royalist hierarchies leveling society into poverty and war are so numerous as to be the main themes of history.

To the extent that it refuses to progress with liberalization and democracy, modern "Communist" China with its capitalism is reenacting the age-old reflex of attempting a version of the subtle absolutism described in Plato's *Republic*, where a collection of "wise people" and a philosophical leader think they have the experience and understanding of past errors to finally get it right. Unless they provide balanced opportunities for the democratic impulse to flourish, they are doomed, and the rest of the world will be severely affected — unless there are good international economic and political systems in place to encourage China on the path of transformation. This is a key time in history; if it appears that the ancient Platonic addiction is being successful, disguised in such a powerful and ancient culture, it could bring about a wave of reversal in the world, where a kind of self-centered gambling fever could take hold, where our hard-won freedoms would be at stake. It is a terrible irony that communism could yet destroy our communities. It is a measure of our addiction that the United States has got itself into such indebtedness to a potential Plato's Republic of China. This dependency reminds me of the gambler and his casino.

From the logic of asymmetry we can infer a theory of economic liberty and justice for all. Every society continually must work to find that balanced and creative sense of direction. Adventures are guaranteed.

As for the value of money, if true value is a River of Asymmetry, where the waterfall and the pond turn the millwheel, then it's the nature of money to require that it be invested so as to open up grass-roots opportunities worldwide, in order for a nation's money to retain its value.

Nature gives back when we invest in her, whether it's an investment of our energy, time, or money. The more we care for each other, the better it is for us individually. The only surprising thing about that is that now our science confirms it with the knowledge of nature's asymmetry.

The twentieth century, at a terrible cost, has supplied us with valuable evidence. The communist symmetry of equal boxes for each citizen is closely related to the chaotic capitalism that protects unnatural divisions of wealth. There are times when we share a pie together in reasonably equal portions, and there are times when we can appreciate the success of individual achievements. Through competition we can find this sense of direction as we partake in the success of our heroes, as we do at the Olympic games, in the spirit of good sportsmanship.

Here is a thought experiment: If we remove competition from the scene, we are left with cooperation, whereas if we remove cooperation we are left with no transactions, in fact, no relationships at all. This is because the open-endedness in the Field of Action happens via relationships that connect. They connect and compete. But the *connection* is fundamental, whereas the disagreement and conflict of disconnection is not. Contractual relationships are reached in a market of haggling competitiveness. Remove the haggling and the contract is still there. Remove the agreement and there is no market.

In trade, all relationships are asymmetric. What does this mean for the globalization of Earth? Many things can be deduced from the asymmetry of market relationships, many of which my colleagues are investigating as regards interplanetary trade. On Earth, where you are just in the process of discovering Earth-like planets outside your solar system, implications of asymmetry for globalization are of immediate importance, if you are to survive the oppressive effects of inequality of wealth and runaway industrialization on your climate. "Comparative advantage" is a concept that was first formally described by your economist David Ricardo. Without going into the complexities, I will leave you with the following comment for further conversation and encouragement to consult the works of Paul Krugman.

In the absence of perfectly homogeneous economic symmetries in the goods and services of supply (perfect — but impossible — ubiquity and replication of hamburgers, for example), nature's fundamental polarity ensures an ongoing opportunity for variety from region to region. Within this variety, regions have specialties (and not only in the food and drink that are of particular interest to the likes of me). Trade between regions is generally advantageous to all concerned, when it takes proper comparative advantage of these specialties by opening them up to more customers. There is more variety available to all, as compared with the conditions that would prevail within a region left only to its own resources.

There is however the countervailing pressure of a reduction in variety that develops with global trade. While preferences for variety push in the direction of more variety, economies of scale push in the direction of less variety. This raises the specter of a global monoculture, with corporations — which are not democracies — wealthier than most countries, leading to unbalanced economies and governments attempting the impossible. Free trade must be fair to survive, and in order to be fair it must reflect an understanding of where the value is — where the River of Asymmetry turns the millwheel, not of oppression but of social justice, building community. Otherwise we will be caught in the attempted paradox of a global monoculture poisoning its own multicultural roots. Do not expect other planetary cultures to bail you out anytime soon! It can be a long way from A to B.

So to round off this introductory discussion, the absence of absolute finality means that there is ultimately no perfect equilibrium in economics. Things will always tend away from perfect equilibrium, even as they tend towards it. The economy is more like a river with towns along its banks, or a tidal estuary. Stability in markets is about community in a natural environment, both regional and global.

*  *  *

Back for a fairly brief note. Now that the ARC edition of *Unicycle*, has enjoyed enough polishing and discussion and the eBook emerges, one of the finest examples of data collection in nature's economy has been organized and published, entitled *Capital in the Twenty-First Century*, by Thomas Piketty. I must now add a further temptation to those resisted in the preface to *Unicycle*'s eBook edition. *Capital* is a gift of labor to the world. And an irresistible invitation. But I must wait before I delve in any detail into the way nature's asymmetry validates the value judgments of *Capital*. Nature does have an ethics, according to the Transformation Proof. A fundamentally moral reason for measures to counter the unmerited growth of inequality is available. The projections of Piketty's book judged to be pessimistic — those being the rise of patrimonial capitalism and its aristocracy — are also for many people wildly attractive but illusory symmetries of power. But I must leave it at that for now and hope for the opportunity to continue to support, with the logic of change, Thomas Piketty's recommendations. An international wealth tax is definitely a good idea, along with a sustained effort to discover the vast hidden treasures of tax havens and stop them from generating a false paradise with hell on earth.

## 37. Asymmetric Evolution, by Extraterrestrial High School Teacher

In the introduction, Samuel mentioned the evolution debate that is taking place on planet Earth. The Transformation Proof disproves creationism. The instinctive and very understandable sense that things are not fundamentally random is used by advocates of creationism or "intelligent design" (ID). Instead of the one-off creation by a single Creator, Creation is happening now, as ever, in a multifarious way.

But I cannot leave it at that. One of the most important decisions my high school students have to make in biology class on our planet is what body to choose. There is quite a lot of controversy at the school board over the question of having to make such a decision at such an early age. On the one hand are those who maintain that to delay only puts off the higher education made possible after the choice of a new body. Others maintain that the risks of forcing such a mature decision on "kids" jeopardizes their chances of further education. As a biology teacher, it often falls to me to help out with the decision-making process. We try to study models of possible lifeways that come with one body or another. Like everything in nature, bodies can be categorized by species, ethnicity, and so forth. No two are exactly alike.

The choice of a body brings with it natural consequences, like the software that comes with a computer. If, for example, one of a pair of twin bodies is chosen, the wearer of the body will be in a new relationship with the one in the other twin body. And then there is the rest of the family, the family's income, medical history, genetic programming, and so forth. Although we can do a great deal with the programming of a chosen body, we cannot undo the choice without losing the body. This death or loss of body is not the dire thing that afflicts the inhabitants of your planet. The bodies worn up to the high school level are sometimes called "provisional," and have special adaptations to facilitate childhood. This is our way, the choice we have earned through the same advances in technology that will one day be put to use on Earth, though the cultural differences will certainly show up in your own distinctive styles and ways of life.

For us it can be compared to buying your first car. There are so many to choose from, and we all have sufficient funds to give ourselves a democratic opportunity. If one of us opts for a Ferrari, for example, while another goes for a Volkswagen Beetle, it is by choice and not for lack of funds. But there may be considerable lack of judgment.

Once ensconced within your "automobile," a whole range of features are automatically engaged. The sound system is right there, operating by default and can be changed at the touch of a button, the turn of a knob, so to speak. A whole technology is continuously monitoring and adjusting your relationship with the road. Traction and balance and breaking and acceleration are all taken care of and available for your decision in driving pleasure to varying degrees, depending on the make and style of the car you have chosen. You get the picture. You have to live within defined parameters, but they are empowering as well as limiting.

Of course you have an inner body. Someday your technology will find out the connections between the inner body and the outer garment, or to continue the metaphor, between the driver's body and the car where that body is seated. We can do a great deal on our planet in the way of autobody repair, but much is still unknown to us about the inner body and beyond, going inwards through the layers of the maze. We do not know how many layers there are to the individual, for example.

When the inner body is damaged or is unravelling, we sometimes use a simulator to check responses. Inside the simulator the person is "off the road" and safe, even though it seems to them that they are driving their vehicle. The simulator has given us many interesting philosophical discussions that have led to breakthroughs. You have the beginnings of something similar in your recent discoveries of stimulating parts of the brain to observe the results. It is a common error in the early stages of this science to assume that there are no further layers to the brain's physical appearance, as they cannot be located without the technology. The result of the misidentification is often the belief that the "body" as you know it has a limited, shall we say Darwinian, life, which I will briefly address in the following pages.

In the process of our own learning, we realize more about evolution, which brings me to the controversy on Earth. Understanding the situation on Earth helps us to gather more information about our own development. Evolution is learning about habitat in a profound and often automatic way, and planet Earth, however remote it may seem, is part of our habitat. As the anthropologist knows, if we as a society deny or do not study other cultures, we become culture-bound, narrow, and ignorant.

This raises some key issues I would like to address. For simplicity I will refer to the book by Daniel C. Dennett, *Darwin's Dangerous Idea: Evolution and the Meaning of Life*. Prof. Dennett, having written what John Gribbin of the *Sunday Times* refers to on the back cover as "the best single-author overview of all the implications of evolution by natural selection available," is just the person to help me, whether or not he might like it — but I think he would, given his deep-rooted rationalism and love of the search for the truth. I will begin with a quote.

> Darwin's central claim is that when the force of natural selection is imposed on this random meandering, in addition to [random] drifting there is "lifting"[34]

He goes on to show that this "lift" is the key to species design. This design is said to be carried out by algorithms in action.

> Love or hate it, phenomena like this exhibit the heart of the power of the Darwinian idea. An impersonal, unreflective, robotic, mindless little scrap of molecular machinery is the ultimate basis of all the agency, and hence the meaning, and hence consciousness, in the universe.[35]

Here I will just pause to point out that the randomness fallacy is another version of the fallacy of absolute neutrality of the automata. Neutrality that lacks any kind of bias, preference, or asymmetry is therefore a fiction of pure symmetry. We are clearly at odds with the premise of Darwinism as described:

> Darwin's dangerous idea is reductionism incarnate, promising to unite and explain just about everything in one magnificent vision. Its being the idea of an *algorithmic* process

makes it all the more powerful, since the substrate neutrality it thereby possesses permits us to consider its application to just about anything.[36]

Now on to the following explanation, where I seem to detect in passing a note of irony in the writing.

> Once upon a time there was no mind, and no meaning, and no error, and no function, and no reasons, and no life. Now all these wonderful things exist. It has to be possible to tell the story of how they all came to exist, and that story must pass, by subtle increments, from elements that manifestly lack the marvelous properties to elements that manifestly have them. There will have to be isthmuses of dubious or controversial or just plain unclassifiable intermediaries. All these wonderful properties must have come into existence gradually, by steps that are barely discernible *even in retrospect*.
>
> Recall that in the previous chapter it seemed to be obvious, maybe even a truth of logic, that either there had to be a First Living Thing or there had to be an infinite regress of Living Things. Neither horn of the dilemma would do, of course, and the standard Darwinian solution, which we will see over and over again, was this: in its place we described a finite regress, in which the sought-for marvelous property (life in this case) was acquired by slight, perhaps even imperceptible, amendments or increments.
>
> Here is the most general form of the schema of Darwinian explanation. The task of getting from the early time when there wasn't any x to the later time when there is lots of x is completed by a finite series of steps in which it becomes less and less clear that "there still isn't any x there, not really," through a series of "debatable" steps until we eventually find ourselves on steps where it is really quite obvious that "of course there is x, lots of x." We never draw any lines.
>
> Notice what happens in the particular case of the origin of life if we try to draw the line. There are a slew of truths — no doubt largely unknowable in detail by us — any one of which we could "in principle" identify, if we wished, as the truth that confirms the identity of Adam the Protobacterium. We can

sharpen up the conditions on being the First Living Thing however we like, but when we then get in our time machine and go back to witness the moment, we find that Adam the Protobacterium, no matter how we have defined it, is probably as undistinguished as Mitochondrial Eve. We know as a matter of logic that there was at least one start that has us as its continuation, but there were probably many false starts that differed *in no interesting way at all* from the one that initiated the winning series. The title of Adam is, once again, a retrospective honor, and we make a fundamental mistake of reasoning if we ask, *In virtue of what essential difference* is this the beginning of life? There need be no difference at all between Adam and Badam, an atom-for-atom duplicate for Adam who just happened not to have founded anything of note. This is not a *problem* for Darwinian theory; this is a source of its power. As Küppers puts it (1990, p. 133), "The fact that we obviously are not in a position to give a comprehensive definition of the phenomenon 'life' speaks not against but indeed for the possibility of a completely physical explanation of life phenomena."[37]

Now to make the following points:

1. This is where we get down to the nitty-gritty of how Darwinians might think that a mechanical operation changed into a conscious process — when the "robot" came to life and woke up. As a fan of Mary Shelly, I cannot resist the temptation to ask, Are the Darwinians today, deep down somewhere, playing God?

2. The Darwinian argument of the awakening robot is dependent on the assumption that there can after all be an *absolute beginning* and that it is possible because there is no essential difference between specific things. This we have asymmetrically disproved, backed up, ironically, with all the evidence of nature's asymmetry, as described in Frank Close's *Lucifer's Legacy: The Meaning of Asymmetry*. It is no good claiming there was no First Living Thing and then claim that life did begin somewhere. The even chance of it being Adam or Badam will not work to obscure the assertion of an absolute beginning.

We find that the modern Darwinian reasoning tends to be founded on the same absolutism, even in its relativistic guises, as that of its strident religious opponents and their God. Incredibly, even more surprising, perhaps, than the absence of the word "asymmetry" in the index of Mario Livio's aforementioned book on the "language of symmetry," no such reference appears in the index of Dennett's book on nature's supposed behavior, apart from a couple of pages under the word "chirality."

This silence on the subject of asymmetry, the one fundamental characteristic common to all of nature, speaks volumes about the deep absolutist connections between many Darwinians and their supposed religious opponents, where things descend into a religious war of words. That being said, the side with the greatest respect for the scientific method, for reason and evidence, is clearly in the lead. I believe some of you call it "the reality-based community."

3. The above Darwinian argument of the robotic coming-alive program depends on the disqualification of a conscious retrospective view. To disqualify consciousness is to assume your conclusion that consciousness could be absent in the early stages of evolution. Consciousness is given an absolute beginning, a priori, later along the timeline of the machine's development. This symmetry of beginning is mutually exclusive with any consciousness or anything at all, as we have explored in our stories and essays.

Dennett proposes two identical individuals of sorts, Adam and Badam. He then says that because life did not begin in an identical Badam, if we remove the later-known fact that life did happen in identical Adam, then we cannot say that it began in Adam either — unless we look back with consciousness. This is an invisible (unconscious) sleight of hand in reasoning that we will now attempt to trace more thoroughly.

Let us work though the passage from the top, dissecting as we go with our asymmetrical blade.

* * *

"Once upon a time there was no mind, and no meaning, and no error, and no function, and no reasons, and no life."

This is what is being assumed and also what Darwinians need to prove and their opponents disprove.

\* \* \*

"Now all these wonderful things exist. It has to be possible to tell the story of how they all came to exist . . ."

Dennett would agree, I think, that he means "it has to be possible to tell the story" in order for the current version of the theory of natural selection to survive.

\* \* \*

"And that story must pass, by subtle increments, from elements that manifestly lack the marvelous properties to elements that manifestly have them. There will have to be isthmuses of dubious or controversial or just plain unclassifiable intermediaries. All these wonderful properties must have come into existence gradually, by steps that are barely discernible *even in retrospect*."

Here we find the author feeling for that open-endedness that defines the asymmetric infinity. But he misses the polarity of the asymmetric reasoning and lapses into absolutism.

\* \* \*

"Recall that in the previous chapter it seemed to be obvious, maybe even a truth of logic, that either there had to be a First Living Thing or there had to be an infinite regress of Living Things."

Although he is cautious about being too categorical, we find the argument ensnarled in the common paradox in thinking about infinity. This results in this particular form of the same old false choices that rear their horns in other fields and labyrinths, if you will pardon the schoolteacher's play on words.

\* \* \*

"Neither horn of the dilemma would do, of course, and the standard Darwinian solution, which we will see over and over again, was this: in its place we described a finite regress, in which the sought-for marvelous property (life in this case) was acquired by slight, perhaps even imperceptible, amendments or increments."

Here the argument opts for a finite beginning, and that is that. We have a confusion that recalls Plato's ghost in the intervals of a number line. A finite but (dare we say "infinitely"?) imperceptible regress to the point to the acquisition. The ambivalent "change of mind" refuses to say which it is going to be: a finite line or a line to imperceptible infinitude?

\* \* \*

"Here is the most general form of the schema of Darwinian explanation. The task of getting from the early time when there wasn't any x to the later time when there is lots of x is completed by a finite series of steps in which it becomes less and less clear that 'there still isn't any x there, not really,' through a series of 'debatable' steps until we eventually find ourselves on steps where it is really quite obvious that 'of course there is x, lots of x.' We never draw any lines."

To say "we never draw any lines" is, I dare say, broad-brush and confusing, as the drawing of finer and finer lines (with their increments of focus and definition) is being described almost in the same breath as "we never draw any lines." The importance and meaning of attempting to draw an absolute line is overlooked. What the author says, confusingly, is that no absolute line is being drawn — except, presumably, the line (whatever shape it takes) where x begins. Such is his ancient paradox: the "line" is absolute, but not — summoning the "ghost" that haunts mathematics, as described by Samuel.

Dennett asks us to "Notice what happens in the particular case of the origin of life if we try to draw the line."

It is already not clear what is meant by "the line," because the logic of asymmetry is missing.

\* \* \*

"There are a slew of truths — no doubt largely unknowable in detail by us — any one of which we could 'in principle' identify, if we wished, as the truth that confirms the identity of Adam the Protobacterium. We can sharpen up the conditions on being the First Living Thing however we like, but when we then get in our time machine and go back to witness the moment, we find that Adam the Protobacterium, no matter how we have defined it, is probably as undistinguished as Mitochondrial Eve."

Here we are getting a definition of a line that is being "sharpened up." But as we go back in time to look at the line, we find it to be "undistinguished." We don't need to know the story of Mitochondrial Eve to follow the current argument. We have a line that is sharpened with pertinent definitions as much as we like but is still not usefully sharp, which is ever more self-contradictory the more we sharpen it up. Our definitions and conditions are eroded as we hone them. So it is still not clear what is meant by "the line."

\* \* \*

"We know as a matter of logic that there was at least one start that has us as its continuation . . ."

Okay, this start is an absolutely finite line. We have a continuum with an absolute beginning, an impossible paradox by the logic of asymmetry.

\* \* \*

"But there were probably many false starts that differed *in no interesting way at all* from the one that initiated the winning series."

We are being presented with the possibility of absolute beginnings that, in retrospect, went nowhere, as far as our subject, x (or life), is concerned. These absolute starts came to an absolute end even as they began, a case of the impossible paradox of pure, point symmetry.

The same pure symmetry is being used to claim that the false starts may have differed in no essential way from the one that was not a false start. And again, there is confusion about drawing a line of distinction between objects that are supposed in some way to be different but not different.

Certainly, one would think that the origin of life would qualify as "essential," especially as this is of the utmost pertinence. How can Dennett disqualify this essential characteristic as being of no interest, especially while being interested in it? He is shifting his position in a paradox. He wants to go back in a time machine while not going back in time.

\* \* \*

"The title of Adam is, once again, a retrospective honor, and we make a fundamental mistake of reasoning if we ask, *In virtue of what essential difference* is this the beginning of life? There need be no difference at all between Adam and Badam, an atom-for-atom duplicate for Adam who just happened not to have founded anything of note."

In a sleight of hand that is often unconsciously made in reasoning that assumes pure symmetries into its language, the Darwinian has attempted to remove the problem of why the origin of life in Adam is of no interest by saying it is only interesting in retrospect. It is only interesting (and therefore an interesting difference with respect to Badam) from the point of view of life and consciousness. Even if we grant this favor of removing life and thereby remove the glaring self-contradiction of it being a major difference between Adam and Badam, between what or whom there is supposed to be no difference, we are still left with their undifferentiated, absolute symmetry.

But can we grant the petition to disqualify life in this search for the answer to the question of its origin? Can we say that the reality that Adam did in fact become the honored beginner has no bearing on his nature at the time? What sort of reality is this? A relativist reality that changes with one's point of view? It would seem so, mixed with a scientific objectivism. Scratch an objectivist or absolutist and you are bound to find the relativist and vice versa.

But leaving aside issues of "what is reality?" where else is the sleight of hand in disqualifying the retrospective knowledge that identified Adam from Badam? The objective for the Darwinian has become one of discovering how life came out of mechanical behavior. They want to conjure life from the machine. They need to say that at the time that the machines, Adam and Badam, were in operation, there was no life, but that life began with one of them. They need to draw an absolute line between life and no life, in the machine Adam. They need two Adams; one that is essentially a machine (or like an ideal template) and one that is essentially alive. This is the problem with Platonic thinking; it puts divisions into objects, including living ones, and Dennett does show an affinity for Plato ever so often in his book. Whether it be the object and its ideal form or the body and soul, the lack of asymmetric thinking leads to irrational and confusing divisions.

The irony is that by assuming symmetry into their thought processes, Dennett and Darwinists generally are too often closer to the believers in the ideal God than they are in opposition to them, closer than they would like to admit. So when the Bible thumpers rant about the soul, the Darwinists overreact, effectively joining the thumping behavior. Referring back to our examples of our teen bodies in cars, this built-in denial of open-endedness and connectedness makes it difficult to seriously hypothesize physical living layers of body merged within the outer body and brain, keeping an open mind.

So the conjuror of life picks one of the two Adams (not to mention the Badams) while appearing to have only one in all. This is not very dissimilar in pattern from the religious person who picks one god before many as the only one, while attributing to it highly personalized characteristics and laws, effectively making it one of many. The logic of asymmetry holds that the concept of "only one" is a self-contradiction, similar to the paradox of an absolute origin of life.

\* \* \*

"This is not a *problem* for Darwinian theory; this is a source of its power. As Küppers puts it (1990, p. 133), 'The fact that we obviously are not in a position to give a comprehensive definition of the phenomenon "life" speaks not against but indeed for the possibility of a completely physical explanation of life phenomena.'"

Here the issue of the two Adams is unconsciously sidestepped. The lack of a comprehensive definition of life is not the question that needs answering. The problem is that no matter how comprehensive the definition might or might not be, the Darwinian argument blunts it with paradox. In citing this quote, Dennett shows that Darwinists have not understood the problem in this area.

We could add that the issue of a comprehensive definition of life raises the subject of universals, which has already been addressed from an asymmetric perspective by my friend Samuel at the end of Chapter 6. Küppers' example of the lack of an absolutely comprehensive definition of life is to favor the absence of a universal without understanding universals. This leaves us an asymmetry that does indeed speak against the "completely physical explanation of life phenomena," as presented by the Darwinian argument in question. In a way, by misunderstanding the truly "physical," the Creationists and Darwinists are rather closely related. As we have seen, consciousness is an all-pervasive physical reality. Consciousness and matter are the same.

## A Handful of Consciousness

The fact is that no matter how simple the machine was, or how subtle it becomes, and no matter how many add-ons it gets, and no matter how much or how little perspective we have on it, the machine will always be just a machine — unless the mechanical parts were *already* forms of physical consciousness and therefore somehow alive.

But Darwinians say, as Dennett plainly words it:

> Let's be clear on the argument. There are those who feel that we are debased by the whole idea of a collection of unconscious atoms and cells being connected together to create consciousness. They also feel that it is self-contradictory to hope for awareness itself to develop from no awareness whatsoever. Many of these offended folks, if I may frame them so, feel that it is more likely that a supreme Creator did it. The particle and cells people, if I may frame them so, try to use reason to discount what they feel is nothing but a fairy tale involving a character called God who is often associated with a talking snake, which does nothing to enhance the credibility of the creation story. Some stories are preferred by some over others, but the problem remains.[38]

This is another example of the false choice that arises where absolutism is found. My grandfather, a Midwestern off-world farmer, more than once looked at us children and asked: "Which would you rather do or go bug huntin'!"

I'll never forget that lesson, and I've been unraveling it ever since.

In conclusion I'd like to make the following points in applying asymmetric thinking to Darwinian questions.

\* \* \*

1. Anthropologists might imagine that one of the earliest and most universal observations by humans might go something like this: Here we are, moving shapes, muscle and bone, like the branches of trees and the rocks and stone. All around us we see things, material things on the move. We touch them, smell them, get to know them. Some are extremely slow, but even a mountain will shake and sometimes erupt. Some things just seem to be asleep all the time. But everything seems

to be moving like we are (and when we look at them as we move), and we are alive. Even when we die, we do not really stop; our bodies decay; we may even separate from the body as a tree loses its leaves, and the soul moves in the forest, like the wind.

This idea has never gone away. Though we may disparage it with terms like "animism," loosely speaking, or with more exotic and scholarly words, it is based on honest observation. It is a good and durable working hypothesis. It has been challenged again and again, notably by Platonic philosophers and worshippers of supernatural deities, where an absolutist division is established, and the gods are not nature oriented but exist *supernaturally* — above and beyond nature. On one side is the ideal, the soul, the perfect god, and so forth; on the other is nature and by association the "impure," the body, etc. This is all too familiar to us now. But while we may find it easy to understand an argument that says "everything, including matter, is consciousness," it is not so familiar to imagine that our thoughts, our consciousness, may be physical, just another way in which matter and energy behave — that material objects are far more amazing than we have been culturally programmed to credit them for being. After all, matter, like the body, has been deemed second rate, even corrupt, in a historically overwhelming, religious cultural context. Scientists often react and try to raise up materialism overreachingly, as do many of the Darwinians. In the reaction, they bring into their arguments the absolutism of their opponents and its concomitant relativism.

\* \* \*

2. How do species tend to evolve one way rather than another? Asymmetric preferences, as yet not fully acknowledged by Darwinian theory, are capable of providing trends of development. The logical polarity of nature's asymmetry would require inconsistent events such as mutations to accompany the closely exact copying that happens when DNA is read by the biological copying mechanisms. Mutations would not achieve the absolute of a purely chaotic random extreme. Nature's asymmetric polarity would turn them back before they attained the impossible absolute. They would partake in nature's sense of direction and variety.

\* \* \*

3. The two Darwinian ideas:

a) Speciation — the logic of asymmetry has a contribution to make by inferring that this variety of pattern occurs because of the interplay of the polarity of change.

b) Natural selection — this is held by Darwinists to involve the pressures of Malthusian competition on species, but, according to the asymmetric reasoning, this pressure is not the necessary factor for natural selection.

Darwinists observe that genetic changes are amplified by inheritance to build advantages that work to alleviate Malthusian pressures. But the asymmetry of natural selection takes place in response to the call of the River of Life from within the habitat. This is a natural instinct imbedded in the very atoms of the universe. Selection does involve a destination, a sense of direction and cooperation. Life is not designed by the "blind watchmaker" of Darwinian lore.

Competition happens because life is a creative process where problems are not yet solved and solutions lead to new questions. This leaves room for competition for answers. But it is the asymmetric and specialized open-endedness that allows opportunity to evolve and diversity to develop. Life's polarity will not allow the diversity to collapse into a monoculture without those asymmetric polarities reviving it. There is a guiding force that has degrees of free will. Even so, reactions and imbalances do obstruct and distort natural instincts and the growth of civilization. However, when these obstacles are overcome, the creativity continues to develop and evolve with new diversity to refresh the habitat — or what might be left of it.

Technological innovation has been shown to directly offset, so far, the predictions of Malthus; evolution also provides innovation with improvements in design that offset the Malthusian environmental pressures.[39] Darwinism would have it the wrong way round, where the adverse pressures are the requirement of evolution. Fundamentally, life evolves in a polarity that works in spite of these pressures, not because of them. The genetic mutations happen as the result of the polarity that kicks in to balance the near-symmetry of repetition.

The algorithms that Darwinians indicate as the operators without foresight, supposedly giving eventual birth to design and life itself, are themselves a part of the same polarity as the genes produced algorithmically. The impossibility of absolutely exact repetition means that the repetitive algorithms must be accompanied by something that looks very random and directionless, such as the "random drift" of Darwinian theory. This drift in what Darwinians call "design space," the space of all possible designs, is contrasted with the "lift" that is natural selection that can lead to increasingly complex designs and life forms. But the drift and lift can together be understood as a manifestation of the asymmetric polarity of nature's evolutionary changes.

To the delight of those of us who love the purely aesthetic contemplation of nature's variety, the creativity of asymmetric polarity allows us to deduce that such astonishing variety can happen for no more reason than its beauty, without denying the practical considerations involved in evolution.

Pursuing a recent article in *Newsweek*, one has to wonder how your recent discoveries of the Lamarckian effects, where the experience of parents can change the functioning of the DNA of offspring, will affect the evolution of biological science on Earth.[40]

\* \* \*

4. I would like to quote the following excerpt from the online *News at Princeton*, "Evolution's New Wrinkle: Proteins with Cruise Control Provide New Perspective," by Kitta MacPherson. Notice how a new understanding of nature's asymmetric polarity can enhance the discovery of the natural feedback control described in the article.

> "The discovery answers an age-old question that has puzzled biologists since the time of Darwin: How can organisms be so exquisitely complex, if evolution is completely random, operating like a 'blind watchmaker'?" said Chakrabarti, an associate research scholar in the Department of Chemistry at Princeton. "Our new theory extends Darwin's model, demonstrating how organisms can subtly direct aspects of their own evolution to create order out of randomness."
>
> The work also confirms an idea first floated in an 1858 essay by Alfred Wallace, who along with Charles Darwin co-discovered the theory of evolution. Wallace had suspected that certain systems undergoing natural selection can adjust their evolutionary course in a manner "exactly like that of the centrifugal governor of the steam engine, which checks and corrects any irregularities almost before they become evident."

In Wallace's time, the steam engine operating with a centrifugal governor was one of the only examples of what is now referred to as feedback control. Examples abound, however, in modern technology, including cruise control in autos and thermostats in homes and offices.

. . . . .

Various researchers working over the past decade, including some at Princeton like George McClendon, now at Duke University, and Stacey Springs, now at the Massachusetts Institute of Technology, fleshed out the workings of these proteins, finding that they were often turned on to the "maximum" position, operating at full tilt, or at the lowest possible energy level.

. . . . .

Chakrabarti and Rabitz analyzed these observations of the proteins' behavior from a mathematical standpoint, concluding that it would be statistically impossible for this self-correcting behavior to be random, and demonstrating that the observed result is precisely that predicted by the equations of control theory. By operating only at extremes, referred to in control theory as "bang-bang extremization," the proteins were exhibiting behavior consistent with a system managing itself optimally under evolution.

. . . . .

The scientists do not know how the cellular machinery guiding this process may have originated, but they emphatically said it does not buttress the case for intelligent design, a controversial notion that posits the existence of a creator responsible for complexity in nature.

Chakrabarti said that one of the aims of modern evolutionary theory is to identify principles of self-organization that can accelerate the generation of complex biological structures. "Such principles are fully consistent with the principles of natural selection. Biological change is always driven by random mutation and selection, but at certain pivotal junctures in evolutionary history, such random processes can create structures capable of steering subsequent evolution toward greater sophistication and complexity."[41]

Nature's asymmetric polarity happens in the absence of absolutes. The absolute paradox of pure randomness cannot achieve the continuity necessary to the separation required between poles of any kind, let alone "bang-bang extremization." The cellular machinery that redirects feedback control from extreme polarities is an expression of nature's ubiquitous asymmetry.

* * *

5. Lastly, I would like to say a word about the "optimal" as compared to the "selected option." The optimal should be regarded as the good. The social Darwinism of "survival of the fittest" is shown to be inadequate in the fundamentally creative context of the equal opportunity of the open-ended continuum. It is well understood among Darwinists that there are many errors of reasoning in trying to transform their evolutionary theory of natural selection (or the selected option) into a sociological theory of the optimal. An asymmetric approach pulls the rug out from under any sort of social Darwinism from the get-go.

* * *

By the way, on our planet we have a physics course that is often taught at university level where physics is explored as a kind of psychology, were we discover the realm of the possible, and natural disasters are like great predators on the food chain, where there is an exchange of energy. We are still learning where to be when, and how to be there in time.

In this course, the question of entropy often arises when speaking philosophically of creativity in physical form. Looking at entropy from the point of view of the life sciences, Prof. Dennett quotes the psychologist Richard Gregory.

> Time's arrow given by Entropy — the loss of organization, or loss of temperature differences — is statistical and it is subject to local small-scale reversals. Most striking: life is a systematic reversal of Entropy, and intelligence creates structures and energy differences against the supposed gradual "death" through Entropy of the physical Universe.[42]

The Second Law of Thermodynamics, being described statistically, has the inbuilt "ghost" assumption of pure randomness discussed by Samuel in this book. One might say there is even a relationship between this ghost and what is referred to as "Maxwell's Demon."[43] The bottom line to the question of entropy is the definition of boundaries and infinity. The Second Law of Thermodynamics depends on absolute isolation. This has given rise to anomalies not entirely unlike those in other areas of study where "absolute finality" is assumed into the language without knowledge of its paradoxical meaning.

The asymmetric leakage from "absolute isolation" is one of the ways physics joins the life sciences.

## 38. Philosophical Habitat, by Interplanetary Inhabitant of No Fixed Abode

In the absence of absolute symmetry in the universe, we are encouraged by nature to be individuals in fundamental harmony, living in community, where horizons are found in assisting each other's opportunities. In the universe of (impossible) absolutes, in denial of the importance of such horizons of individual opportunity, we are more like minuscule, almost insignificant specks relative to a gigantically hierarchical universal environment — cogs in the cosmic machine. Viewed more as a living maze or a winding River of Life where the furthest reaches are intimately connected with the inner currents, the entire universe can be seen as a habitat, rather than something largely alien.

We have explored how absolutism, oblivious and in denial of nature's asymmetry, automatically tends to prefer hierarchies of power. The edge of the waterfall can be a slippery place. It is a beautiful threshold that can hold the attention with a magical fascination, inspiring romantic notions and real poetry. The climactic seduction of such a threshold, where nature is in definitive but elusive transition, is like a porthole on the edge of adventure. The trees over the stream are reflected in otherworldly images and beguiling colors — before the water breaks up and the images are shattered and scattered over the rocks in the cascades. It is like the light through the stained glass of a place of worship. Surely God is there, one might assume. Here we see both His peaceful and wrathful nature. Surely there is a place just beyond that threshold or just beyond the successive falls upstream, where the Absolute exists on an almost unimaginable throne.

Then, as things keep opening up, the artists and musicians and writers, architects, craftspeople, mathematicians, and even the scientists go to work, embellishing that divinity — or they are elaborately prohibited with lists and laws from engaging in some aspect of such behavior. Either way, it's the same invisible hand attempting in varying degrees to close the one, great, impossible circle — while some wonderful works are created along the way.

As Peter Woit points out in *Not Even Wrong*, "One of the main principles of general relativity is what is called 'general coordinate invariance,' which means that the theory doesn't depend on how one changes the coordinates one uses to label points in space and time."[44] It is understandable that a scientist must have a frame of reference — a habitat for numbers — that doesn't slop around frivolously but allows us to draw consistent conclusions that relate to other areas of nature's manifold presence. The question I would ask is: Just how absolute does the independent foundation have to be to satisfy the requirement of invariance? Must every last degree of possible invariance or change be squeezed out of the cornerstone? How much territory must the theory claim before we can relinquish creativity to new understanding, and new thresholds of change are allowed?

This is but another aspect of the question I ask of the worshippers of the perfect God: How much wisdom do you require of your source of inspiration and guidance? If the repository of wisdom went to the roots of time and the universe, would that be enough? Would such wisdom disqualify itself in your life if it declared itself not to be infallible and not to have everything sewed up with perfect knowledge?

An all-knowing god preempts your creativity because there is nothing left to discover. Even the discovery of creating something new is preempted, since it would already be old hat to the omniscient and much-admired deity. Even your most intimate fountain of creativity, your soul, would be nipped in the bud — your very soul would be preempted from happening. The innate creativity of a child in the expression of its young personality would be denied. Look to the creativity of your children, your people, and within yourself, where the Muses find ways to inspire. Be inspired by nature. Discover the Muse in each other!

The Transformation Proof allows a tightening up of our frame of reference that is sufficient to the purpose at hand, without going over the falls and disintegrating into self-contradiction. It is not a Theory of Everything, more of an unfolding. It clears up the confusion between extremely near symmetry and absolute symmetry. It allows us to have science without destroying our habitat. It allows us to have romance without falling into denial of facts and figures. It gives us a sense of direction that is community oriented, without losing the sense of adventure often lacking in closed circles.

What to call this philosophy? you might wonder. Is it some sort of democratic pantheism? Is it like the deism held by some of the Founders of the United States? Is it Pagan? Atheism, loosely considered? Science fiction, perhaps, with its combination of logic and mythology? Paganism involves the worship of more than one god; this is not worship; it's democracy, therefore not Pagan as such, though it sees our mythologies as often inspired, including monotheism. If deism requires a First Cause, it misses the mark. But we cannot be sure what is meant by "First Cause" to each individual.

The inferences made from the Transformation Proof and backed up by nature's asymmetry could be claimed as pantheistic and some good fiction could come of it. Though it was not the intention of the authors, it may fall out under that broad and confused label. To quote Michael Levine in the online *Stanford Encyclopedia of Philosophy*:

> There are probably more (grass-root) pantheists than Protestants, or theists in general, and pantheism continues to be the traditional religious alternative to theism for those who reject the classical theistic notion of God. Not only is pantheism not antithetical to religion, but certain religions are better understood as pantheistic rather than theistic when their doctrines are examined. Philosophical Taoism is the most pantheistic, but Advaita Vedanta, certain forms of Buddhism, and some mystical strands in monotheistic traditions are also pantheistic. But even apart from any religious tradition many people profess pantheistic beliefs — though somewhat obscurely. Pantheism remains a much-neglected topic of inquiry. Given their prevalence, non-theistic notions of deity have not received the kind of careful philosophical attention they deserve. Certainly the central claims of pantheism are prima facie no more "fantastic" than the central claims of theism — and probably a great deal less so.[45]

The authors of this book have faithfully tried to follow the reasoning to discover where it might lead. Because pantheism includes absolutist as well as relativistic positions, the label is mainly useful as a way of finding common ground between what may otherwise be very different philosophies and religions.

To say that this philosophy is "pantheistic naturalism" may sound a bit redundant, but it is naturalistic in that it considers the term "nature" to be sufficiently inclusive of all there is. The term "supernatural" would therefore not have anything to designate, apart from being useful to imagine the impossible and the fictitious, and the fiction is not to be underestimated. Naturalism on its own, whichever way it is parsed these days, does not really convey the interpretative power of myth and inspiration from regions hitherto regarded as supernatural, though it does ensure the inclusion of science. Pantheistic rationalism, perchance?

Panpsychism, ancient and curiously inclusive, has regained traction in academic circles, perhaps for steering clear of declaring for deities not thought to be worth one's career.

This project came together with some friends of a publisher who has had a lifelong interest in the relationship between fiction and nonfiction. They created this book where I, as no more than one of the supposed characters, am bringing it to a conclusion. In doing so, in the context of this book, I am unavoidably cast in the light of a question with many possible shades and colors, such as: Who am I? How real am I? Where do I come from? And what do *I* know?

Or to quote the four basic questions of Tantra: Who am I? Why am I here? Where have I come from? Where am I going?

Which brings to mind the Zen story of the chaotic but honest fellow who is seen galloping wildly around on his steed and when asked by a passerby, "Where are you going?" answers, "I have no idea! Ask my horse!"

Do I flit about the world peering into people's lives like Shakespeare's Oberon? Are there any rules about that? The possible barrage of profound questioning inspires me to tell stories and often to remain anonymous or use pseudonyms — and to introduce myself only at the conclusion, where I can make ready my escape.

\* \* \*

One of the main conclusions that follows from the absence of absolutes is that there is fundamentally democratic civilization flowering continuously in diverse parts of the universe and that the leadership that cultivates this widespread life, from the grass roots and beyond, by its very nature also encourages us here to be inspired towards true civilization in deep harmony with nature. We are discovering that we can do so because nature is profoundly so itself. The inspiration shows up in our daily lives when we try to do the right thing and find the way. But the conditions in which we find ourselves are all too often close to impossible.

As the inspiration of being part of a greater truth filters through the connections that we can infer but have yet to understand in more detail, it must do so in ways that are recognizable, whether by fairy tales or religion, fiction, art, music, or a good movie, a job well done, or something your child said, a moment in the garden, science and technology — the ways are limitless and continue with our soul creativity. One of the most impressive ways that this creativity shows up is in the sheer determination and perseverance in improving — whether more or less directly or indirectly — the habitat we all share.

On Earth, we have witnessed an explosion of inspired science and technology. But we now have to account for an imbalance in the way we are reacting to it. The more we are able to find the balance, the better we will be at securing ourselves amidst the powerful forces of nature, instead of being at the wrong place at the wrong time. This will, of course, take time, and will require some impressive science applied through political cooperation and social change, but it can be done if we have the balance of heart and mind — the polarity of soul to let love's logic lead the way.

Theologians can spend a lot of time over the question of "good and evil," trying to excuse God for allowing people to suffer natural disasters. A better use of time would be to work on ways to minimize the impact of these events and progress as a civilization that knows how to live with nature. We are like the little child who is still figuring out where its body is.

\* \* \*

Faced with the often-stultifying cycles of the mind, many turn inward to mysticism, a main component of religion, though mysticism per se is often considered apart from the mythology that accompanies religious traditions. This would-be mystic is empowered by nature's polarity to ride away from the extreme chaos of the mind, sometimes referred to as the "drunken monkey." But the mystic typically falls into a variation on the same error as religion in general, of assuming there is an essential symmetry of existence "beyond the mind" and within the self or soul. This does not mean that some of the main vehicles of mysticism — meditation and yoga, for example — are not liberating. They are, as the increasing empirical evidence shows. But the would-be mystic tends to compartmentalize the mind. The denial required in the continuous attempt to "close the circle" and find "the center within" comes with a compartmentalization that allows the typical patterns of behavior observed by sociologists and anthropologists who watch and wonder at people of faith in every culture.

One moment the faithful are engaged in rituals of love and humility and the next thing you know some if not many of them will be attempting to enforce their faith on others, using a wide range of excuses, scholarly and otherwise. The more symmetrical, monotheistic, and hierarchical the mindset, the more evident the compartmentalization. This makes it easy enough for the hypocrisy of the wealthy churchgoers who, for example, praise the poverty of Jesus on Sunday and then turn a cold shoulder to those who are denied the opportunities to help create the sound habitat that is their natural right. This "boxification" of the mind can be mitigated in many stronger people of faith, who have more supple minds and souls and are able to shoulder the responsibility that is so easily shirked by others who use the ready-made denials and excuses of the belief system they enjoy. And there is a lot to enjoy in belonging to a religious group; there is a high romance involved in being able to believe what the soul knows deep down to be a fantasy. It is a suspension of disbelief that allows the benefits of fiction, art, music, inspiration. But there are risks. The compartmentalization is nature's way of giving us a break, but of course when the mind takes a break, things can go awry. To go with the unicycle imagery, long-term balance requires that we put the unicycle aside now and then. The many forms of monotheism are specializations of a specialty that require extra-special balance. The gifts to society can be invaluable, but sometimes the cost is too high.

The Bible is a handy grab-bag of excuses for everything from slavery to genocide to incest, while containing some of the most inspired literature in the Testaments Old and New. It is the doom of the fundamentalism that takes it only at face value. And a man like Jesus, a thinking man under the rule of Rome, at a time when it was slowly losing its democracy, must have known of the democratic legacy and would surely have been pressed to answer questions about it. The pressure of Rome was just about everywhere in Jesus' world. No statements specifically on democracy have made it into the Bible as we know it; the word "democracy" conspicuously is missing. But the recurring democratic theme of equal opportunity in the consistent Christian message of caring for one's neighbor is clearly present amid the rest of the Bible's claims. All the authors and prophets of the Bible might be described as mystical in some degree, and ever since the dawn of Western democracy around 500 BC, would-be mystics — like Plato — would have been faced with the questions raised by the codification of the democratic impulse. We hear plenty against it from Plato, but the Bible is strangely silent. And yet they are similar in many basic ways.

True mysticism consists in understanding the "edge of the waterfall" and the asymmetric nature of infinity that may flow beyond thoughts and words, but without going beyond the current absolutely. The mystic may want to go beyond the machinations of mind and its occasional reasoning powers. But the last snare of such "transcendence" is the delusion that one can do so and achieve a permanent "enlightenment." There is no such absolute transcendence, not any more than the would-be God can escape the open-endedness of asymmetric infinity — as is, I am assured, already described in this book.

The old saying about enlightenment — "first there is a mountain, then there is no mountain, then there is" — can be understood as an acknowledgment of universal continuity where transcendence is not about finding a place where there is no mind and no reason. It is about creating a healthy habitat of the mind in the maze of life, not a perfected center of being. When the mountain is rediscovered as part of nature's habitat and in some mysterious way alive, then, in a way, it has disappeared with the loss of illusion and reappeared more as it is. It might be referred to as a "reappearance," because the deeper reality is already known and is now known again by one more soul. The mountain's mystery will not, of course, end, not any more than anyone can claim finally to be enlightened. Any branch of Buddhism or Hinduism, when it encourages helping out in the world, demonstrates this understanding.

This philosophy also accords well with aspects of what has become known as the "creative economy," where the three T's can be found: tolerance, technology, and talent that are attracted to the communities that encourage these. In his research, the author Richard Florida has found that in communities where such principles are in use, a diverse and healthy economy tends to be the result. Simply put, people like to live and work in communities where there is tolerance of individual differences, where they can feel free to relax and be creative, enjoy an interesting street life and a home for the soul, where everyone's innate creativity is encouraged.

So communities can attract a diversity of business in a balanced way to improve the habitat, rather than adhering reflexively to the old model of people moving to a mill town or into the artificial circumstances built around an industrial center, leaving the inhabitants vulnerable to desolation if the business decides to move.

Economists have been slow to face philosophical questions of creativity, questions of psychology or of the environment, even to credit them. But these questions of quality require answers that connect ethics and nature.

The cities, towns and villages that have the cafés, restaurants, crafts people, artists, musicians, and writers, along with the self-employed small businesses, where business leaders like to consciously participate in creating the right environment, housing, and environmental habitat for economic well being, these locales discover a balanced and protective cultural diversity and wealth — even though it is still true that the artists, writers, and musicians may be the last to benefit financially. For this last reason alone the struggling artists and musicians, the poets and writers, must be given special investments for the common good, just as businesses sometimes get tax breaks to move to the area and young farmers are helped to provide.

\* \* \*

The concept that economic prosperity is largely dependent on creativity and on its preferred habitat raises the question of the source of creative thought and action. The inferences made in this book from the Transformation Proof, where thoughts are deduced to be physically present in a changing physical aspect of the body — what we might call a "soul" — which in turn is connected fundamentally with an enduring democratic sense of direction in our habitat, align with recent evidence that altruism is hard wired in the ancient brain, along with food and sex.

> The more researchers learn, the more it appears that the foundation of morality is empathy. Being able to recognize — even experience vicariously — what another creature is going through was an important leap in the evolution of social behavior. And it is only a short step from this awareness to many human notions of right and wrong, says Jean Decety, a neuroscientist at the University of Chicago.[46]

This goes well with the conclusion from the Transformation Proof that love leads the way. We develop soul through empathy, which accompanies the polarity of relationships. Certainly the power of love is no less powerful for being physically grounded. Matter and energy can be more amazing than we have imagined, being the stuff of imagination itself. Of all our ideas about what love might be, the continuous offer of equal opportunity in balancing relationships in the midst of the adventure of life cannot be denied — without encouraging oppressive hierarchies of power. The goddess of Justice would therefore inspire us to find the continuing balance where opportunity is opened up to those who need it most and those who attack the balance are stopped, not absolutely but in the right degree, according to the degree of the attack. Thus the rule of law. This leaves open the opportunity for us all to learn and change. The key to successful community, creativity, and habitat is the ability to understand nature's shades and degrees of meaning. This requires the empathy offered by the polarity of soul relationships.

Current research on the human brain is identifying the neurological switches and connections that "light up" when activated in association with a range of stimuli. Illusions and hallucinations can be activated, and responses to external events observed. Following this audit trail will lead to asymmetries where the fundamental continuum can be found flowing through the most closely specified patterns of behavior. The closer the research gets to the nature of the currents that pass through the brain, the more significant the asymmetry of the connections will become. This will lead research to the vision of the larger maze of life and the altruism of the universal habitat.

Meanwhile it is too easy to assume that we are just a complicated bunch of wires. The observation that a specific part of the brain is activated when a person sees a certain pattern does not necessarily mean that the system between the brain and the object observed is closed. If there are further soul "layers" to the brain, we would expect them to light up the observable, activated parts, as the soul interacts with the external environment of stimuli, as energy passes though that part of the brain that we are able to monitor. A rewiring of connections that results in altered behavior does not prove the absence of more fundamental networks that might have been short-circuited.

Likewise, the ability to produce the illusion that a ghost is in the room, for example, by stimulating the brain does not, of course, prove that if someone sees a ghost it must be an illusion projected by the brain. The brain is a lot like a computer in a larger network. Because we can use it to "Photoshop" an image into the room does not mean that the brain isn't able to pick up on the presence of an object actually in the room and load it, share it, even if that image is not seen by everyone present. Some of the same circuits may be activated for illusions as for not, like in the Egg Sequence soon to be described. In fact, the various abilities are different aspects of the same software, though some may be referred to as "paranormal."

It is perhaps extra easy to build an ego while manipulating the brain. The ego, as earlier described in this book, would tend to opt for symmetries to account for our consciousness, such as the "neutral" building block (assigned to Darwin) somehow evolving into our relatively complex and aware selves — or opt for an "absolute Creator" or even the selfish objectivism of the celebrated Ayn Rand, who wrote *Atlas Shrugged*, when we know otherwise from the Titan himself. Neither the pure symmetry of absolutely indifferent, self-centered neutrality nor the God in question will cut it asymmetrically.

* * *

I am beginning to get the feeling that I am about to react to some comments made by the Titan, Atlas. When a giant stirs something up, it's a little hard to leave it alone. The subject of perception in philosophy might seem recondite, but who would be surprised if it turned out to be about as relevant as the way we perceive? I cannot say that I am overjoyed that Atlas has left me the task of describing what the philosopher Simon Blackburn refers to as a "catastrophe" in his handy book which I recommend, *How to Read Hume*.⁴⁷

To further raise the subject with Blackburn:

> It is only when we conceptualize "visual experience" and "the way things are" in terms of either identical or parallel "spaces," inner and outer, that we cannot make a consistent story about how vision [or perception] works. It would be nice if we could seen how to reflect and reason on the process without entrapping ourselves in such an image, but even now the large and controversial literature on the topic proves that it will not be easy.⁴⁸

And again:

> The situation here is much worse than it is with induction and causation. There we have aspects of our nature that cannot be "certified" by reason. We go in for inferences that cannot be shown to be probable. But here, right at the heart of our entire conception of ourselves and our world, we go in for beliefs that can be shown not only to be improbable, but to be straightforwardly contradictory. We cannot help it, and we cannot mend it either.⁴⁹

Then Blackburn quotes Hume: "Carelessness and inattention alone can afford us any remedy."

David Hume died in 1776; he was born in 1711. Blackburn explains that Hume was the greatest British philosopher, that he "was a central figure of what was later recognized as the Scottish Enlightenment, that great flowering of arts and sciences that was pivotal in creating the modern world."⁵⁰ Hume clarified our thinking and presented the problem.

It falls to me in this essay about habitat to address the situation, the "inner" and the "outer," here, so as not to leave a proverbial elephant standing, let alone a herd of elephants, including a mythology to go with them, along with a River of Asymmetry to water them. So before I bring asymmetry into it again, I will outline, with Blackburn's help, the problem Hume clarified as regards perception, the question mark he posed — for Hume had an open mind.

First of all we are faced with that old-time observation that there really do seem to be interior experiences that are distinct from exterior objects of our perception. So what are we perceiving? Are we just seeing (to use vision as an example) a vision that is in fact just internal but appears to be external in some convincing way?

The other famous possibility advanced by philosophers is that the objects are indeed external, but that we perceive them as though we are in a theater, via some medium that always keeps us in a second-hand state of existence, even though the show can be really very good.

Science has given this "show" (if that's what it is) de facto rave reviews, as evidenced by amazing technological progress, without having to go so far as to solve the problem faced by philosophers on the question of perception itself.

Also, in that the scientist deals with observation and experimentation with objects, using technology to extend our ability to look into nature, the "theater" has become an amazing scene in itself. In a curious twist, the reviews can be spun so as to recommend the philosophy that it's all in the mind of God or some demon, after all.

Meanwhile Hume has already rejected both suppositions: both the "double existence" associated with the philosopher John Locke and its counterpart of the "single existence" in the mind of God, associated with Bishop George Berkeley.

The idea that "it's all in the mind" is dismissed on the grounds that nature is too strong for us to maintain it. When the chips are down, we get out of the way of the oncoming object (for example) if we can; we don't believe it's "all in the mind" or even in the mind of God, no matter how much we want to philosophize about it or pray on it.

We are left with what Blackburn refers to as the Egg Sequence.

> But now the trap is sprung. On the one hand, we have to do justice to the phenomena, here illustrated by the subject in the Egg Sequence, that force us to distinguish experience and its normal object, the "body," which in this case is the actual egg. On the other hand, we cannot tolerate the theory to which this leads, the story of the double existence. But we cannot put up with anything else either, since the only theory of "single existence" on hand is the intolerable Berkeley.[51]

Though I concur with the sentiment on Berkeley who would have us stand in the face of the intolerable, still, the Bishop's position is not soundly refuted with reason, without asymmetry. Readers who have got this far in our book will enjoy some interesting correlations with Berkeley.

Back to the Egg. What, then, is this disquieting sequence that forces us into the theater of duality and despair, where all our "careless" clowns (if we hope for any comedy) are either intrinsically sad (or perhaps cynical) in the catastrophe of human reason or entirely devoid of any reason whatsoever? I will quote Blackburn to get the actual words, including those I have italicized, which should by this time in this book ring asymmetric bells.

> So imagine a person in a rather unusual situation. He is facing a nicely illuminated egg, against a black background, which he sees perfectly normally.

This is the standard situation where the egg *might* be assumed to be observed directly, without any theater or intervention. Perception here is itself as though invisible, revelatory of the egg.

> However, he shuts his eyes occasionally for short intervals, and then reopens them. It has been arranged that at some of these intervals, unknown to him, the egg will be substituted by a hologram of an egg, arranged to look *indistinguishable* from the original egg. And at other intervals a skilled neurophysiologist will stimulate electrodes that have been planted in his visual cortex to generate in a third way an *indistinguishable* visual experience, so that when he opens his eyes it will again be as if there is the illuminated egg against a black background, only in that case there will be no egg, nor a hologram of one. Let us call the sequence of these three situations, the Egg Sequence.[52]

The conundrum seems to team us up with John Locke, to theorize that there is a double existence. This also nicely tees everything up for Hume to take a convincing swing at the object, whether it is there or not. (Didn't golf originate on the Scottish moors?)

Allow me to add a few more italics.

> The subject's visual experience is *indistinguishable* whenever

he opens his eyes, but the external layout of things is very different. Only in the one case is there an egg there. Yet since the cases are *indistinguishable*, from the subject's point of view, it is also natural to think of an *identical* visual experience, or "perception" in Hume's terminology, produced in the three varying ways. After all, the subject cannot tell, just by looking, which of the three situations he is in. He knows how he is seeing things — as if there is an illuminated egg in front of him — but there are different ways the world might be, compatible with this being how it appears. Once we say this, however, the problem of perception opens up. It is by means of such experience that the world is disclosed to us. Yet how can experience have this power if, as just suggested, the same experience can coexist with widely different surrounding layouts of the world?[53]

Asymmetric sequencing solves the problem. The experiences in the sequence cannot be identical or repeat exactly in any way, so they cannot be absolutely indistinguishable. There is something about each experience that can be perceived to give it away as different from the others. What does it take to be able to pick out such individual characteristics under the circumstances? It may take more than a casual glance. It might require special training or equipment. But it is possible; the discernment can be achieved, because the reality is continuous throughout the experience and connects it with any and all objects. There is an audit trail; the truth can be found. Regardless of whether in some instances we might lack the ability to perceive the differences, the premise of identical eggs is broken. The power of the Egg Sequence depends on indistinguishability in every case; the perceptions must be fundamentally identical.

According to the Transformation Proof, the Egg Sequence assumes an impossibility that is mutually exclusive with observed asymmetry. So we are not compelled to face the intolerable Berkeleyesque fantasy, though we can tip our hat to the bishop for providing us with fiction. The catastrophe is averted. Objects do exist; they are perceived in many ways. Our perception of them can be distinguished and characterized without unduly affecting the nature of the object in its own right. Nature is quite up-front about it. Far from being forced to be in her companionship only by adopting a state of "carelessness and inattention" to reason, we are given opportunities to enjoy detail to the highest degree. Our habitat can be cultivated to provide characterful opportunities that as rationalists we have perhaps been afraid to dream of and that have been left to the romantics, who understandably rebel at inhabiting a second-rate reality — one that they are known to try in vain to escape, like the tragic hero.

Simon Blackburn expresses a natural asymmetric approach when, after a brief discussion of the various unsatisfactory attempts to deal with Hume's conundrum, he concludes that (my italics):

> A better kind of approach, I believe, would be to stay relaxed about the *identity* of the experience in the three phases of the Egg Sequence, but to insist on the primacy of the veridical case in a different way. The proper function of the visual system [for example] is to enable us to know how things stand. It makes us into good instruments for detecting eggs, their position in relation to us, and their visible properties. It is no problem that it is sometimes fooled... Vision's success lies in its selecting for us the features that we need in order to navigate our way around our environment...

He continues as quoted earlier,

> It is only when we conceptualize "visual experience" and "the way things are" in terms of either *identical* or parallel "spaces," inner and outer, that we cannot make a consistent story about how vision [or perception] works.

So as soon as we assume those absolute identities and exact repetition into our reasoning (as did David Hume), our reasoning demonstrably breaks down. Although the significance of the asymmetries escaped him, Hume showed us the dead ends we encounter in reasoning without recognizing them. Blackburn continues to say,

> It would be nice if we could see how to reflect and reason on the process without entrapping ourselves in such an image [of absolute symmetry between the phases of the Egg Sequence], but even now the large and controversial literature on the topic proves that it will not be easy.[54]

In the absence of absolutes, we can further deduce that no two people can ever perceive exactly the same thing, while without nature's asymmetry no one could distinguish anything at all, for it is this open division among us that gives us the creative potentials of exquisite discernment and shared overlapping experience.

\* \* \*

Humans have, in varying degree, an addiction to absolutism — in both its chaotic and hyper-organized forms — that often makes their world a living hell. When stress is running high, especially, a final answer is often relished. Stress is habitually high in very hierarchical (sorry) societies, where oppression and denial automatically cling, or in more democratic communities that are being pressured from the outside. A powerful predilection for absolutes encourages, in ways large and small, eventual crises and instability that build excuses for further hierarchies of power in a potentially self-reinforcing cycle that can end in near-absolute collapse.

In the absence of an all-knowing God or savior to grant a miracle of deliverance, we tend to make one up, including delusions of release at the "end of the world." This builds powerful institutions of worship. It can become increasingly difficult to even think in degrees and shades of meaning in such an environment. Creativity goes into decline along with education. The weak who buckle first to the easy, absolutist answers are then upheld as strong by the ignorant, and those who are able to endure and persevere have to "support the world." Sometimes they are worshipped as martyrs, thus building the sort of hierarchy they worked to dismantle.

When Isaac Newton figured out a consistent way to explain the relationships of orbiting bodies, the absolutist mind was taken aback yet again. Old ideas had been changing over the centuries, especially since the Renaissance. Even before those Renaissance centuries (when the rediscovery of ancient ideas crept across Europe), back as far as the so-called Dark Ages, breakthroughs in mechanics were revolutionizing society, as wind and water mills turned cranks and shafts to transfer energy and grind flour and increase productivity. But when Newton's calculus so succinctly organized our understanding of such vast regions and orbs that had been matters of religious mythology for so long, it was a threshold. The tendency of the absolutist mind was to deal with the change by imposing another absolute. This time a "Newtonian clockwork universe" was assumed, much against his scientific temperament of discovery. Given time and money, everything could be predicted, it was widely thought. Meanwhile civilization was again receiving the gift of reason. But when reason and evidence seemed to fail — as David Hume pointed out — to supply a deducible ethics, there was the reaction in the form of Romanticism, bringing us poetry, but also the worship of the hero, the over-glorification of the emotions, cutting reason loose in many ways and belittling democratic ideals as incapable of producing anything more than the mediocre and commonplace.

A roughly parallel development of science and romanticism brought about the current situation addressed in *Zen and the Art of Motorcycle Maintenance*, where the conflicted philosopher rides a product of science that embodies romance and adventure. He travels in nature and society. The thing is, in the broad sweep of history, the romantics have overpowered the rationalists to a dangerous degree, economically and politically, and controlling where the money goes. The degree of worship in the US today, for example, expresses a deep romanticism involving the Christian mythology, among others. This threatens the stability of our democracy to the point where even the numerous democratic impulses within the stories of Jesus himself (whose appeal is that of a highly romantic figure) have been sidelined in favor of self-enrichment and bonding between groups who attack with potent wedge issues of narrow doctrine. Just because David Hume and others did not figure everything out right away? Why should they have? Everything will never be figured out right away to satisfy our absolutist desires.

The modernist movement challenged authority and the post-modernists bring us back again to our introduction (which, I am reliably assured, promises a resolution regarding relativism). All this turmoil of ideas and expression has accompanied the greatest horrors know to humanity and inhumanity.

The Romantic Movement is still with us, empowered with technology. It is high time for some popular emphasis on reason. Without reason we lose the heart and the true emotions. Reason cannot be relegated to the specialist who dutifully provides the next generation of technology.

By the way, what a terrifying prospect it must be for kids to face the fact that they might want to be "wonks," "nerds," "geeks," or any of the latest names that social pressure might exert! Such labelling should be relegated to the school dustbins, along with the other more recognized, destructive epithets, instead of being regarded disingenuously. (Prof. David Anderegg's book, *Nerds*, is an enlightening analysis.)

Nature is showing us what happens when we become absolutist with technology. The long-term weather is changing in ways that challenge the most hopelessly romantic survivalist.

\* \* \*

This brings us back to the Truth Wars and the way the relativists trade backdoor secrets — unconsciously or not — with their absolutist neighbors, the objectivists. These backdoor crosscurrents also offer hope of agreement between liberals (who are typically identified with relativism) and social conservatives (who are typically identified with absolutism). The hope is in awareness of a truth that some of us like to call the River of Asymmetry or Field of Action. These are just a few metaphors; there are many others and many other lifeways and languages to express the asymmetric truth.

This does not mean to imply that the asymmetric path is just somewhere in the middle. The relativist and the objectivist (to use another word for absolutist) are not symmetrically opposed — one reason why there is more emphasis on absolutism in this work. The problem, as mentioned in the introduction, is that we humans have had a hard time finding some locale from which to achieve a standard outside our individual awareness — a place that can be respected as having a true perspective. (Yes, I am human.) Philosophers ever so often give up on the quest for truth, and sometimes it fades into a cliché, but by its nature it cannot go unacknowledged for long and must resurface, as in Simon Blackburn's *Truth: A Guide* — lately the best place to pursue this subject to gain a good idea of the landscape of our journey, with the following asymmetric landmarks in mind.

As Blackburn says, the objectivist is often caricatured as a blow-hard who insists that there is no problem, really. The facts are the facts. We should get responsible and face them as they are, for that is how they are: "as they are" — in a manner of speaking.

The relativist is often caricatured as insisting that the blow-hard has his truth in his or her manner of speaking and others have theirs. The objectivist waxes romantic with emotion, as does the relativist.

There is a recent twist that Blackburn highlights. Nowadays relativism has (unconsciously or otherwise) gone on the offensive in the form of the fundamentalist. Where once it was the domain of the skeptics to be respected for meditating on life's paradoxes from a dignified distance, now fundamentalism can be interpreted as a nod out the backdoor to the relativist neighbor, saying, yes, it's now all a matter of opinion and the one with the most money and the greatest number of supporters takes territory from the others. It's a free-for-all. Besides, says the Bible-thumping moralist (the relativist wolf in sheep's clothing), you relativists are really objectivists in disguise, because in saying "it's all relative" you are not only exhibiting perfect, objective, absolutist symmetry by allowing all positions evenly, but you are also in absolute symmetrical opposition with my position, which I am setting forth on no uncertain terms!

Relativist philosophers have tried to come to the rescue with the idea that they do not directly object to the objectivist. Instead they back away from such symmetry, they say, to a safe distance and plant their flag on more subtle ground.

The relativist, in his more "cunning" (or accepting) aspect of backing away from symmetry, must distance himself by degrees from something specified to some degree. The more the relativist tries to specify what is happening, the more of a specific connection he is making with the objectivist, by characterizing the distance between them. His problem is to say he is NOT an objectivist without sounding too absolutist.

Without invoking the asymmetry of nature's polarity, he will perforce argue himself into the corner of the opposite non-pole from the objectivist.

There is no escaping the symmetry of self-refutation by distancing himself in this way.

The more he leaves the degree to which he backs away unspecified, the less heat he can reasonably put into any argument in favor of his position. He waters himself down. He gets accused of being wishy-washy and overly accepting.

He can respond that at least he has the strength to live with uncertainty and face the unknown, in the absence of an absolute truth. He has a point there, in that the absolutist can so easily buckle under pressure and opt for the simplistic and often ill-considered answer, especially where good education and old-fashioned horse sense (the asymmetric instinct for reason) are lacking.

Even so, in backing away from symmetry, the relativist cannot escape the nature of asymmetry, of the balance in the absence of absolutes, where all things are connected with polarity and specificity. The continuity predicts that he cannot accord a different status to his opponent and back away along an *unrelated* line of degrees. In distancing himself, the only hope is to embrace asymmetry, because it is mutually exclusive with the pure symmetry of the objectivist.

Perhaps this is what the relativist is really looking for — and same for the objectivist in good faith. In short, the answer to objectivism is to show that absolutes do not exist and that the very concept self-contradicts. In order to do so, one must abandon relativism altogether.

The objectivist cannot insist that facts are facts and no more, since they are connected in asymmetric ways. It is not surprising that the objectivist is often closely related in temperament with the religious fundamentalist who is not all that concerned with facts; both tend to trivialize the facts by discounting their amazing associations. Meanwhile postmodernism has shown an obsessive tendency towards the trivial pursuit of disconnected fact and detail.

The balance of change provides a reference from within all things, whereby they share truth and being. It will not do to say, "That is your truth only; I have my truth." The universal continuity of asymmetric open-endedness will not allow the absolute disconnection required by relativists and objectivists of all kinds. They both harbor the dream of an absolute disconnect, even if the objectivist disconnect is in the form of an absolute finality, whereas the relativist wishes to disconnect from the absolutist position — hoping, perhaps, for community where everyone is on their own island of "truth." They are both relying on impossible universals.

The universal continuity is asymmetrically specific. It is not a fully generalized thing. Recall the discussion of universals in the introduction where it says, if I may quote the man in the maze: "In order to generalize, we must realize that we are really just leaving off being more specific, leaving a loose end — the very refutation of absolute finality."

Which brings us back to the importance of the degrees of exactitude, the specific open-endedness of asymmetry, found in all the empirical facts, as well as in our thoughts. A specific asymmetric path away from the objectivist position is formed by the footsteps of the relativist leading away from it. Such a pathway, no matter how subtle, will never make a relativistic argument against objectivism without understanding asymmetry. It will only reinforce a backdoor deal.

It is widely recognized that the relativists have not taken the wind out of the sails of their supposed opponents, who have in the last thirty years framed the arguments, soaked them in emotion, and dangerously unbalanced the cultural landscape in the United States, at least. It has all come down to posturing, fashion, and the accumulation of power. So what about democracy?

* * *

Today the words "We hold these truths to be self-evident, that all men are created equal" and many words like them — the legacy of the Enlightenment — are in a challenging cultural context. One that has in a way assimilated them and now mimics them like a usurping virus, claiming superior patriotism, having favored the imposition of "democracy" on others. How will the enlightened words of our Founders endure? Religious leaders are once again claiming just as much right to build religion into the Constitution as the Founders claimed for the separation of powers and of Church and State. The Founders and various supporting factions understood that the challenge of organized religion is as old as history.

A democracy founded in a military revolution and established with military and economic power must evolve and become more deeply rooted, with not only philosophical reason but with a respect for reason that is rooted in the common good and balanced with common sense, especially as science progresses.

Equal opportunity must eventually be discovered in the very foundations of living matter, as an ethic to guide the surprising growth of technological power. Otherwise, we will have nothing but ever more deadly muscles to flex and sabers to rattle at tyrants, as democracy competes as just another belief system.

The rough-and-ready justification given by Churchill's famous remark that democracy is the lesser of evils, and even Russell's insolubility of finding a collection of wise men as a rationale for democracy, cannot compete with ancient forces of myth and literature like the Bible. Unless we break through in our thinking, free societies will be reduced to behaving tyrannically and will fail to encourage the democratic impulse that naturally builds and overthrows oppression. In the absence of absolutes and symmetrical relativism, true progress is possible. But cycles of history will be uncomfortably repeated until we more thoroughly get used to the asymmetry of it.

Philosophy branched out into science. The philosophical is a unifying perspective, even — perhaps especially — in the absence of answers. If we confine this natural human instinct to a specialty, we are lost. We all philosophize. We all have questions. This is respected in a healthy habitat. If we suppress our philosophical nature — and its sense of humor — we oppress the soul. Without the ability to doubt we are insane. When we can no longer question, we have lost the context of our answers, their provenance and meaning. Faith helps us to achieve continuity when it seems broken, but it is now possible to say with reason that no leap of faith should be a substitute for the open-ended quest of the soul, including the adventure and the love that comes its way. To attempt to leap beyond open-endedness is to slam up against the door of hope and everything besides.

By the Transformation Proof we can discover that democracy is at the very heart of nature, even to the atoms, particles, and energies of matter. The democratic impulse is deeply and inexorably favored, though buried by many layers of cultural and physical pressure. We find the democratic impulse in varying degrees in our mythologies. We can find it in the beauty of nature. Democracy should be encouraged in all nations, but never assumed to be achieved once and for all, just as we should never assume we have no ego, as described by Alice and her friends. Neither democracy nor life, for that matter, are maintenance free; this we know from hard experience. Where democracy is more prevalent, the people should not feel so superior that they begin to lose it while attempting to impose it, as we have seen tragically in recent years.

*   *   *

Where there is an addiction to the illusion of absolutes, asymmetric reasoning will often be considered rebellious. But democracy has often been a rebellious thing. It functions like a free country — with its laws written in the negative. You are free to do anything at all, except for certain limited and hopefully clearly defined things that are not allowed. It is not a relativist free-for-all. It is not an absolute. It needs to be improved in the process of change. With a deeper understanding of the ethics of freedom, we discover the genie of asymmetry at work. Conversely, dictatorial moral systems have codes that positively tell you how to live, and if you step outside the system, you are pressured back into the "correct," "proper," or accepted way to be. On the River of Life, the only thing we cannot do is achieve an absolute such as pure symmetry. Near-symmetry breaks in a variety of ways to create a democratic ethic. A certain rebelliousness is involved in maintaining the balance under social pressures that favor the impossible absolute.

\* \* \*

With the flattening of infinity, one can imagine a story where a decentralized god repeatedly bounces off the rim of the asymmetric circle, trying to escape the reasoning and go beyond. The changing boundary is always at least one step ahead, until the god realizes there is no absolute and focuses on expanding equal opportunity for all.

\* \* \*

The day after the salmon barbecue, I stood by as the two couples got in their canoes and set off, one standing in the stern of each canoe, poling upstream to the first carry on the native canoe routes of Maine. After they had disappeared round the bend, I returned to Molly's tea room for a nice cuppa, in anticipation of their return and the completion of the book.

## 39. Snagged by the Imperfect Democratic Tao of Pi

Pi is the relationship between a circle and its diameter. Sounds simple. But it's not really a simple fact that the diameter fits into the circumference 3.14 times — that will not quite do it, will it! — There's a snag. All those decimals in a tangle: 3.141592653... and on and on and on, and will they ever let go! After all that's been said in this book, Murphy's law of land and sea simply advises us that if something can snag, it will snag. A rope round a protrusion, even in calm weather, an electric lawnmower cord on a smooth rock, we have our favorites.

Something obtuse about natural law seems to invite things to snag on things. And so I will venture the thought that, in spite of the trouble, it might be a good thing. Without this unruly attraction, what could connect? Not that everything that connects need be called a "snag," but the point is that the snag was not the destination. Had we someplace in mind? some objective that was presumed snag-free?

The surprising thing about pi is that we are alerted against thinking the circle is perfect, that it will come clean. The decimals of pi are a string of red warning lights. Endlessly imperfect! That the circle will not close absolutely is re-enumerated in all sorts of ways, no matter how we pull on it — but it does get our attention. It's got traction.

In the absence of perfection, the circle connects with things; it snags many things in the real world and in the imagination. But it can be unsnagged if we find where it connects, so we can stop pulling on more decimals, stop counting pi, and be aware of something else. How many decimals must we endure before we cave and admit that there are no absolutely perfectly symmetrical circles, no absolutes at all, in fact, in the absence of any perfectly, finally, straight lines for diameters? Pi calls out echoingly that infinity is a snag, mathematically, metaphorically, and otherwise. It is snagging the loftiest physicists. Where the rubber meets the road, pi provides useful traction when viewed realistically.

Experimental science has not found any pure symmetry in nature, at all. Walk outside and find me just one thing that does not imperfectly imply circularity — even in your ruler.

Just when you think you can identify symmetry in a flower, in a leaf, there is a snag, one of the petals is askew, and that is a beautiful thing — nature's true balance. Another beautiful aspect of pi is its call to democracy. We can share the democratic pi(e) in a balanced way by getting inspired by nature's gifts. How does the circle snag democracy? The number pi snags the mind into the natural world, in spite of our presumptions and with no need to be familiar with the snagger. Individuals are brought together, not into a monoculture of symmetrical banality, but into a potential flourishing of character, one and all.

This notion of a dancing, changing, balancing polarity in circles is of course not new, and is renewable in time. The ancient understanding of the polarities of the Tao have long been applied to relationships of a circle, where Yin and Yang move round each other. So do not be snagged by an illusion of some ideal symmetry in the famous Yin-Yang symbol! As the *I Ching*, the *Book of Changes*, foretells in the natural cycles of the lines of its well-weathered hexagrams, absolutes are overturned, preemptively snagged, I would add. The connections between the seasons and the livelihood of the people had deep and long-recognized roots in the planet, way before it was widely known to be round.

The vital questions of how to live and behave as humans among the forces of nature, what is right and wrong and what works and what fails in life, these issues have long focused the mind as it developed. Does nature have a moral compass? Should we follow it? If so, how? But these questions have begun to look dated, and we have become jaded. We need to be snagged by more democratic pi all round (puns included)!

## 40. Nature's Democratic Counter-Pressures

One important conclusion we can make in the logic of asymmetry is what Lola repeated loudly in a vital moment recently: "Counter-pressure!" As expressed more than once in this book: The more pressures build into a fixed pole or central position, the more counter-pressures will develop away from the impossible symmetry. Poling upstream in a canoe requires the skill to find the eddies and counter-currents to help lift the canoe in a fluid stairway. Moving out of control in the other direction, whitewater building all round, we almost succumbed to a snag, to be sucked under the fallen branch like novices. Rendered even more philosophical, we turned the crisis into a last takeaway for this book.

Nature has no choice but to avoid poles of pure symmetry — perfect absolutes — whether cosmically indirectly or with unsettling immediacy. This key principle, as mentioned, follows from the Transformation Proof and the evidence of experimental science. If democracy has been on the defensive about being boring and lacking in aristocratic flair, lacking in superheroes among the "humble masses," mired in dread mediocrity, the multifarious pressures inherent in nature's democratic polarity say otherwise. Instead of the water analogy, consider the Wheel of Fire. This is the inability to let go of the circle that will never close with perfection, leaving one with increasingly unfulfilled desire, until ego explodes. Plenty of drama in a democracy, where it's all about balance.

Because we were just able enough to be flexible and not panic with the poles and paddles, we survived a well-known danger in watery regions, where egos are too often extinguished. We let go just enough, working together, and the river let us go downstream.

The flourishing of the circles of democracy, not just their survival, will depend on prioritizing opportunities for those who need a chance the most, who are living closest to snags and dead ends, in areas of the economy and community with the "lowest asymmetry," requiring of its denizens the greatest balance. We must learn from them about social pressure, stress, and they must be given the most care and attention, including the allocation of funds, investment, opportunity.

Aristocracies have never needed democracy like the people need it. Hence the famous words, "We the people . . ." The benefits of equal opportunity should get round to the rich and powerful less directly than the emergency where the poor are concerned. The fact that democracy is asymmetric and what that means needs repeating in creative ways. The more the congestive social pressures that constrict natural liberties and rights with symmetries of poverty, where the circle is closing in on people, trapping them into eventual enslavement, the more immediately relief is required from the wealthy at the other pole — especially via representative government. In order for the systems of a democracy to sustain hope and progress, they must be organized for aid and rescue by the central government, in polarity, for balance and the health of all.

North American Beaver
Courtesy Maine Department of Inland Fisheries and Wildlife

# Notes

1. European Space Agency and the Planck Collaboration, www.esa.int/spaceinimages/Images/2013/03/Planck_enhanced_anomalies, March 21, 2013. For more on the CMB asymmetry see also Charles Q. Choi, "How Did the Universe Get So Lopsided? How could the cosmos have become so skewed?" Scientific American, www.scientificamerican.com/article.cfm?id=how-did-the-universe-get-so-lopsided, September 17, 2013.
2. Lee Smolin, *Time Reborn: From the Crisis in Physics to the Future of the Universe* (New York: Houghton Mifflin Harcourt, 2013), 215.
3. Ibid., 226.
4. Katia Moskvitch, "Paradox Solved? How Information Can Escape from a Black Hole" http://www.space.com/24899-black-holes-stars-information-paradox.html, March 04, 2014.
5. https://en.wikipedia.org/wiki/First_observation_of_gravitational_waves.
6. Philip Goff, *Galileo's Error: Foundations for a New Science of Consciousness* (New York: Knopf Doubleday, Kindle ed, 2019), 123-4.
7. David O. Solmitz, *Piecing Scattered Souls: Maine, Germany, Mexico, China and Beyond* (Solon: Polar Bear & Company, 2011), p. xiii. This book also contains the description by Walter M. Solmitz of his experience as a prisoner at Dachau in 1939. This is a particularly important report, as it shows one aspect of how the Nazis changed from a pretense of civilized behavior into the deepening horrors that followed. This is a window into the way any society can fall to the internal attack of the dictatorial attitude.
8. The allegory of the cave is found in Plato's *Republic*, where Socrates tries to distinguish fundamental reality as changeless "Forms" in the light of day, as compared with the changing images, sounds, and shadows in the firelight of the cave.
9. Dennis Overbye, "A New Clue to Explain Existence," New York Times, www.nytimes.com/2010/05/18/science/space/18cosmos.html?src=me&ref=homepage, May 17, 2010.
10. Fermilab Press Release: "Fermilab scientists find evidence for significant matter-antimatter asymmetry," www.fnal.gov/pub/presspass/press_releases/CP-violation-20100518.html, May 18, 2010. Title of Fermilab report: *Evidence for an Anomalous Like-Sign Dimuon Charge Asymmetry*.

11. David Chalmers and Andy Clark, "The Extended Mind," *Analysis* 58: 1: (1998): 7–19.
12. Robert B. Laughlin, *A Different Universe: Reinventing Physics from the Bottom Down* (New York: Basic Books, 2005), 80.
13. Ibid., 76.
14. Ibid., 76–77.
15. Frank Close, *Lucifer's Legacy: The Meaning of Asymmetry* (Oxford: Oxford University Press, 2000), 166.
16. B. Sidney Smith, "Infinity: You Can't Get There From Here!" Math Academy Online/Platonic Realms, www.mathacademy.com/pr/minitext/infinity/index.asp. There is an interesting connection between the Transformation Proof and Kurt Gödel's Incompleteness Theorem, which has yet to be fully explored and is outside the scope of this book. Daniel C. Dennett gives a clear insight into Gödel's theorem in Chapter 15 of *Darwin's Dangerous Idea*. The Incompleteness Theorem presents us with what we have been calling a "Platonic infinity," with an ever-escaping "Gödel sentence." Dennett describes some interpretations of what this might mean, including Gödel's own view. Asymmetric infinity would not require that there always be a Gödel sentence. This relates to there being a largest number in any asymmetric series (see Chapter 22, "Samuel's Essay: The Largest Number Proof, Etc.").
17. Ibid.
18. Ibid.
19. Ibid.
20. Peter Woit, *Not Even Wrong: The Failure of String Theory and the Search for Unity in Physical Law* (New York: Basic Books, 2006), 139–141, but the issue is thematic through the book.
21. Adam Frank, "Is the Universe Actually Made of Math?" Discover Magazine, http://discovermagazine.com/2008/jul/16-is-the-universe-actually-made-of-math/article_view?b_start:int=0&-C=.
22. Ibid.
23. Sam Nelson, "Theorems and Theories," http://www.esotericka.org/cmc/tth.html (2004–2010).
24. Frank, "Is the Universe Actually Made of Math."
25. Woit, *Not Even Wrong*, 166.
26. Frank, "Is the Universe Actually Made of Math."
27. *The Thousand and One Nights* represented in our story of genies in bottles does not in every respect keep to the stories translated by Richard Burton!
28. "There was a paper published in Science this February, and what it showed was that if you do an experiment with a photon, put it in the apparatus, that what you do right now actually changes an event that already occurred in the past." Quoting Robert Lanza. Pamela Weintraub, "Fighting for the Right to Clone," *Discover Magazine*, http://discovermagazine.com/2008/

sep/19-fighting-for-the-right-to-clone.
29. Khayyám, *The Rubáiyát*, Ernest E. Laws, quatrains 119 & 126.
30. Aquilah's musings are so far supported by scientific experiments.
31. Close, *Lucifer's Legacy: The Meaning of Asymmetry*, 143.
32. Ibid., 228.
33. J. Bradford Delong, *What Happened to Milton Friedman's Chicago School?: Reactions to the Financial Crisis of 2007–2009*, MTI-CSC Economics Speaker Series Lecture, Jan. 7, 2009, http://delong.typepad.com/sdj/.
34. Daniel C. Dennett, *Darwin's Dangerous Idea: Evolution and the Meaning of Life*. (New York: Simon & Schuster, 1996), 125.
35. Ibid., 203.
36. Ibid., 82.
37. Ibid., 200.
38. Ibid., (?)
39. Thomas Robert Malthus, 1766–1834, author of *An Essay on the Principle of Population*.
40. Sharon Begley, *Sins of the Fathers, Take 2*, www.newsweek.com/id/180103).
41. Kitta MacPherson, "Evolution's New Wrinkle: Proteins with Cruise Control Provide New Perspective," *News at Princeton*, www.princeton.edu/main/news/archive/S22/60/95O56/index.xml?section=topstories, posted November 10, 2008.
42. Dennett, *Darwin's Dangerous Idea: Evolution and the Meaning of Life*, 69.
43. Maxwell's Demon, a thought experiment by physicist James Clerk Maxwell, was designed to show that through a weakness in statistics, the second law of thermodynamics might not hold true.
44. Woit, *Not Even Wrong*, 102.
45. Levine, Michael, "Pantheism," *The Stanford Encyclopedia of Philosophy* (Spring 2011 Edition), Edward N. Zalta (ed.), http://plato.stanford.edu/archives/spr2011/entries/pantheism/.
46. Shankar Vedantam, *Washington Post*, www.washingtonpost.com/wp-dyn/content/article/2007/05/27/AR2007052701056.html?hpid=topnews, May 28, 2007.
47. Simon Blackburn, *How to Read Hume*, (London: Granta, 2008), 39.
48. Ibid., 43–44.
49. Ibid., 40.
50. Ibid., 1.
51. Ibid., 39.
52. Ibid., 35.
53. Ibid., 36.
54. Ibid., 43–44.

# Selected Bibliography

Anderegg, David. *Nerds: Why Dorks, Dweebs, Techies, and Trekkies Can Save America and Why They Might Be Our Last Hope.* New York: Penguin, 2011.
Blackburn, Simon. *Truth: A Guide.* Oxford: Oxford University Press, 2007.
Blackburn, Simon. *How to Read Hume.* London: Granta, 2008.
Blyth, Mark. *Austerity: The History of a Dangerous Idea.* Oxford: Oxford University Press, 2013.
Burton, Richard Francis. *One Thousand and One Arabian Nights*, Vols. 1–16. Charleston, South Carolina: Forgotten Books, 2008.
Chalmers, David, and Andy Clark. "The Extended Mind." *Analysis* 58: 1: (1998): 7–19. Also: www.philosophy.ed.ac.uk/people/clark/pubs/TheExtendedMind.pdf.
Close, Frank. *Lucifer's Legacy: The Meaning of Asymmetry.* Oxford: Oxford University Press, 2000.
Dawkins, Richard. *The God Delusion.* Boston: Mariner Books, Houghton Mifflin Company, 2008.
Dennett, Daniel C. *Darwin's Dangerous Idea: Evolution and the Meaning of Life.* New York: Simon & Schuster, 1996.
Durell, Fletcher, and E. E. Arnold. *A First Book in Algebra.* New York: Charles E. Merrill Company, 1928.
Feynman, Richard P. *The Meaning of It All: Thoughts of a Citizen-Scientist.* Reading MA: Perseus Books, 2005.
Florida, Richard. *The Rise of the Creative Class: And How It's Transforming Work, Leisure, Community and Everyday Life.* New York: Basic Books, 2002.
Fox, Justin. *The Myth of the Rational Market: A History of Risk, Reward, and Delusion on Wall Street.* New York: Harper, 2011.
Goff, Philip. *Galileo's Error: Foundations for a New Science of Consciousness.* New York: Pantheon, 2019.
Hackett, Robert. *The Computer Maverick Who Modeled the Evolution of Life: Nils Aall Barricelli showed that organisms evolved by symbiosis and cooperation.* https://nautil.us/the-computer-maverick-who-modeled-the-evolution-of-life-234936/. *Nautilus*, May 30, 2014.
Herrigel, Eugen. *Zen in the Art of Archery.* New York: Vintage, 1999.
Hofstadter, Douglas R. *Gödel, Escher, Bach: An Eternal Golden Braid.* New York: Basic Books, 1999. Some of the key ideas in *Gödel, Escher, Bach* are addressed via the discussion of Daniel C. Dennett's description of

consciousness in *Darwin's Dangerous Idea*.

Johnston, Basil. *The Manitous: The Spiritual World of the Ojibway*. New York: HarperCollins, 1995.

Laughlin, Robert B. *A Different Universe: Reinventing Physics from the Bottom Down*. New York: Basic Books, 2005.

Livio, Mario. *The Equation That Couldn't Be Solved: How Mathematical Genius Discovered the Language of Symmetry*. New York: Simon & Schuster, 2005.

Mazzucato, Mariana. *The Value of Everything: Making and Taking in the Global Economy*. London: Penguin, 2019.

Newton, Isaac. *Philosophiæ Naturalis Principia Mathematica*. London 1687, translated by Andrew Motte, 1729.

Piketty, Thomas. *Capital in the Twenty-First Century*. Cambridge: Belknap Press, 2014.

Pirsig, Robert M. *Zen and the Art of Motorcycle Maintenance*. New York: Harper Perennial Modern Classics, 2008.

Rifkin, Jeremy. *The Empathic Civilization: The Race to Global Consciousness in a World in Crisis*. New York: Tarcher, 2009.

Russell, Bertrand. *A History of Western Philosophy*. New York: Simon & Schuster, 1967.

Smolin, Lee. *Time Reborn: From the Crisis in Physics to the Future of the Universe*. Houghton Mifflin Harcourt, 2013.

Wilhelm, Richard and Cary F. Baynes, translators. *The I Ching or Book of Changes*. Princeton: Princeton University Press, 1967.

Woit, Peter. *Not Even Wrong: The Failure of String Theory and the Search for Unity in Physical Law*. New York: Basic Books, 2006.

## The Author's Story

Born in Los Angeles, California, Paul Cornell du Houx grew up among several Western countries. Graduating from Winchester College in the UK, he attended Amherst College in Massachusetts, where he majored separately in economics and French. His honors thesis identified the aesthetic mysticism in the works of Gustave Flaubert. This led to his early attempts to bring cross-cultural insights to clarify a crisis some economists saw in the utilitarian way mainstream theory was moving. He decided to investigate the marketplace firsthand, rather than take the well-worn academic path that one day would lead the world economy into the Great Recession and largely unprepared into the 2020 pandemic. Clearly, capitalism has gone begging for something more than money.

While looking for answers, Cornell du Houx wrote currency reports for the MSA consultancy newsletter in the London Square Mile, audited companies for PwC, studied law at the Inns of Court, sold computers, and with his patented improvements on an electrical connector got involved in a start-up.

Attracted to the succinct form of the ancient sutra, the author began gathering ideas in the late seventies under the *Yoganomics* portmanteau, written as a conversation piece, in the spirit of his storytelling grandfather, a Kansas farmer with a talent for making up words and combining disparate ideas with comedy.

Eventually, Cornell du Houx developed the math proposed in *Unicycle* that lets us read the ethics of natural law within the environment. In 2020, he finally rewrote *Yoganomics* accordingly.

Somewhere along the line, he penned *What the Farmer Told the Bard, a Novel of Erotic Panpsychism*, involving runes encoded in a Shakespeare monument and some Pagan deities from the Bard's comedies.

In 1991 Ramona and Paul settled with their children in Maine. The publication of books, art, and the news magazine *Maine Insights* led to founding the Solon Center for Research and Publishing (501c3) and EOPA Code Blue Water Solutions (501c4). Gallery Fukurou at 20 Main St., Rockland, Maine, opened to the public in 2018.

The independently founded project Elected Officials to Protect America (ProtectingAmerica.net) joined with the Solon Center to combat climate change, with the help and leadership of military veterans.

It is the author's hope that the sense of a deep democracy in nature, which inspired Native American communities and merged with our Founders' Enlightenment vision of natural law, will help bring hearts and minds together in time.

www.ingramcontent.com/pod-product-compliance
Lightning Source LLC
Chambersburg PA
CBHW020323170426
43200CB00006B/249